CULT INSANITY

CULT
INSANITY

A Memoir of Polygamy, Prophets,
and Blood Atonement

IRENE SPENCER

**CENTER
STREET.**

New York   Boston   Nashville

Author's note: Some individuals' names have been changed to protect their identity.

Unless otherwise indicated, all scripture quotations are taken from the official scriptures of The Church of Jesus Christ of Latter-day Saints. The quotations from Brigham Young and others regarding blood atonement were retrieved from http://www.realmormonhistory.com/blood_atonement1.htm and http://www.utlm.org/onlinebooks/changech20.htm.

Center Street
Hachette Book Group
237 Park Avenue
New York, NY 10017

Visit our website at www.centerstreet.com.

Center Street is a division of Hachette Book Group, Inc.
The Center Street name and logo are trademarks of Hachette Book Group, Inc.

Printed in the United States of America

First Edition: August 2009
10 9 8 7 6 5 4 3 2 1

Library of Congress Cataloging-in-Publication Data

Spencer, Irene, 1937–
    Cult insanity : a memoir of polygamy, prophets, and blood atonement /
Irene Spencer. — 1st ed.
    p. cm.
    Summary: "Irene Spencer tells the full story of her brother-in-law
Ervil LeBaron and his unimaginable reign of terror and violence
in their polygamist community"—Provided by the publisher
    ISBN 978-0-446-53819-0
  1. LeBaron, Ervil M.   2. Church of the Firstborn of the Fullness
of Times.   3. Church of Jesus Christ of Latter-day Saints.
4. Mormon Church.   I. Title.

  BX8680.L48L422 2009
  289.3092—dc22
  [B]
                                                            2009012068

I honor my son Steven R. LeBaron for the courage he displayed in the Los Molinos raid.

To my children, Donna, Andre, Steven, Brent, Kaylen, Barbara, Margaret, Connie, LaSalle, Verlana, Seth, *and* Lothair, *who are my best friends, and make me proud.*

Rich Hall Photography, February 2009

My heart goes out to all of my family and those unfortunate souls who were blood atoned. *Their shed blood will continue to seep through the pages of history.*

PREFACE

Cult Insanity refers to all religious extremist, authoritarian dogmas, practices, and crimes that control, exploit, and disempower individuals, robbing them of their god-given agency, freedom, and potential. These mind-control tactics are instituted and played out within diverse religions and religious cultures. I have personally witnessed these things in Mormon fundamentalism. The shocking degree of mind control and disrespect for human dignity is real, as are its destructive effects upon the human spirit.

Dehumanizing behaviors typical in cults are defended in the name of "religion" or "religious freedom." Yet they indicate mental illness—the real issue at the core of cult dynamics. We should question abusive behaviors, because they invariably indicate a warped personality. The destructive nature of religious fundamentalism arises from pathology and mental illness acted out upon others while asserted as "divine revelation" or "divine authority."

Countless reports about the LeBaron fundamentalist cult have appeared in print since the Church of the Firstborn was founded in 1955. In my files, hundreds of news articles, spanning decades, detail such stories.

One excellent book about the LeBaron story is *Prophet of Blood: The Untold Story of Ervil LeBaron and the Lambs of God,* by

Dale VanAtta and Ben Bradlee, who interviewed me about my experiences and quoted me in sixteen places. I was a primary source along with dozens of others who lived the story.

Another good, more recent book is *The 4 O'Clock Murders: The True Story of a Mormon Family's Vengeance* by Scott Anderson, which used some material from *Prophet of Blood* reflective of some of my experiences.

Journalistic works such as these two books contain a wealth of research, details, and interviews that go far beyond or may differ from information in my experience. They present a detached, objective, third-person perspective combining numerous points of view.

However, my work is a personal memoir that reflects a first-person, firsthand experience inside the LeBaron group. My perspective is based on my life among the LeBarons from 1953 to 1986 and with the Church of the Firstborn since its inception in 1955. My story is my account rather than a scholarly work. I can't speak for others or their perspectives. This is just how I saw things.

Descriptions of events, persons, and information in this book are taken predominantly from my life experiences within the LeBaron communities as well as within other fundamentalist Mormon cultures, including the Allred and Short Creek communities. I have had the benefit of many conversations with my Aunt Rhea Kunz, my late husband Verlan M. LeBaron and our family members, and friends Marilyn Lamborn, Fay Falk, as well as members of the Church of the Firstborn, all of whom I lived with or knew intimately for three decades.

Secondary sources I consulted include Verlan's book, *The LeBaron Story*, and a few details from *Prophet of Blood: The Untold Story of Ervil LeBaron and the Lambs of God* by Ben Bradlee and Dale VanAtta, as well as *The 4 O'Clock Murders: The True Story of a Mormon Family's Vengeance* by Scott Anderson.

However, ultimately, I am responsible for the material in this book.

ACKNOWLEDGMENTS

My heartfelt thanks to:

God—for His faithful protection for delivering us from Ervil.

Hector Spencer—my husband, for sharing his love with my children and me for the past twenty-one years. Thank you for your constant dedication, encouragement, and the countless hours of research and proofreading. Your extraordinary patience has made this all possible!

Donna Goldberg—my beautiful daughter, who has been my pillar of strength. Your sacrifices, devotion, love, and passion have propelled me into fulfilling my purpose in life. I'm so thankful you were the first of my children to break the generational cycle of Mormon fundamentalism. It's a joy to see my posterity following in your footsteps.

Thomas J. Winters—the best literary agent an author could possibly hope for.

Debby Boyd—the best executive assistant ever! Thanks for believing in me and being my number-one cheerleader!

Rolf Zettersten—of Hachette Book Group, and the staff, for investing in my dreams. Your faith has empowered me.

Michelle Rapkin—for her enthusiasm, validation, and editing skills.

Maxine Hanks—who validated my voice as a writer. I'll be forever grateful for your encouragement. You are not only a mentor, but my friend.

Rebecca Kimbel—who had the courage to take a new path after generations of polygamy. She is not only my sister, but my friend, mentor, and advocate. Thanks for your unconditional love and wisdom.

Brandy Goldberg Biglow—my granddaughter and personal assistant, who does it *all*! I can't imagine living without your talent and multitasking skills. I appreciate your confidence in me as an author and speaker. Thanks for making me look good with your bubbly spirit and striking beauty!

Men never do evil so completely and cheerfully

as when they do it from religious conviction.

—BLAISE PASCAL

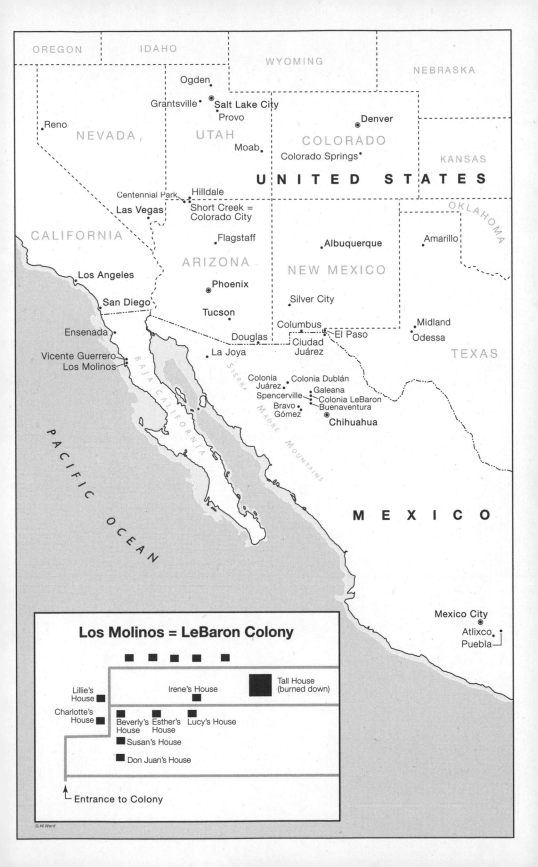

CULT INSANITY

CHAPTER ONE

Ervil LeBaron, often referred to as "the Mormon Manson" who ordered the deaths of at least twenty-eight family members, friends, and church members—and who had threatened to kill my husband and me—was my brother-in-law. I was married to his brother Verlan LeBaron for twenty-eight years.

I married Verlan without my parents' permission or knowledge. They had warned me against getting involved with the LeBarons, saying there was "insanity" in that family. As a teenager raised in fundamentalism, however, I was sure God had told me I was to be Verlan's wife. So I ran away and became the second of ten women who shared Verlan and called him "husband." During those years, which I have recounted in *Shattered Dreams,* I mothered fourteen of his fifty-eight children and lived in terrible poverty, raising or scrounging for our own food, wearing clothes the thrift stores couldn't sell, and doing most of it without electricity or indoor plumbing. Everywhere I go, people ask me how I could have willingly involved myself in a lifestyle that was so difficult, unfulfilling, and abusive. To answer that question, I need to give a bit of a history lesson. And mind you, I heard this lesson repeated over and over from the time I was very young, so I never questioned its validity or worth. I was a fifth-generation plural wife, so I had no real reason to believe the practice was anything other than God's plan for my life.

There are an estimated fifty to one hundred thousand practicing polygamists today throughout the western United States, Canada, and Mexico. Joseph Smith, the founder of Mormonism, practiced polygamy in the 1830s and 1840s, marrying at least thirty-three wives (some historians say he had more). He officially introduced polygamy in 1843 with a revelation from God, which later became section 132 of the Doctrine and Covenants, a Mormon scripture.

Many of his followers were appalled, including Brigham Young, who stated that upon hearing of the new doctrine, he "desired the grave."

Believing, however, that Joseph Smith had truly heard from the Lord concerning this principle, Young pushed his inhibitions aside and eventually married at least twenty-seven women. (Some historians claim it was a greater number.)

Brigham Young taught that plural marriage was the better mode of marriage for all concerned. Theoretically it enabled every woman to marry the man of her choice. There'd be no spinsters. There would be no "houses of ill repute." Every woman could have a respectable husband who would honor her.

In 1875, the U.S. government ramped up its efforts to abolish polygamy. The Latter-day Saints (LDS) Mormon Church properties were confiscated and many leading polygamists were fined and imprisoned.

Wanting their territory of Utah to gain U.S. statehood, the Mormons knew they'd have to abandon polygamy. Therefore, in 1890, the president of the LDS Church, Wilford Woodruff, signed and issued a "manifesto," which supposedly put an end to the "Principle." The government returned the confiscated properties to the church but denied statehood to Utah because polygamous marriages were still being performed by Mormons. As early as 1885, a safe haven of eight colonies had been established in Chihuahua and Sonora, Mexico, where the polygamists continued to carry on their religion, and after the 1890 manifesto, a few of the LDS officials secretly sealed many men to plural wives. As proof of this, in 1903, the LDS stake president in Mexico, Anthony W. Ivins, performed my grandparents Byron Harvey Allred and Mary Evelyn Clark's plural marriage, which was considered legal by the church. A second manifesto had to be issued by the sixth president, Joseph F. Smith, in 1904 to actually stop these marriages in the church. From that time forward, any member who entered into a union with more than one woman would be immediately excommunicated.

So, after that second manifesto of 1904, even two of the LDS's governing twelve apostles, Mathias Cowley and John W. Taylor, were punished because of polygamy. Most Mormons received the manifesto as the "word of the Lord," but a small minority rebelled. They still believed plural marriage was their ticket to heaven. They didn't think God would change the rules just so Utah could become a state! If they did not continue the practice, they feared damnation. So, polygamy went underground, and the polygamists began referring to themselves as "fundamentalists."

A few devout men determinedly kept plural marriage alive, regardless of the consequences—excommunication from the LDS Church and the possibility of being imprisoned.

In 1929, Lorin Wooley gathered quite a number of polygamists together. He then set up a "Council of Friends," which designated him as the presiding member. The seven men on the council were Lorin Wooley, J. Leslie Broadbent, John Y. Barlow, Joseph W. Musser, Charles Zitting, LeGrand Wooley, and the young Louis Kelsch.

As a child, I knew this story almost by heart. We had to understand the importance of this council. These men were given the commission to keep plural marriage alive, to help us all live in obedience to God's command. We memorized their names so we would know who we could contact later when we desired to enter into plural marriage.

Upon Lorin Wooley's death, J. Leslie Broadbent presided over the small group until he died shortly after his appointment. John Y. Barlow then took his place and promptly filled the two deceased members' positions by choosing LeRoy Johnson and Marion Hammon.

When I was a child, Louis Kelsch was our neighbor. We were taught to honor and revere him because of his important calling. We all loved him and even called him Uncle Lou. He had seven faithful wives and dozens of children who became my playmates. Four of his sons grew up and married four of my sisters. Uncle Lou was my father's best friend. Within our community, Uncle Lou was hailed as a prime example, a dedicated stalwart man who would lay down his life for his religion.

Also, Charles Zitting, a practicing polygamist with five wives, was a close neighbor. Children from the Zitting and the Kelsch families attended public school with us.

John Barlow died in 1951 and was succeeded by the elderly Joseph Musser. I'd met him on several occasions with my father. He was exalted as a "true champion of the gospel" and published the cherished *Truth* magazine, which polygamists looked forward to reading every month. The heads of all polygamist households faithfully read and expounded its teachings to their children.

My sisters and I read his magazine, savoring every word. Musser wrote eloquently about the sacrifices the polygamists had endured throughout the years. His writings buoyed us with resolve to carry on the sacred principle.

When Musser suffered a stroke and remained ill from its

effects, certain members of the Council of Friends questioned his ability to lead.

My uncle Rulon Allred (my mother's brother) was a naturo-pathic doctor who treated the sickly leader for months. Out of the blue, Musser called and appointed Uncle Rulon to the council. Bickering began among the members, and some accused Musser of being partial toward Uncle Rulon because of his extended care to their failing leader.

The council was further shocked when Musser surprised them by choosing Margarito Bautista, a Lamanite (a Book of Mormon Native American) from Ozumba, Mexico, to be an apostle. Educated in Mexico, Bautista had attended school in the Mormon colonies. He joined the LDS Church, where he received a calling to work in the temple in Salt Lake City. After intensive study, he recognized the changes that were taking place. His dissatisfaction came mostly from seeing the mutilation of the sacred garments. He knew they had been given by divine revelation from God. The pattern, cut, length, marks, strings, and collar all held symbolic meaning, and only those Mormons in good standing could receive them. He witnessed several other changes and decided to separate himself from the LDS Church. At age fifty, he returned to Ozumba, where, in a short period of time, he married several women; some of them were only fourteen or fifteen years old.

When the other members of the council refused to accept All-red or Bautista, Musser flexed his power by dissolving the council. He then formed another one, designating my uncle Rulon as his successor.

I remember the arguments and confusion among my relatives and friends, expressing their sorrow that Musser's actions had split the fundamentalists apart.

At his death in 1954, Musser had about a thousand polygamists who upheld his appointment of Uncle Rulon, whose group later became known as the United Apostolic Brethren.

Those who refused to accept Uncle Rulon's position as presiding elder clung to the men in the previous council, whose followers constitute the members in Short Creek, Arizona, today, now known as Colorado City.

They had filled Musser's place with Charles Zitting, but Zitting died a month later.

Hungering for power, LeRoy Johnson decided he would lead the group. He won them over after claiming that Christ had personally visited him. Those in the Short Creek group began to worship "Uncle Roy." One believing couple actually had a daughter who from birth was promised to him in marriage. At town celebrations and parties, the weak and shaky octogenarian leader was driven through the town. Throngs of devout members sought a special place on the periphery to wave to him as though he were the pope.

The adulation for the feeble leader heightened as each year passed. Every home displayed an eight-by-ten photo of their beloved prophet as though he were Christ. A plaque was hung in every home that read THE KINGDOM OF GOD OR NOTHING, indicating they were willing to die for what they believed.

In the early 1950s, there were an estimated thirty thousand polygamists in the U.S. About fifteen thousand followed either my uncle Rulon or LeRoy Johnson. The remaining numbers became independents. My father, Morris Q. Kunz, was one of hundreds of independents strung throughout the western United States and Canada.

Alma Dayer LeBaron Sr., who became my father-in-law, was the founder of Colonia LeBaron in Chihuahua, Mexico. After he died, two of his seven sons, Joel and Ervil, and their mother, Maud, plus a few others were baptized into the Allred group. A branch of that church was established in Colonia LeBaron, and

Alma Dayer LeBaron Jr. became bishop under the supervision of Margarito Bautista.

For a while, Ervil remained firm in the fundamentalist beliefs, but, oddly enough, two years later, in 1953, Joel asked to return to the Mormon LDS Church, from which he had been excommunicated. He was baptized by Bishop LaSelle Taylor, with Hector Spencer as the witness.

EVERY FUNDAMENTALIST GROUP has its own particular rules and mode of dress, and the members blindly follow their leader. Though some of their practices differ concerning the act of procuring wives, every group is convinced that they are a "peculiar people." (This idea comes from 1 Peter 2:9 in the Bible: "But ye are a chosen generation, a royal priesthood, an holy nation, a peculiar people; that ye should show forth the praises of him who hath called you out of darkness into his marvelous light.") Their sense of being persecuted emboldens them to believe they are God's only righteous people, chosen because of their dedication and adherence to plural marriage.

Though ostracized by the LDS Church, most fundamentalists believe the LDS Church is God's true church, which will someday be put in order. All groups wait expectantly for the One Mighty and Strong. Many feel that it will be Joseph Smith himself who will return to finish his work, setting God's house in order.

Four of my sisters were members of the Short Creek group. I yearned for them, often writing letters. When no reply came, I heard that they had been forbidden to associate with me because I had followed Uncle Rulon, not their leader, LeRoy Johnson.

I spent hours pondering the situation. I was in Mexico, separated from my twenty-nine siblings, my father, my mother, and my extended family. Loneliness overwhelmed me. My only comfort was my husband and half sister Charlotte. I longed to be a part of something, to have a social life, but mostly I wanted to have something to believe in.

In 1953, when Verlan married me, he had received Uncle Rulon's permission, who then appointed one of his members to perform our marriage. Uncle Rulon was pleased that we were loyal to him. He told me he had faith that Verlan would vindicate the LeBaron name.

I've seen radical polygamists' thirst for power. I've known several claiming to be the One Mighty and Strong. There were many fundamentalist splinter groups. Seeing men vying for power is like playing "Button-button, who's got the button." It amazed me how every leader seemed to use the same scriptures to prove his right to wield power over other people's lives.

THE LEBARONS CLAIMED that the highest priesthood office remained hidden from the LDS Mormons. They taught that Joseph Smith secretly passed this mantle on to his adopted son Benjamin F. Johnson, who in turn gave it to his grandson Alma Dayer LeBaron Sr., known as Dayer. He began his work as a loyal LDS Mormon, but after much study he became convinced that the LDS Church had given up the "saving principle" of plural marriage. He eventually married five women.

Dayer and two of his wives, Maud Lucinda MacDonald and Onie Jones, were excommunicated from the church because they became polygamists after the manifesto.

Maud gave birth to thirteen of Dayer's children: Irene, Ben, Wesley, Lucinda, Alma, Jenny (died in childhood), Esther, Joel, Ervil, Floren, Verlan, and twins Mary and David (died at birth). All the LeBaron children were baptized into the Mormon LDS Church even though their parents were excommunicated. Joel and Ervil became Mormon missionaries in the Mexican mission. However, while there they were excommunicated, along with two brothers, Ben and Alma, for promoting the fundamentalists' beliefs.

For several years, they had lived in Colonia Juárez, one of the eight Mormon colonies in Mexico. Dayer worked a few months at a time in the States. His second wife, Onie, became unwilling to carry on without him. Unable to handle the poverty and loneliness, she divorced Dayer and returned to Laverkin, Utah, with her six children. Ervil and Verlan remembered Aunt Onie kindly and kept in touch with her six children throughout the years.

We had been taught that the LDS Church was the only true church of God, but in 1890, when the church abandoned plural marriage, a great number of followers disagreed and felt the church was out of order. Section 85 of the Doctrine and Covenants spoke of the One Mighty and Strong who would appear in the last days to set the house of God in order.

The LeBarons, embittered by the rejection from their neighboring Mormons, felt spiritually superior. Shortly before his death, Alma Dayer LeBaron Sr., who claimed to hold the priesthood mantle of Joseph Smith, proclaimed he had had a vision. In it, the Lord told him that through his sons the whole world would be blessed.

Because of this prediction, Ben became the first son to make the claim to be the One Mighty and Strong. He tried to prove it before spectators in downtown Salt Lake City. Ben stopped his dilapidated black pickup at a red light. He wanted to impress a police officer whose car idled directly behind him. Ben despised authority. He had been at the mercy of every kind of authority all his life. He decided to prove to the smart-aleck cop behind him who had the most power. To the amazement of everyone stopped at the light, blond, six-foot-two, curly-haired Ben sprang from his truck, walked smack into the center of the intersection, lay down on the pavement, and then holding his long lean body stiff as an arrow, began doing push-ups. He counted, "One...two...three...four..." The light changed to green. Impatient onlookers blared their horns as Ben continued, "Ten...eleven...twelve...thirteen..."

The cop frowned as he got out of his car, asking his partner, "Do we have some kind of a nut here or something?" He stooped down close to Ben's face. "What are you trying to prove?" the officer asked disgustedly, holding his billy club on Ben's right shoulder.

Red-faced, straining for air, Ben paid no attention to the policeman—and never broke rhythm. The pandemonium from the blaring horns and angry citizens didn't faze him. He went right on counting, "Ninety-seven...ninety-eight...ninety-nine....one hundred!"

As he stood up, Ben's big silly grin insulted the officer, who asked a second time, "What are you trying to prove?"

"I did one hundred push-ups. That's more than you can do," Ben bragged. "So, that proves that I am the One Mighty and Strong."

Shortly thereafter, Ben was admitted to a mental institution. The following is an excerpt of a letter he wrote to my uncle Rulon from the Utah State Hospital.

They don't think I am sick mentally. They are holding me for believing in polygamy... you may think that I am kidding, but I always hear the voice of the Lord all the time. I never make any mistakes. I am as infallible and perfect in all my ways, as a little child is. I don't think so. I know so. The Lord has told me.

Strange as it may seem, he soon had two brothers following him, Ervil and Alma.

Ervil traveled to Ciudad Juárez on a mission for Ben. Ervil had convinced his prophet brother that a pamphlet needed to be published. The truthfulness of Ben's claims would be proven from the holy scriptures, then printed and distributed among the Mormons. Ervil had the smarts, so he declared himself the mouthpiece for Ben, just as Aaron had done in the Bible for his brother Moses. Ervil composed every page of the pamphlet. His only regret was that since he was the ghostwriter, Ben received all the honors.

Ervil and his brother Alma then enthusiastically distributed the pamphlet to the Mormons, declaring their brother Ben as a prophet of God. "Let it be known to every nation, tongue, and people, unto whom these words come, that God, the Eternal Father, by the power of the Holy Ghost, has given us a sure knowledge that our brother Benjamin T. LeBaron is...the Prophet unto whom all the nations of the earth must listen to in order to establish world peace and that by his word the Kingdom of God will be established upon the earth. We declare this solemnly in the name of Jesus Christ, and do not lie, God being our witness. This we prophesy by the power of the Holy Ghost and in the name of Jesus Christ."

Besides these two brothers, Ben's first and only convert was Joe Marston from Utah. No sooner had Joe been converted than God informed Ben that Joe was to become the sole supporter of the cause, which meant it would be his obligation to support Alma's and Ervil's families also. Joe felt like he had been slapped in the face by Ben. No God in his right mind would ask him to make such a sacrifice, especially when he was told to leave his own family in Mexico and return to the States so he could support everyone else. He had been taught from the Bible that every man should sit under his own vine and fig tree, and any man who would not support his family was worse than an infidel.

Joe had raised his eyebrows, questioning Ben when he'd claimed to hear the word of the Lord every ten minutes. In fact, the Lord revealed to Ben that his four young daughters should comb their hair according to the Lord's wishes. One daughter's hair would be parted down the middle, one parted on the left, one parted on the right, and one had her hair brushed straight back with no part at all. And, all girls had to have their hair braided.

Shortly after hearing the revelation regarding his new responsibilities, Joe left quietly during the night, taking his wife and their two children back to the States.

After Joe Marston abandoned Ben's congregation of three, the LeBarons were left alone. Depressed over Joe's rebellion, Ben suffered yet another mental breakdown.

Having witnessed Ben's ramblings, plus seeing firsthand that the devil had crowded God completely out of their new prophet, Alma and Ervil apostatized, but they held on to the Mormon revelation that the One Mighty and Strong would soon return. Their only hope was to live worthily, believing that someday in the near future this foretold prophet of God would return and set the house of God in order.

Ervil was disillusioned with his bipolar brother. Ben's weird ramblings became an embarrassment to him. Ervil had lost faith that his brother was the long-awaited foretold prophet who would set up God's kingdom.

After the fiery testimony that Ervil had distributed in Oaxaca, Mexico, he capitulated, severing all ties with his brother Ben.

We lived in such poverty that toilet paper was a luxury we could not afford. Ervil willingly donated Ben's now useless pamphlets to be used in the outhouse. The glossy printed pages were a bummer to use. For about a year, we tolerated the slick paper. I jokingly told all the brothers that when future publications were necessary to please use Charmin toilet paper.

Ben's claim marked the beginning of the LeBaron brothers' struggle for power and authority. And as time passed, I began to wonder if my parents' assessment of the LeBaron family was true after all.

CHAPTER TWO

I first laid eyes on Ervil Morrel LeBaron on August 28, 1953, when I arrived in a dust-covered pickup at the isolated LeBaron ranch in Chihuahua, Mexico. We drove past the corrals where Ervil was milking cows with Verlan. When Verlan realized I'd arrived, he beelined ahead of Ervil to welcome me home. Ervil didn't know I was his brother's second wife; Verlan wanted to keep this secret from his family. However, two brothers, Floren and Joel, knew of our marriage because Verlan had sent them to El Paso, Texas, to meet me and Floren's wife, Anna, and her two children at the bus station and bring us home.

Ervil joined his brothers at the truck. He was strikingly good-looking. His chiseled chin, blue eyes, and dark hair often drew second looks from women. And most people looked up to him—literally; he was two inches taller than his blond-haired, blue-eyed, six-foot-two brother Verlan.

American visitors were rare—maybe two or three a year—on the LeBaron ranch. I could sense Ervil's hunger for social contact, but Verlan suggested he finish the milking and leave for home, and we could visit tomorrow. It was late and Verlan knew we needed to retire. Nevertheless, I felt Ervil's disappointment.

Charlotte, a beautiful brunette, was my half sister and Verlan's first wife. She had moved from Provo, Utah, to Mexico to the isolated ranch with Verlan. I had married her husband on July 3, 1953.

We walked down the dirt path to where Charlotte and Verlan lived. The small clearing was surrounded by mesquite bushes. Just northeast of the house were two large cottonwood trees that stood out in the stark, barren view, their branches providing the only shade in sight.

I could not believe that the first two adobe buildings I saw near the corral were the "ranch." I felt I'd been lied to. There was just no way anybody in his right mind could call this isolated barren land, surrounded by mesquites, a ranch. I bristled at the thought of having to accept this primitive farm as my home and refuge.

The weather-worn adobe on the house was unplastered; the windows lacked glass in the wooden frames. A rickety, old wooden screen door sagged, partly hiding a homemade open door. Upon entering the house, I was shocked to see rough cement floors and bare, unadorned walls; there was no sink, no plumbing, only a table and four chairs, a cupboard, and wood cookstove in one corner near Charlotte's bedroom door, from which she came out to welcome me.

Verlan and I stepped back outside. He walked over to the only source of water I could see, beckoning me to follow, and began pumping the water from a cast-iron, long-handled pump that looked as though it had been borrowed from a John Wayne movie. I washed myself as best as I could in the cold gushing water, using a bar of soap, trying to rid myself of the dust that powdered my body. (The ride over the dirt roads had blown dust into the open cab, completely covering me from head to foot. My hair looked like a powdered wig. It wasn't quite the impression I had hoped to make on my new family, but it was definitely dramatic!)

Verlan could see my disappointment as I washed up, but he laughed, making light of the awkward situation. "We don't have electricity, but, see, we do have running water."

I stiffened at the shock of the cold water as I held my unbraided hair under the pump, gasping. Nevertheless, I lathered my hair, making sure I rinsed out all the accumulated dirt. I wrapped a towel around my head, flipped it back, and resumed washing my bare legs and feet.

Feeling at least somewhat refreshed, I followed Verlan back inside. By then night was falling, so he lit a coal oil lamp that sat on the wooden kitchen table. Then he led me into a small bedroom off the kitchen to the right. The only pieces of furniture in the room were a metal bed with woven springs and no mattress and a white painted kitchen chair beside the bed to be used for a nightstand. Verlan lit the wick on another lamp, then carefully replaced the glass chimney.

"This will be your lamp and your room," he told me. "And don't worry about the bed. The springs are woven. When you throw a blanket over them, you won't even miss the mattress."

My eyes scanned the bare adobe walls. There were no mirrors, pictures, or anything at all to beautify the rough adobe. It didn't matter that I didn't have a dresser; I owned just two changes of clothes, three bras, and a half dozen pairs of panties. I'd keep them in my small suitcase.

Meanwhile, Anna had gone with Floren, and Charlotte had retired to her bedroom.

It was such an awkward situation for me. I felt like an intruder in my husband's home. I cried to him when we finally settled down, and we quarreled over the situation. I demanded he find me some quarters elsewhere so I could have privacy, but he informed me that my sister and I would be living in the same three-room adobe house permanently.

He felt guilty about making love to me when he was in the same house with his other wife, so he refused—and preached to me instead. Verlan was only twenty-three, naive, and filled with dreams of grandeur. Attempting to make sure I understood his resolve, he said, "You're the key to my salvation, Irene. I'm in plural marriage now, and with your help I hope to obtain at least seven wives. If I do, I could possibly have fifty children." As his hopes rose, mine deflated. I asked myself if I was just a tool in furthering his quest for godhood. He gave me a *peck* good night, and, devastated to say the least, I quietly cried myself to sleep.

Humiliation flooded over me when I saw my sister the following morning at breakfast, especially when I knew she assumed I had made love to our husband in her house.

Later that day, I happened to overhear Verlan and Ervil's conversation from my bedroom off the kitchen. Ervil seemed to have a one-track mind. He quizzed Verlan for all the information he could get. "What's Irene doing down here?"

Verlan responded, "She's here to keep her sister company so she won't get too lonely."

"How old is she?"

"Sixteen. Actually sixteen and a half," he corrected himself, hoping it would later justify his marrying me at such an impressionable age.

"Who's responsible for her?" Ervil pried further.

"I am. She's under my jurisdiction."

Boy, was Ervil ever relieved. He thought he had found out all he needed to know. Euphoric, he leaned toward Verlan, who could see the excitement on Ervil's face as he smiled broadly and announced, "Last night, God gave me a revelation. Irene is to be my second wife!"

"Oh, no she's not!" Verlan snapped. "She's already mine."

Ervil flushed with embarrassment. "Aahh!" he sputtered, grasping for words. "I was just jokin'. Just jokin', that's all."

I always remembered that this was Ervil's first false revelation.

ANNA, A CONVERTED GERMAN GIRL from Utah, endured the craziness and hardships of Mexico just long enough to give birth to her third child, her second by Floren. She'd been married previously and brought a five-year-old son into the marriage. I envied Anna's spunk and convictions. When she left, she told me that a year in a foreign country with poverty and constant threats of polygamy made her departure easier.

I CONSIDERED MYSELF more or less the middle child, since I happened to be the thirteenth of my father's thirty-one children. Four generations of my family before me had practiced polygamy, so I thought plural marriage would be a piece of cake. After all, that's all I'd ever been exposed to.

Joseph Smith, the founder of the Mormon Church, claimed an angel with a drawn sword appeared to him, stating that if Smith didn't live in polygamy, he and his people would be destroyed. In the Doctrine and Covenants 132:61, I read "And again as pertaining to the priesthood—if a man espouse a virgin, and desire to espouse another, and the first give her consent, and if he espouse the second, and they are virgins, and have vowed to no other man, then he is justified; he cannot commit adultery with that which belongeth unto him and to no one else."

Verse 62 states, "And if he have ten virgins given to him by this law, he cannot commit adultery, for they belong to him, and they are given unto him; therefore he is justified."

I'd wrestled with my beliefs. I wanted a love of my own, someone who needed and cared for me. In my heart I longed to be the
apple of my husband's eye. I shuddered at the thought of another
woman fulfilling my husband's sexual needs. Yet, I'd been indoctrinated to believe that I had to give up all my "selfish" desires to
become a goddess. By living in plural marriage, I could one day be
exalted. I would give my husband numerous wives, which would
qualify him to become a god and rule over his own earth.

I respected Charlotte for her faithfulness and determination
in upholding polygamy. She held such a strong belief in plural
marriage that she told Verlan that if he wouldn't live that law of
the gospel, she wouldn't marry him. I wondered how she could
have actually given me to her husband in a ceremony, allowing
me to also be his wife. Even more, I wondered if I would be able
to do the same when the time came.

I WAS ALMOST a thousand miles from home, wondering if I'd ever
return to Utah to see my family again. As I mentioned, I'd actually
married Verlan without the knowledge of my father and mother;
both were very much against the LeBaron family. My father ranted
on and on each time I'd see him, insisting the LeBarons had insanity in their family. I was so hurt by his judgmental accusations that I
avoided him. My mother had divorced him when I was six. She bore
her own heartache and emotional scars from living in polygamy.

My relatives gossiped about Mother's failure to keep God's
commandments and the fact that later she'd married a "gentile"
(anyone who was not Mormon). To them it was unforgivable. I'd
been persuaded by my aunts that she had failed God by leaving
my father. I questioned if she would ever be exalted, having broken her marriage vows. I'd been taught that all women needed
a man to make it into heaven. A woman's husband was going

to be her savior. He would take her hand and lead her through the veil into heaven. By divorcing my father, my mother had no one to save her. Though I had seen her unhappiness and tears, I was all the more determined to step up to the plate and show God that I had it in me. Therefore, I didn't confide in my parents; I was married in a secret ceremony. I did, however, tell my older brother Richard, who promised to defend me and tell my mother that I had married Verlan and moved to Mexico.

REALITY HIT ME IN THE FACE when Verlan took me on a tour of the ranch. I hated what I'd seen of Mexico—sandy, barren hills and valleys full of mesquites. It was hard for my brain to compute the reality of the landscape. I'd held visions of a sprawling ranch, as I'd seen in Utah, with luscious green alfalfa fields, a large barn, and a big farmhouse surrounded by a white picket fence. The four other adobe buildings that I could now see looked worse than anything I'd seen in even the poorest parts of my hometown. The dry, hot August air was stifling. There wasn't a hedge or flower in sight.

I met Alma's wife, Luz, and Ervil's wife, Delfina. The two women chattered in Spanish, and I couldn't understand a word. Verlan interpreted the conversations. Both women were kind, but I detected suspicion in their eyes. They didn't know about my marriage to Verlan, and I was sure that any single girl on the ranch was a threat to them.

From across the yard, on the north side of the clearing, we heard incoherent jabbering coming from a small, two-room adobe hut. Before I could get too upset, Verlan quickly explained that the noises came from his sister Lucinda, who was detained in her own private cell. "She once was a plural wife who lost her mind several years ago. Come and meet her. She won't hurt you."

I'd never witnessed such an appalling situation. Lucinda, in her mid-thirties, half naked, and with uncombed, matted red hair, reeked with a foul odor. Seeing her jolted all my senses. How, I wondered, could anyone live in such a filthy cage? Could she ever get her mind back while living in such atrocious circumstances? I quickly withdrew, walking briskly ahead of Verlan. He caught up with me, laughing. "Hey, she won't hurt you. In fact, she said you were pretty."

Verlan's brother Alma had seen us from his adobe house close by. He was the only brother living there whom I hadn't met yet. As he sauntered toward us, I stood still waiting, with my hands on my hips. When Alma was close enough, he reprimanded me before Verlan had time to introduce me. "Nice girls don't put their hands on their hips," he said. And without further ado, he continued on his way.

"Is he crazy too?" I asked Verlan.

"Oh, no." Verlan laughed apologetically. "He's just a little different." He paused a moment before continuing. "I guess I'd better tell you before someone else does." He flushed a bright red as he spoke. "A couple months ago, Alma was deceived by our cousin Owen from Canada. He claimed that flying saucers were coming down to take both of their families to heavenly realms. Owen convinced his own two wives and children, and Alma, to run around the ranch naked. They paraded through the orchard then up on the foothills. Finally the Lord told Owen that the group should congregate on the roof of Alma's house and await the arrival of flying saucers. Joel was humiliated and in shock over their actions, so he notified the authorities."

Seeing the surprise on my face, Verlan tried to comfort me. "Hey, the police showed up before the saucers did." He laughed again. "Please forgive Alma. Since Owen returned to Canada, he's repented and seen the error of his ways." I couldn't help but wonder if maybe Alma still had a loose marble or two. I felt spooked around him. I began to understand why my father and mother did not want me in the LeBaron family.

OUR ONLY RECREATION was held five miles south of the ranch at Spencerville. My mother's second cousin, Aunt Sylvia, as we addressed her, was the second wife of Carling Spencer. They had lived in Mexico for eight years, where she cared for her aged husband and their dozen children.

Aunt Sylvia's poor living conditions troubled me. I watched as a pot of beans began to boil on her kitchen stove. She held a chipped blue enamel cup in her hand, which she used to scoop up the dead weevils as they floated to the top of the water that covered the beans. The longer the beans boiled, the more weevils floated to the top of the kettle. My stomach felt queasy, and I fended off my urge to vomit.

When Aunt Sylvia saw my ashen face, she laughed apologetically. "A little weevil won't hurt any of us. In fact"—she chuckled again—"it's a good source of protein. We're just lucky to have beans to eat."

Her undernourished goat produced only a pint of milk a day. Every bit was fed to the baby. The other small children watched eagerly as the baby was fed its cereal. When a blob of food fell onto the high chair tray, the hungry youngsters took turns licking it up. Aunt Sylvia didn't even own enough utensils or dishes to feed all the family at once. They had to take turns using what few small bowls she owned.

I watched Aunt Sylvia make wash soap from the fat of a butchered burro. Her kids were ragged, yet she kept them clean. I never heard a complaint from this woman. She showed gratitude for even the fresh air she breathed. Her one luxury was a small grape arbor that loaded with concord grapes each summer. Her kids kept them picked, hardly giving them time to ripen.

Though poor indeed, nonetheless, she graciously opened her home each Sunday for the four LeBaron brothers—Ervil, Alma, Floren, and Verlan—and their families, as well as others from the community, to meet together for worship. (Joel and his wife, Magdalena, lived in the mountains, too far away to join us.) We'd hook up horses to a four-wheeled wooden wagon, taking a pot of cooked beans and some homemade bread. We would hold Sunday meetings and then eat lunch together.

I'd longed for recreation, for social interaction, but when Verlan started courting Aunt Sylvia's seventeen-year-old daughter, Lucy, at the meetings, I literally wanted to die. At every opportunity, she shared her love for Verlan with the crowd, making sure both Charlotte and I knew she had been in love with him since she was ten. Verlan had asked Lucy to marry him before he proposed to Charlotte, but she'd refused. She told Verlan she *knew* she was to be his third wife. Therefore, she encouraged him to find two wives and then return for her, which he did. Lucy became wife number three in May 1955. My spirit had been broken by the poverty and hardships in Mexico. But when Verlan married Lucy, my heart broke as well. Less than a month after her wedding, Verlan brought her to our three-room adobe house to live with Charlotte and me.

CHAPTER THREE

From what I'd seen, Ervil did very little physical work on the ranch. When I mentioned it to Verlan, he told me that from the time he could remember, Ervil had always given orders and bossed his brothers around. With resentment in his voice, Verlan shared with me how Ervil gave commands to his siblings to draw heavy buckets of water from the well and water the orchards by hand. While they sweated away in the hot sun, he relaxed in the shade of a tree, sleeping or reading the scriptures. Many times he would walk through the orchard, following them around as he expounded pertinent Mormon beliefs. Ervil felt menial work was beneath him, but he kept tabs on the brothers, prodding them to keep working throughout the day, while he daydreamed of greater things. He would milk the cows only when he was forced to in an emergency or if his brothers weren't there.

When I suggested to Verlan that it was an injustice for Ervil to be so lazy while he slaved away, Verlan explained that Ervil thought he was better at delegating than digging ditches or carrying heavy buckets of water.

Ervil wore out his welcome with me when he'd come to my house and preach incessantly, no matter if I was busy or not. He'd follow me around when I went to the well for water, or to haul in wood for the stove, never offering a helping hand. He was too busy expounding the scriptures. It wouldn't have been so bad if he had just spilled out what he was trying to say and get it over with. But he'd tell me a story and then retell it in different words, quizzing me between sentences to determine whether I understood. "I'm not stupid," I'd tell him. "I certainly don't need you to explain it to me three times. Really . . . I got it the first time."

He never seemed to pay attention to my replies, and he would simply continue on with his rhetoric. I wondered if he preached to me just because he liked listening to himself talk and maybe to convince himself how knowledgeable he was.

Ervil's tall six-foot-four frame, and long legs and arms, made it almost impossible for him to find clothing in the right size. In the early days his Levi's were always too short. He rolled up the long sleeves on his shirt because the sleeves didn't extend far enough for him to be able to button them at his wrists. My eyes were often drawn to his sockless feet and ankles. One time, when his jeans were ripped in the crotch, though embarrassed, I brought it to his attention, offering to fix his pants. He apologized for exposing himself, explaining that he owned no shorts. On that occasion and another, I had him step into my bedroom and remove his torn Levi's. He handed them out through a crack in the door. I mended them and gave them back. In a way I pitied him, wondering why Delfina didn't mend for him; but I soon discovered she had no sewing supplies, a luxury the couple simply couldn't afford.

ERVIL'S DISSATISFACTION WITH HIS MEXICAN WIFE, Delfina, was constant. He complained to Verlan and me that he'd married beneath himself. The fact that his wife was a professing Catholic convinced him that God himself felt displeasure toward her. "After all," he announced, "the Catholic Church is referred to in the scriptures as the 'great and abominable church.'"

Even Verlan shook his head as Ervil continued. We couldn't believe how disparagingly he spoke of his tall, pretty wife and her beliefs.

"In a way," he said, "it's not her fault to be counted less worthy." He looked at me as he continued enlightening me. "It says in the Book of Mormon that the Lamanites—you know those are the Mexicans—became wild...full of adultery and filthiness. We've been taught that we can upgrade the race by marrying these native women, and producing 'white and delightsome children.'" He laughed. "We'll build up the race all right. We need people in the Kingdom of God, so if we can't convert 'em, we'll produce 'em. That's how we'll raise up righteous believers." He sounded determined. "I always wanted an American wife"— he glanced at me longingly—"but I never had the opportunity to court one." He looked at Verlan and said, "You were sure lucky, Verlan, because when you went to BYU you had a chance to find an American woman."

Relentlessly, he kept on telling us more than I wanted to hear. "The Mormons in Colonia Juárez mistreated us, didn't they, Verlan? We were ostracized because our father continued to live polygamy long after the Mormons gave it up. The LDS Church excommunicated our father when he married Aunt Onie. It was really hard on our family to be the town misfits. We were snubbed and shunned. Even during our school years, other Mormons were forbidden to associate with us. We had no sleepovers, we were never invited to any birthday parties, and we definitely never had the chance to court their daughters. These Mexican women are difficult to get along with. I could never imagine Delfina living in the same house with another woman like you and Charlotte do, Irene."

Changing the subject, he looked at me and said, "Yesterday, Delfina came home from your house crying."

"Why?" I cut in, surprised. "Did I offend her with my broken Spanish?"

"No." He laughed. "She got upset while she was visiting you in your bedroom. She swears she saw a pair of Verlan's pajamas tucked under one of your pillows. She says she knows something is going on between you two. If I admitted the truth and told her you were married to my brother, I'd have hell on my hands for sure. These Catholic women are so hotheaded and controlling. She'd never consider nor allow me to take another wife."

I could sense the jealousy in his voice. "Verlan, I can't believe you're so lucky. Two Americans...and both believers." He shook his head regretfully. His eyes met mine as he spoke. "I'd give anything to have two pretty wives like you and Charlotte."

His seething jealousy soon prompted him to take action.

Ervil revealed to us that three months earlier, he had met a Mexican girl in the mountains, pretty twenty-one-year-old Maria de la Luz, whom he had enjoyed flirting with. He had met her at a corn festival, where she reigned as queen. He lowered his voice confidentially and said, "I feel led by the Lord to go to the mountains and find her. If I can convert her to Mormonism, I'll ask her to marry me and become my second wife."

The next day, Ervil lied to Delfina, telling her he was going to do some missionary work in the mountains and to not expect him to return for at least two weeks. Disappointed and dejected that he was leaving her for so long, she walked him up to the main dirt road, where he caught a bus.

Two weeks later, while filling my water buckets at the cast-iron pump, I spotted Ervil with a pretty Mexican girl approaching the house. I couldn't believe my eyes. He'd actually done it!

I trudged back to the house with my heavy buckets as the

couple followed me inside. I positioned the buckets on the counter. Ervil introduced his shy bride. "This is Maria de la Luz, but I want her to be called Mary Lou."

I smiled, welcoming her into the house. Charlotte joined us from her bedroom; extending her hand she made the woman feel welcome. Ervil laughed nervously. "I'm depending on you both to keep quiet about this. I took this woman to Ozumba by bus, where I had her married to me by Brother Bautista's priesthood authority. I hope I can leave her here with you guys for a while until I can break the news and convince Delfina that this is the will of God."

Both Charlotte and I were surprised. According to our Mormon teachings, a man was supposed to get permission from his first wife to marry another one. It was her duty to place the new wife's hand in her husband's, thereby approving the marriage. I wondered how Ervil could be so brazen and insensitive to force his religion and plural marriage on his unsuspecting wife.

Ervil left his bag of soiled clothing with Mary Lou, requesting that she wash them, and he headed home to Delfina and their three small children.

Who was Ervil to impose by putting us in this awkward situation? Why would he get another wife when he couldn't take her home?! I knew it wasn't Mary Lou's fault, but her presence was a disruption to our demanding, though lifeless routine.

I could see Mary Lou felt like a fish out of water and I sympathized with her. It had been less than a year since I had arrived to live with Charlotte in secrecy. Although I completely identified with her situation, I was caught between a rock and a hard place. If Charlotte and I were accomplices in hiding Mary Lou from Delfina, we would be left without any friends, because I knew that Luz, Alma's wife, would side with Delfina. I wondered how long it would be before Ervil broke the news to her.

Ervil met Verlan coming from the corrals to the house, carrying a bucket of milk. Verlan spoke as he set the bucket down on the path, "I'm surprised to see you back. It's been two weeks, and I was wondering how long you'd be gone."

Ervil blurted out joyfully, "Well, Verlan, I've caught up with you. I have two wives now. I just left Mary Lou Vega at your home until I have the courage to tell Delfina. I need to work on her a few days to get her converted."

"Boy, you sure work fast," Verlan said. "What will you do if Delfina doesn't accept her?"

"Well, God definitely instructed me to marry her, so I'm sure he will help me explain my actions to Delfina."

"Good luck," Verlan said, picking up his bucket of milk.

As though Ervil was speaking to himself he said, "I don't know about my Catholic wife. She's never been touched by the Holy Ghost, and she needs to be in order to deal with plural marriage."

When Verlan brought in the milk for Charlotte to strain, he welcomed Mary Lou, asking her to join us in our evening meal of boiled pinto beans and hot tortillas. While we ate, Verlan began explaining the difficult situation to the new bride, trying to give her hope. "When Delfina gets over having a tantrum, we'll all get back to normal. I know it will be hard on her to accept you. She has fought the principle of plural marriage ever since she got married. But," he added, trying to justify Ervil's actions, "he has never lied to her about plural marriage. He always told her that he would live polygamy someday. So, in a way, he has tried to prepare her."

While Mary Lou offered to help Charlotte wash up a few dishes, Verlan had me accompany him outside in the dark to the woodpile. I'd barely extended my arms for him to start stacking the chopped mesquite branches in them, when, from the distant darkness, we heard strange cries through the night. "Is it an animal howling?" I asked, frightened. Bracing ourselves, we both listened.

"It's Delfina," Verlan exclaimed. "It sounds like she's lost it. Let's go over there before she flips out."

The incessant, wailing cries of sheer agony troubled me.

Her bloodcurdling screams of anguish wrenched my soul. I'd never heard anyone cry out in such wretched despair. Verlan ran ahead. I followed at his heels as the wails grew more distressing. Outside Ervil's two-room unplastered adobe hut, we both encountered Delfina thrashing violently, trying to free herself from Ervil's grasp. "Let me die!" she screamed again and again. Trying to get away from Ervil, she grabbed Verlan for security and comfort. Verlan's consoling words were drowned out by her sobbing gasps of complete devastation.

In spite of the darkness, I could see Delfina's wild, wounded spirit. Her countenance made me think of a frightened, snared animal trying to free itself. By now, I, too, was crying tears of sadness. I could barely tolerate polygamy and I was the product of four generations. How could Delfina, who had never been taught this principle, even begin to comprehend it? I wondered, because I was still trying to come to terms with it myself.

Verlan ordered me to go home. He wanted to spare me the pain of witnessing Delfina's mental breakdown. He could tell by her bizarre behavior that this wasn't going to be resolved anytime soon. Obediently, I started for home. Verlan's crazed sister, Lucinda, had joined in the unintelligible commotion from her nearby cell. I heard her garbled ranting mingled with Delfina's, like an eerie chorus. Disconcerted, I stopped walking and stood still.

"Go on home!" Verlan commanded. "Do what I tell you!"

Traumatized and shaken by the event that had just taken place,

I obediently headed for home down the rocky path. It was my night with Verlan, so I crawled into bed, anticipating his return. Tears flowed...tears of anger...tears of hopelessness. Why is it, I asked myself, that the gospel brings so much pain to women? Between God and these men, I concluded, a woman had no recourse. It was always their way or hit the highway.

I heard Verlan entering the kitchen. He went into Charlotte's room to tell her about Delfina's breakdown. He briefly told her in English so the new bride would not understand. He had decided to let Ervil deal with Mary Lou tomorrow. He kissed Charlotte good night, then wearily came to bed with me.

Disheartened, he said, "I had to help Ervil force Delfina into the rock feed house. She was so violent, actually spitting and biting. We shoved her inside to keep her under control. I guarded her while Ervil went to his house to get a couple of blankets and a pillow for her to sleep with on the cement floor."

"Is she going to be okay?"

"Yes, the door is chained and padlocked so she can't escape. Boy, did she ever put up a fight. I hope by morning she'll get a hold of herself and come to her senses. It'd be a shame if we had another Lucinda on our hands."

Too shocked by the frightful experiences and overwhelmed with grief, I barely kissed Verlan good night and turned over. It suddenly occurred to me that out of three plural marriages, two women were already locked up. Statistically speaking...things were *not* looking good!

After a week of incarceration, confined in the darkened room—the only light came from between the cracks in the door—Delfina showed no progress at all toward recovery. She jabbered incoherently, mumbling through her tears in utter hopelessness. Ervil asked his brother Alma to drive Delfina and him four hours south to Chihuahua City to Delfina's parents' home. He figured they might have some idea as to what to do with her. "I can't deal with her right now, especially when I'm still honeymooning with my new wife. I want no part of the dilemma," he informed Alma. Ervil took their three small children with them so his mother-in-law could care for them.

Before Ervil and Delfina left, he explained to Verlan the urgency of getting her out of the colony. He knew now that Delfina, like Lucinda, was possessed with several demons. He claimed he had actually had to fight off a few of them as he restrained her. "It's easy to understand that when a person gives in to their jealous spirit it gives Satan a chance to take them over. This is really Delfina's fault because she wouldn't accept the gospel, so I'm going to let her family deal with her."

In Chihuahua City, Ervil stayed long enough to make sure his wife was admitted to a mental hospital. We had no idea it would be nearly five months before she returned home.

CHAPTER FOUR

I was eight months pregnant with my second child. Having lost my first baby in a home delivery, I longed to be delivered by a doctor in Casas. I voiced my fears one day to Verlan in Ervil's presence. I thought maybe if Ervil heard my concerns he would speak up, defending me. I asked Ervil, "Don't you think it's better for me to go to the hospital than to take another chance on losing my baby?"

Verlan cut in. "You know there's no need to worry. Every mother on earth has gone through the pain and uncertainty of childbirth. I promise you will be okay." Then he joked, "Believe me, you don't need to worry, because it will all come out in the *end*."

Mr. Know-it-all Ervil, who seemed to be the ultimate authority on any and every subject butted in. "Having a baby is no big deal," he said, looking directly into my eyes. "I've seen Delfina give birth three times. It's no worse than getting your finger smashed."

I became riled. How dare he take my fear so lightly! Where was his compassion? He seemed so insensitive; I couldn't help but lash out at him. "Well," I said sarcastically, "the next time

Delfina has a baby, we'll *both* be there. And every time she has a labor pain, I'll personally put your thumb on an anvil and smash it with a hammer. Each time you scream out in pain, I'll tell you, 'It's no big deal!'"

Ervil was shocked. "You're so outspoken! I wonder how Verlan allows it."

I hated to be put down, but I could see I was outvoted, so I stomped off to my bedroom, where I had a good cry. I wanted to argue with both brothers, but I knew I would be in big trouble with Verlan if I continued to voice my opinion. Since not being obedient invariably caused repercussions, I decided to remain silent. I feared he would make me forfeit my night with him as punishment. He didn't appreciate my sarcasm, especially in front of his brothers.

How clear it became to me, as my tears flowed, that women have no rights! It looked to me as though we were just the breeding stock that kept the movement expanding and alive.

WE SAW MY BROTHER-IN-LAW JOEL only every month or so. He dropped by the ranch while hauling loads of produce from the mountains where he lived with his wife, Magdalena. He bought and then resold beans, potatoes, and corn. It was a real pleasure to see him each time he came. He had such a pleasant personality and always seemed so upbeat.

On the other hand, I always felt very uneasy around Ervil. I deliberately stayed away from him. Somehow, I knew he would still try to take me for his wife if he ever got the chance. He was far too friendly, so I avoided him whenever possible.

I'd never felt really close to Alma either. He was nice enough, I guess, but he was just so odd.

Needing someone to converse with, I turned again to poor,

crazy Lucinda. At least she didn't judge me. Since she couldn't remember much or tell a story straight anyway, I went up to her window often—her door was locked. The interior of her adobe hut was appalling. The dirt floors stank of urine and excrement. Only one room had roofing. The other had a meshed web of chicken wire, tightly nailed down over it to keep her in while the sun could shine in for light.

More often than not, I'd find Lucinda stark naked, sunbathing. At times she'd act so irrational that deep down I really was afraid of her, but my heart went out to this neglected soul. She needed someone she could depend on, so I made my visits to her almost daily, in spite of my misgivings.

One particular day, I stood close to the barred window of two-by-fours and greeted her with a friendly smile. Six months pregnant, I decided to share the news with Lucinda, hoping she wasn't incoherent. I smiled as I rubbed my bulging tummy with one hand, displaying the good news. "Look, Lucinda," I bragged contentedly. "I'm going to have a baby."

She laughed, flipping her matted strawberry blonde hair without responding. Without warning, she became angry and screamed, "You stole my cold cream and never gave it back!"

"No," I said, lowering my voice to calm her. "That must have been your sister Irene or someone else. It wasn't me."

She shook the wooden bars with her large strong hands, laughing, almost sneering at me. There was a wild animal look in her eyes.

"Lucinda, I've never done anything to hurt you," I said, trying to calm her.

Before I could back away, I felt the joy and words wrung out of me. Lucinda had thrust her long freckled arms through the bars and grabbed me by the throat. Her deadly fingers were choking the breath out of me. I fought to release myself from her imprisoning clutches. She laughed crazily, grinning with sheer delight, shrieking, "I am going to kill you and you'll be resurrected tomorrow."

Frantically I pried her long fingers away from me and, exhausted from the struggle, leaned on the adobe hut just long enough to get my breath, then ran to the corral where Verlan was milking the cows.

He had heard the commotion. He could see I was crying as I approached, yet he still asked, somewhat irritated, "What is it this time?"

"Lucinda grabbed me by the throat!" I cried, still gasping. "She said she'd kill me and I'd be resurrected tomorrow!"

Verlan just laughed while he checked the bruise marks on my neck. "Stay away from her, Irene. It looks like she's still plenty dangerous." And he went right back to his milking.

He might have been used to Lucinda's madness, but I was so upset I went two full years without talking to her again. During all this time she'd call out to me as I walked across the yard. Traumatized by her actions, I refused to go anywhere near her.

CHAPTER FIVE

Lucinda had once been a second wife to John Butchereit. Shortly after the birth of her third child, she suffered a nervous breakdown. Her German husband, not wanting the Utah authorities to discover he was married to her, asked her father, Dayer, to come rescue her and their children and take them to Mexico. Because this was only the latest in a string of mental breakdowns she had suffered since the age of sixteen, her brothers gave up hope of her ever recovering.

The twins—Joseph and Joan—and Maudie, were Lucinda's three children. They grew up on the LeBaron ranch, where they lived with their grandmother Maud. Later she decided to go to the States, where she could earn money as a piano teacher and help support Alma, Ervil, and Lucinda.

After their grandmother's departure to Las Vegas, Lucinda's children were passed back and forth between Alma's and Ervil's wives. The kids essentially became slaves to their uncles' families. They carried heavy buckets of water to both houses from the well, about fifteen yards south of their adobe huts. Joseph chopped the mesquite branches, stacking them for firewood.

Daily he herded thirty or more goats up to the rocky, cactus-covered hillsides, where they scrounged for sustenance.

The colony had no electricity, so the children—all of us, really—suffered from the heat in the summer and the cold in the winter. The homes had no indoor plumbing or running water, but flies, mice, rats, cockroaches, and pesky bedbugs could be found at every address.

The children visited their insane mother, Lucinda, regularly, taking her a plate of food three times a day. They hauled her water to bathe with and to drink. They were used to seeing her naked, sunbathing in the one room that wasn't roofed.

Maudie and Joan tended to the babies, washed dishes, and scrubbed clothes and pressed them with heavy irons that were heated on the stove. They had very little time for play, and, even worse, while they worked they listened to Ervil's and Alma's endless hours of rhetoric...polygamy and priesthood, priesthood and polygamy.

Verlan told me when Maudie and the twins were young, he chanced upon the three playing under a tree in the nearby orchard. He thought they were probably playing "house" or "cowboys and Indians." He listened for a moment, hearing them bickering among themselves as to what role each should play. Verlan said Joseph got hot under the collar because he insisted that he, not Joan, should be Jesus Christ. He said, "I'll be Jesus Christ this time, and you can be the One Mighty and Strong. And, Maudie," he added, "you can be the Holy Ghost."

Maudie piped up, whining in her own defense, "It's not fair! I had to be the Holy Ghost last time."

When I arrived at the ranch, I learned that the twins had never been to school. Verlan informed me that his mother had been trying to teach them to read. Their text was the Book of Mormon.

Wanting to help further their education, I offered to listen to Joseph read. He never missed a word for the first three paragraphs. "I, Nephi, having been born of goodly parents..." He read on until he got to the fourth verse.

"Go ahead," I said. "Let's continue."

He ducked his head in embarrassment. "I don't know that verse yet."

It was then that I realized he couldn't read at all. He had memorized the verses as he listened to Grandmother read to him.

When I began reciting nursery rhymes to the children, they giggled and laughed excitedly, begging to hear more. I soon learned that they had never heard a nursery rhyme in their lives. They were mesmerized by my rendition of Cinderella, Sleeping Beauty, and other fairy tales. Though I was only five years Joseph and Joan's senior, they respected me and soon adopted me as their mom. Still today, they call me Mother and introduce me as such. My heart really went out to these poor, abandoned children.

CHAPTER SIX

As far back as the family could remember, Verlan's father, Dayer, had claimed Joseph Smith's priesthood mantle, which his grandfather, Benjamin F. Johnson, had supposedly handed down to him. The final one to hold the mantle would prepare the people for the Second Coming of Jesus Christ and lead them into Christ's presence.

Frequently, the older boys, Ben and Wesley, who lived in Salt Lake City, had cajoled their aging father, each vying for the coveted mantle, hoping to have it conferred on them.

Once my uncle Owen (Rulon's younger brother) wrote to Floren. In the letter, he stated that Dayer had no authority and never would. Floren claims that he read the letter to his sickly father as he lay in bed, to which Dayer responded decisively, "I want you to understand that I do have some authority through the mantle my grandfather conferred upon me. The day will come when we will take the lead over the Allreds and everyone else."

Eventually Joel claimed he had received the mantle just before his father passed away on January 19, 1951. In early September 1955, thirty-two-year-old Joel boarded a second-class bus in the mountains, intending to come to the ranch to visit his brothers.

Shortly after he had taken his seat, he got the surprise of his life. Jesus Christ appeared to him and in no uncertain terms told him to go to Salt Lake City and incorporate a church in which he would be the One Mighty and Strong. It was to be called the "Church of the Firstborn of the Fullness of Times." After personally having a one-on-one with Jesus, Joel thought he knew what was required of him. He was cautioned to tell no one about his miraculous encounter or the instructions he'd received. I often wondered if Christ knew the future slogan "Save the Fuss and Ride the Bus."

Our first hint that there was trouble in Utah's land of Zion was a letter Aunt Sylvia received. Our Sunday gathering was interrupted when she read the shocking words to us. According to the eyewitness who had penned the letter, Joel's countenance had become black and he had started a church. In fact, the next paragraph depicted Joel as a man gone mad. The writer declared that Joel had been cursed by the Lord himself. Just like in the Bible, Joel had been given the curse of Cain.

The room buzzed with statements of disappointment, disbelief, and judgment.

"Joel, of all people!" Aunt Sylvia commented. "Starting a new church? Why, he always seemed to be the least religious of all the LeBaron boys."

Ervil and Verlan voted to adjourn the Sunday meeting. "There's no use to even pray this morning," Ervil stated matter-of-factly. "I'm sure with the displeasure God's feeling toward this sinful act of Joel's, our praises and petitions wouldn't ascend to God's throne." They all knew Joel could not be the prophet that would usher in the millennium.

Verlan hurried us to the horse-drawn wagon to escape our weekly gathering. He was shocked, appalled, and also questioning Joel's sanity.

Our five-mile ride over dirt roads only compounded our sorrow. Every time the wagon wheel hit a rut, we felt the jolt to our very bones and each bump felt like a punch in the stomach. Verlan was quiet, so I had time to think.

My esteem of the LeBaron brothers seemed to be falling faster than the temperature ever could. The two years I had lived among the LeBaron clan had intensified feelings of great dissatisfaction in my religious life. Not only were Joel's claims a disappointment, but so were his older brothers Wesley's and Ben's. Before my marriage in Salt Lake City, I'd personally seen Ben bodily thrown out of my uncle Rulon's fundamentalist meeting because he had stood up and shouted to the crowd, announcing publicly that he was God's anointed prophet, the long-awaited One Mighty and Strong.

I couldn't understand how both Ervil and Alma had been convinced of Ben's profession to be favored by God. Both brothers grew up witnessing Ben's recurring mental breakdowns. Throughout their childhood, they had often heard Ben claim that a voice in his head guided him. It was incomprehensible to me how two brothers had defended Ben when he claimed to be the Lion of Judah. They often heard him roaring like a lion to demonstrate how powerful he was. Thank goodness Ervil and Alma became disillusioned when none of Ben's prophecies materialized. But then Alma had embarrassed the family two years earlier when he had paraded around the ranch nude with his cousin Owen, and then waited for flying saucers to take them into heaven.

That Sunday evening, Alma and Ervil came to our home to discuss the disgracefulness of Joel's claims. Ervil, taking the floor first as usual, ranted as he pounded his fists on the kitchen table. Charlotte, Lucy, Verlan, and I could see his disgust (Lucy had barely married Verlan).

"Joel's nuts!" Ervil stated. "He holds no special priesthood. How can he claim to be the great prophet of God? I am so crushed over this devastating news. I feel worse than if I had received word that Delfina and all my children were killed in a car wreck."

Alma jumped up from his chair, taking his place beside Ervil. He pounded his left hand with his right fist, bellowing, "He absolutely has no power at all! I was once deceived by Ben, and it will never happen to me again." His smirk vanished as he announced, "A smart rat doesn't get caught in the same trap twice."

Verlan agreed with his brothers. "Joel is making outlandish claims that will continue to disgrace our family. Thank God our dear father is dead. He's probably turning over in his grave at what Joel is professing."

We women remained silent. We were too confused to articulate our feelings. Besides, even if we had wanted to speak, the three brothers didn't pause between their sentences. Still, I couldn't help remembering how even Mother Maud had said it was impossible for her husband, Dayer, to have given Joel the mantle to succeed him, because Dayer had been much too sick before his death to anoint anyone.

Later, both Charlotte and I begged Verlan to move us back to the States, where we could live a normal life. I didn't want any entanglement in any other priesthood authority. After generations of polygamy, I felt I could not be wrong; we had the truth. I felt the Mormon Church was God's true church. Though it was out of order because it had given up plural marriage, I felt someday we'd all be members of it when the church was put back in order again. I would not waver from my faith. I wanted no part of Joel's new church or his claim to be the prophet that would gather and redeem the elect from the four corners of the world.

A FEW NIGHTS LATER, through the darkness, Verlan's voice startled me. "Irene, you and Lucy wake up." I turned over as he struck a match and removed the glass chimney from the oil lamp. "C'mon, girls, sit up," he ordered. He lit the wick, turning it up a little higher so the lamp would burn more brightly, then he replaced the chimney. When my eyes adjusted to the light, I realized Charlotte and Floren had entered the room with Verlan.

"What's going on?" I asked, concerned. "Is something wrong?"

I could hear the excitement in Verlan's voice when he answered. "No, Floren just returned from the States and he wants to share something with us." Verlan grabbed two wooden chairs from the kitchen for Charlotte and Floren to sit on. Verlan instructed Floren to position himself next to me at the head of the bed, where he could sit and see better from the lamp's light.

Floren began. "Listen carefully, all of you, and don't say anything until I'm finished. Joel has received a revelation from God." Floren's shocking words hit me like a thunderbolt. "Thus saith the Lord, unto my servant Rulon C. Allred..."

Good grief, I thought. *Don't tell me Joel is actually receiving revelations from God. Why doesn't God respect Uncle Rulon enough to give the revelation directly to him?* I felt my heart falling to the floor with each word. I could see that my mother's misgivings about the LeBarons were coming true. Floren continued:

"I have called my servant Joel F. LeBaron out of the land of Mexico, even as I called my servant Moses, that through him I might deliver my people from bondage...And I call you by mine own voice out of the heavens to be a counselor to my servant Joel...Whereby my people may gather to the place I have appointed to be a land of Zion unto them, even the place known as Colonia LeBaron...The time has fully come spoken of by mine holy prophets, when I have set my hand again the second time to gather my people to Zion...that my people might be prepared to be caught up into the clouds while fire and brimstone are rained upon the face of the whole earth, to the utter destruction of the wicked and ungodly. Even so, amen."

When he finished reading, I was completely nauseous. *First it's Ben who received daily revelations, but never wrote them down. And now, here is Joel, blatantly declaring the word of God to the whole world.* I cringed. *What on earth will Uncle Rulon think when he hears that Joel is claiming revelation for him?* Floren's enthusiastic rendition convinced all of us that he believed every word of it. The final warning, *all will be caught up in fire and brimstone*, unsettled me.

All of us were in shock except Floren. He grinned proudly. "Isn't this wonderful? When Joel first read this revelation to me, a sense of joy went through me. After all the years of prejudice and ostracism we LeBarons have endured, this revelation proves the favor of the Lord. Father said it would be his boys who would help usher in the Kingdom of God, so Joel does have the mantle!"

Numb with disappointment, I slid down in bed, pulling the covers over me.

"Well, you can all sleep on this and we'll discuss it tomorrow," Floren said, folding the revelation and tucking it in his shirt pocket. Floren left Verlan alone with us three wives. None of us said much.

Verlan shook his head sadly. "I am as shocked as you girls are. This will be one more strike against our family." He fell to his knees beside the bed for prayer, and Charlotte joined him. Lucy and I lay quietly as Verlan made supplication to God, explaining that we did not understand what was taking place. He finished the prayer, saying, "We need guidance and mercy. Amen."

CHAPTER SEVEN

I'll never forget Joel's return to the ranch. I could see his skin was not black, but after what we had heard, his manners were suspect. I scrutinized his every move. I would focus on his facial expressions, then mentally judge every word he uttered. I'd tell myself repeatedly, "He sure doesn't look like a prophet to me." He really wasn't educated or well read. How could God set up his kingdom with a guy who looked like a hayseed that had blown in from the sticks? Searching desperately in my mind to find any godly qualities I could attribute to him, I came up short. I wondered if Abraham and Moses were such common men. I tried to be open-minded, but when he ate lunch with us, I was absolutely shocked. How a prophet of God could take large gulps of milk from his glass, swish it around his mouth to clean his teeth, then swallow it was beyond me. Maybe what he lacked in social graces would be replaced by God's holy anointing.

We were taken aback when Joel solemnly confided in his disbelieving family that he had stood in the presence of heavenly beings.

When my stunned mind finally registered his claim, I asked him, "How did you know they were real?"

"Oh, it was easy," he said nonchalantly. "Each one of them offered me his hand and introduced himself." He continued, hoping to enlighten me further. "If a resurrected being appears, you must give him the acid test. Joseph Smith taught his followers this secret. If the heavenly being is resurrected, you will be able to feel his hand, but if the being is from the devil, you'll feel absolutely nothing."

I couldn't believe how fast Joel's church took shape. He soon convinced his mother, Alma, and Ervil that just before his death, Joel's father had blessed him with the priesthood office that had come down from Joseph Smith to Benjamin F. Johnson, his adopted son, then to Alma Dayer LeBaron Sr., who had given this so-called mantle to Joel.

On April 3, 1956, 120 years after the supposed mantle was given to Joseph Smith, the new Church of the Firstborn of the Fullness of Times was formally organized with: Joel the prophet, Alma the bishop, and Ervil the mission president, later becoming the patriarch. They proceeded to research every scripture and historical event that backed up Joel's new teaching. Soon, they published a tract called *Priesthood Expounded*. In it, their mother, Maud, and Ervil testified that they had witnessed Joel's receiving the mantle that made him the One Mighty and Strong, somehow forgetting that they had observed no such thing.

The tract stated that Joel's father called him to his bedside and gave him a very strict solemn charge. He then put all his earthly affairs in Joel's hands. He put him under a covenant and made him promise to carry on the work his father had commenced and to build on the foundation he had laid. Dayer said to him, "When I die, my mantle will fall upon you even as the mantle of Elijah fell upon Elisha, and even as the mantle of my grandfather fell upon me; and you will have to round up your shoulders and bear it because there is no one else qualified. I have tried to qualify your older brothers, but have only met with rebellion and opposition."

After having said these things, Dayer told Joel that great things would be required of him, but the Lord would uphold and strengthen him and give him wisdom to solve the many problems that would come before him in carrying out his life's work. He also gave him the promise at that time that "he would not fail."

I knew these claims were absolutely false because Verlan had explained his father's last days to me, stating that at least a month before Dayer's death, he was partially paralyzed and bedridden. Maud and her two granddaughters had spoon-fed the old man because he was completely incapable of even raising his arms. Though this was the case, and they knew it, Maud and Ervil allowed their testimonies to be published in the revised edition of *Priesthood Expounded* (pages 57–58).

No one was more shocked than I was when I read their account. I blew up at Verlan as I refreshed his memory. Verlan, his mother, Maud, and I had stood by my wooden gate, where Verlan had told her Joel was in Salt Lake City, claiming he held the "scepter of power," which his father had given him. Tears ran down her cheeks as she listened. After a moment she had said to Verlan, "He must be crazy! You've got to go to Salt Lake and bring him home. If he's making these claims, then I must have another Ben in the family. You and I both know that your father was far too sick and paralyzed to give anyone anything. So, Joel's making false claims."

Verlan agreed that his family was contradicting what they had first declared.

AS SOON AS JOEL INCORPORATED THE CHURCH of the First-born of the Fullness of Times, in Salt Lake City, he received the revelation Floren had read to us, but it was the only one he ever recorded. Joel claimed the revelation was from the Lord God himself and was directed to my uncle Rulon Allred, who had several thousand followers. It was meant to convince him and his group to follow Joel and gather in Mexico to the new ensign, a model community for the world.

Naturally, when Uncle Rulon received the revelation, he ignored the outrageous instructions. He considered it just one more piece of evidence of insanity in the LeBaron family.

NOEL PRATT WAS JOEL'S FIRST CONVERT outside the family. The LeBarons had been acquaintances with his father in Colonia Dublán. He helped Joel and Ervil formulate sixty tricky questions, which became Joel's challenge to the world and backed up his priesthood claims, such as who is the promised seed of the prophet Joseph Smith, through whom the kindred of the Earth are to be blessed? He claimed that if anyone could answer his questions and prove him to be wrong, he would retract his claim to be God's newly appointed prophet.

Verlan was not excited about it. Charlotte, Lucy, and I just knew he couldn't be a prophet like Moses as he claimed.

Before long, because of arguments over religious interpretations, Noel felt he could no longer trust Ervil. He was both one of the first converts, and one of the first defectors, of Joel's church.

WHAT A COMMOTION BILLY WISER caused. He was the second convert to be baptized in the emerging church. Joel's father had prophesied that God would send people from the four corners of the earth to help build up Zion and prepare people for Christ's Second Coming.

Accepting Billy into the new church only verified Joel's role as a true prophet. It was actually Ervil who had converted him. While driving with Alma, he felt impressed by the Lord to stop for a hitchhiker ahead of them. With the forty-year-old disheveled stranger sandwiched between the two brothers, they learned he was a convicted forger who had served his time and was now traveling with no particular destination in mind. Ervil invited him to go to Mexico with them.

They were both jubilant that after twelve hours of driving they had found this man who had been humbled by his sufferings in prison and was now so interested in and open to the teachings of God. Billy was especially elated when Alma revealed the law of plural marriage as a requirement for being a god.

"I hope this principle of having to accumulate numerous wives doesn't shatter your faith," Alma joked.

Billy laughed. "That won't be too hard. I've lived with many different women. Of course none of my relationships panned out. I'll commit, though—if obedience is a requirement for women also. But," he said, shaking his head doubtfully, "no woman ever obeyed me before."

Upon their arrival at the ranch, Ervil asked Alma to drop Billy and him off at his mother's.

After introducing Billy, Ervil asked her to give him a place to stay and feed him for a couple of days so he could figure out what duties to assign him. Ervil shared his excitement with his mother about the faithfulness of God. They now had seven members in the newly formed church.

Ervil appointed Billy to be his bodyguard. His new position gave him an exaggerated sense of importance. He was a braggart, a rough, crude character who toted a .38 pistol. I distrusted the ex-convict. As far as I could see, he didn't have an ounce of godliness in him.

Ervil tried to reassure me. "He may not look like a saint, but God can use him mightily."

It didn't take long for Billy to resent Ervil's cockiness and his constant lies to Delfina and Mary Lou. He began to see Ervil as the con man he really was. After a heated altercation with Ervil, he hitchhiked back to the States, and we never saw him again.

JOEL'S EFFORTS AT PROSELYTIZING were easier than he'd imagined. In Moab, Utah, he'd stopped at a small grocery store for a few refreshments. At the counter, Joel paid and then started a conversation with a bald, rotund, sixty-five-year-old man who was also shopping. Lewis F. Ray, a single, lonely man who longed for attention, listened intently as Joel and he stood outside drinking their Cokes. Joel held nothing back. He announced to the nonpracticing Mormon that he was a prophet of God. Mr. Ray was fascinated by Joel's sincerity, by the fact that he revealed to a total stranger that he was the long-awaited One Mighty and Strong. Mr. Ray, like many dissidents from the LDS Church, had been patiently waiting for this "One's" arrival.

So, Mr. Ray became an instant believer. He begged Joel to spend the night at his house, where the two men packed Mr. Ray's few belongings into a small car. Mr. Ray testified that God had sent Joel to his rescue to help him make his move to Mexico. He voiced his exhilaration that he had found God's anointed.

Mr. Ray was filled with anticipation. He had not only met a bona fide prophet, but he was headed to Zion, where the saints would be gathered. He felt fortunate, knowing that he would escape Babylon before it all went up in smoke, destroyed with fire and brimstone.

Brother Ray boarded with me until his one-room house was built. His wooden floor seemed such a luxury. Everyone else's in town was either dirt or cement. He thanked God he had a Social Security check.

The LeBaron brothers bragged they had converted three out of three strangers.

JOEL PREACHED IN SOUTHERN UTAH, mainly in St. George and Hurricane. With his newfound confidence and his recent revelation in hand to back up his claims, he spent days upon end with a few cousins and acquaintances. He convinced them that the LDS Church had apostatized. A few of those who listened to him were fundamentalists who were considered misfits in the LDS Mormon community because they were practicing polygamy. All had one thing in common: they were awaiting the arrival of a foretold prophet who was the One Mighty and Strong.

Joel held his audience captive for eight to ten hours at a time. He talked about his new priesthood order and the end time prophecies, instilling fear and uncertainty within the listeners. With urgency in his voice, he pleaded with them to flee immediately to Mexico to the LeBaron colony, where God had promised them safety. A determined few became converted. They were told to sell all they had and move to the new Zion.

Shortly after Joel's return to the ranch from the United States, he moved Magdalena from Gómez Farías to Colonia LeBaron, which would be the designated headquarters for his newly incorporated church.

In late summer, we received a surprise visit from Joel's new investigators. They arrived in three different vehicles. All fifteen men came from Utah with one goal in mind: to find out if Joel was truly a prophet sent by Almighty God. My kitchen became the central gathering place. I fed all the men three meals a day. None left the room except to go out back and use the outhouse.

Ervil expounded the scriptures, proving all Joel's claims to each man's satisfaction. Question after question was answered. Joel used the four standard works, the Bible, the Book of Mormon, Doctrine and Covenants, and *Pearl of Great Price*, plus the teachings of the prophet Joseph Smith.

A couple of men expressed their dissatisfaction, seeing how Ervil seemed to be taking control. When Joel tried to answer their questions, Ervil invariably cut in with his own interpretation—and an arrogance that a few did not appreciate. One visitor, David Barlow, paused between words as he directed his question solely to Joel. I could see he was hesitant about asking such a direct question: "Joel, I want a straight answer. Are you the One Mighty and Strong?"

Joel's eyes dropped for a moment, staring at the floor. David spoke again. "Either you are, or you aren't. If you are, why don't you have the guts to say so?"

Joel looked up. We could all see his face was red with embarrassment. "Well," he began humbly, "I happen to be that man, but I don't like to flaunt it. I didn't ask for this job. It was given to me, and I have been appointed by God."

I could see a new fire in some of the men's eyes. This was the first time these men had ever heard Joel utter this claim. Three days of complete indoctrination proved to be a milestone for the new church. All fifteen men pledged their faith and allegiance to their new prophet. They vowed to follow Joel's advice and make the move to Mexico as soon as they possibly could.

Verlan had been skeptical for two years, doubting Joel's continual claims. Yet, he couldn't help but be impressed with his brother's forthright honesty. He had opposed Joel up to this point, but it all changed at the encounter with these converted men. Verlan wondered how Joel had ever convinced the entire group when he so thoroughly lacked knowledge of the scriptures. Therefore Verlan felt it was definitely the power of God that convicted the men. Verlan let his guard down, reconsidering Joel's doctrine. Had he refused to accept Joel's claims because of prior disappointments and fear of further rejection and condemnation from all his friends and peers? He eventually surrendered the reservations he had about his brother.

Verlan had shown his loyalty as a teenager to the LDS Mormons. He had received baptism at their hands. He had been troubled that his mother and father had been excommunicated for living polygamy. Another disappointment came when Joel and Ervil were fulfilling a mission in southern Mexico. Although both were in good standing with the Mormon Church, they were excommunicated, along with Alma and Ben, for teaching polygamy.

Joel later repented, asking to be rebaptized in the Mormon Church. They forgave him, thus allowing him back into their fold. Then, two years later, he was called into a church court for claiming to be a prophet and was excommunicated again. The LeBarons became a bigger embarrassment to the Mormons every day.

Although Verlan loved the LDS Church and he valued his membership, he felt he had to live polygamy in order to gain his exaltation. For this reason, he kept quiet about his marriage to me. When I was in my third trimester with my first child, Verlan had no clue that Dr. Hatch would extract the secret information from me when I went in for a checkup. But, about a month later, Verlan was called in before a bishop's court and then the High Council of the LDS Church and was excommunicated for practicing polygamy. He felt saddened because he had been treated so wonderfully by the Mormons when he lived among them. He had many friends whom he respected and did not want to lose. But following his excommunication, Verlan was deeply humiliated because the LeBarons were the butt of every joke and criticism, especially in his hometown, Colonia Juárez, and in nearby Colonia Dublán. He had been born and raised in Colonia Juárez, had attended Juárez State Academy and BYU, and now lamented not being accepted in those communities.

Now, after two years of intense study, Verlan was convinced that Joel had indeed received their father's mantle and was the promised mighty and strong prophet. Therefore, he decided to be baptized. I was heartsick about the incident. After years of loyalty to Uncle Rulon, I felt that to abandon his priesthood now would be a betrayal.

Lucy joined Verlan in his baptism. Out of sheer jealousy and not wanting Lucy to be favored, I was baptized the following day. A few days later, Charlotte conceded.

BY 1958, IT HAD BECOME EVIDENT that Lucinda needed to be committed to a mental facility. Too many people had complained that her presence on the ranch was not conducive to the growth of the now-flourishing church. Even Joel could see that she should no longer shout greetings, welcoming the saints from her adobe cage day and night upon their arrival. Her jabbering and disheveled appearance repulsed and embarrassed the newcomers.

Many times I had argued with the brothers collectively and individually about Lucinda's being a problem, insisting that her needs were not being met. I knew something needed to be done in order to bring hope into her life. If she lived in a clean facility with other mental patients, she could converse and share good food, music, and social events. All this would surely benefit her mental and emotional health.

The family finally agreed that Lucinda needed to be moved. Maud prepared her for travel, bathing her and packing clothes and other necessities for her daughter.

Verlan knew what this trip would entail, and he was *not* looking forward to being contained in a vehicle for several hours with his sister. He had dealt with Lucinda many times before and knew she was unpredictable and could be uncontrollable. Nevertheless, he and his brother-in-law Floyd Spencer drew the short straws, so to speak, so with Lucinda sandwiched between them in a pickup, they headed for the border at Douglas, Arizona, carrying only Lucinda's few belongings and a couple of plastic gallon jugs of water.

Upon their arrival at the institution in Tucson, they were told Lucinda would have to meet certain requirements before she could be admitted to make sure she qualified for their services. But when three officers came out to the truck to escort her into the building, Lucinda jumped out of the truck. She grabbed one of the gallon jugs of drinking water. Then to everyone's amazement she held it high over her head and hollered hysterically, "I'm Napoleon! See, I'm Napoleon!" As she shouted, she danced with the jug, shaking it and drenching her hair and clothes.

Apparently there's no waiting period for sopping wet, dancing Napoleon impersonators; my sister-in-law was admitted on the spot.

Lucinda spent the rest of her life in the Arizona State Mental Hospital.

CHAPTER EIGHT

One afternoon, Maud, accompanied by Lucinda's two daughters, Maudie and Joan, went to El Valle to do some shopping. The girls had been invited to participate as bridesmaids in their Mexican friend's wedding. Using her fractured Spanish, along with hand gestures, Maud made her wishes known. The proprietor, a short, middle-aged man, was very attentive. He retrieved three bolts of satin material—pink, blue, and yellow—from the high shelf behind the counter. The two girls excitedly unfolded a yard or so from each bolt, asking their grandmother which material she liked best to make their bridesmaid dresses.

"I like the light blue," Maud said, holding the bolt in her left hand as she unwound enough cloth to cover Joan's chest. "Look how nice this color is," she exclaimed. "It will bring out the blue in your eyes. I'll buy enough to make you girls identical dresses."

The proprietor smiled, satisfied, and replaced the remaining two bolts on the shelf. He then measured and cut ten meters of the blue cloth. Sliding the material across the table toward Maud, he asked her in his native tongue, "Do you need anything else?" His rapid speech made it difficult for Maud to decipher exactly what he'd said. She asked the girls to clarify.

Just then, a swarthy Mexican who was standing nearby asked in perfect English, "Could I interpret for you?" His charming smile captivated the women.

"Oh, thank you. I think we can do okay between the three of us," Maud said, laughing.

From the look of the stranger's tan leather jacket and expensive shirt and shoes, it was apparent that he wasn't a local resident. The man was surprised when the fifteen- and sixteen-year-old girls rattled off questions in perfect Spanish, inquiring as to his hometown and future plans.

"I just arrived on a bus from Ciudad Juárez. Eventually I'll go to Mexico City, where I hope to find my family; I haven't seen them for a very long time."

Maud, trusting her instinct, invited the young gentleman to accompany them back to the ranch. "I'm Mauro Gutierrez." He offered his hand to all three, greeting them warmly. "I'd love to accompany you."

"Where did you learn such good English?" Joan asked.

"I've lived in California for the last thirteen years. Actually I'm a wetback." He chuckled. "I had a few domestic problems. My wife called the police and turned me in as an illegal alien. Immediately, I found myself evicted from the U.S."

Concerned, Maud interrupted. "I hope I haven't invited someone who is violent to come with us."

"No, don't worry. My wife was upset because she learned I was having an affair."

Maud paid for the cloth, and Mauro offered to carry it to the bus station a block away.

By the time the bus had traveled the twelve miles to the ranch, Maud felt as if she had known this young man forever. Not only was he exceptionally good-looking, his jovial personality seemed infectious. She quietly cautioned sixteen-year-old

Joan to quit flirting with him. "Remember," she whispered, "he can be no more than a friend to you. He's a *gentile*."

Shortly after Mauro's arrival, Maud walked him over to my little house. By then I had moved out of Charlotte's house to a place of my own with three small rooms. After introductions, she asked if I would invite the young stranger to stay at my home for a few days.

Not wanting to impose, Mauro interrupted. "But not if it's going to be an inconvenience. I'll be going on my way soon," he assured me.

I personally felt that Mauro was a godsend. I longed to have someone who could speak English to visit with. Since I had been isolated in Mexico for three years now with virtually no visitors, his presence was more than valuable to me.

I knew he must be hungry, so when Maud left, I served fresh-cooked pinto beans and corn tortillas to my guest. Like a sponge, I absorbed every word he said. His life was a bit shocking; he talked so nonchalantly about several affairs he'd had. But I immensely enjoyed hearing his life story as he ate. When he finished, he set his plate to one side, cleaning the space on the table in front of him. With his wide, piercing brown eyes, he leaned forward into my face. "Tell me, what is an intelligent young woman like you doing here, living in these conditions?" He sounded disappointed, as if I'd failed him somehow, and his words punctured my pride, almost summoning tears. I too, had asked myself that same question many, many times.

Before I could answer, my brother-in-law Alma showed up at the door. His mother had informed him of the newcomer's arrival, and Alma was as eager as I was to talk with someone new. He entered the house, introduced himself, and shook hands with Mauro. "Do you want to ride around with me in my truck today? We can get acquainted while I check on a few cows in the pasture."

Mauro asked where he could leave his small bag of belongings. He shoved it under the metal cot in a small room adjacent
to the kitchen that I indicated would be his. The two men left. I
was a little nervous after the comments that Mauro had made to
me. Did he think I was nuts living here? I knew Alma had a few
weird ideas, so I hoped he'd keep quiet about my situation. I did
not want him to reveal to Mauro that we were living polygamy.
I wondered if I would be condemned by Mauro upon his return.
Would he be as accepting when he discovered our lifestyle? I
hoped he wouldn't think all of my ideals were in agreement
with Alma's. I'll never forget what happened that evening when
Mauro returned to my house alone. "Hi," I said, welcoming him
in with a smile. "How did your day go with Alma?"

He shook his head as though he wondered if he even dared
share their conversation. "Well, it's been interesting to say the
least." He chuckled.

"What's up? You can tell me. I'm used to surprises."

He hesitated, embarrassed. "I'm still trying to digest the conversation myself, but I'll tell you anyway. I told Alma how I'd
been thrown out of the States for sleeping with an underage girl.
When my wife found out, she blew up and had me kicked out
of the country. Alma told me that my wife didn't understand the
laws of God. He told me the Bible says if you 'entice a maiden'
[become sexually involved], the punishment is that you have to
marry her. I found out that I could have had every woman I've
ever slept with if I'd of just done it in the name of God. Alma
told me that God allows a man to have all the wives he wants as
long as they are married to him by the priesthood." He laughed
at the ridiculousness of it all. "I screwed 'em in the U.S. and
almost went to jail, and now I can come here and screw 'em
with God's permission. Isn't that insane?" he joked.

I was sick inside. I had to agree. It did sound pretty irrational,

especially when an unbelieving gentile explained it so offensively.
I myself didn't understand the whole concept behind it, yet because
my family had lived polygamy for five generations, I didn't believe
it could be wrong. All I knew was that Joseph Smith had received
a revelation from God that we had to live polygamy to gain our
salvation. And I definitely didn't want to go to hell!

I had to clarify my situation before he got any wrong
impressions.

"Mauro," I ventured, hoping to defend myself and sound log-
ical, "I happen to be my husband's second wife. All three of us
live side by side."

His jaw fell. "Tell me it's not true." He looked at me as though
he were questioning my sanity. "Don't you think you deserve to
have a man to yourself?"

I wondered who he thought he was, telling me this after his
confessions of illicit affairs. Instead of answering him, I fed him
homemade whole wheat bread, peach jam, and milk. After he
had gone to bed, I lay in mine, feeling uneasy. Would he try
to seduce me? I'd hoped that I'd said enough to convince him
of my fervent beliefs. Perhaps when he realized my unshakable
faith, he would examine the scriptures himself. Maybe the truth
would be revealed to him.

AS HARD AS I TRIED to keep Mauro away from my niece Joan,
it seemed he was constantly flirting with her. I was actually
relieved when he announced he was leaving for a few days to
Villa Humada, a small town near Ciudad Juárez. He hoped to
find a cousin there who would tell him of the whereabouts of his
six brothers whom he hadn't seen in thirteen years.

I was shocked, three days later, when Mauro got off the
bus by the cattle guard at the entrance of the ranch. He had a

light-skinned, beautiful nineteen-year-old Mexican girl with him. She flipped her short black hair as they walked hand in hand. When he saw me come to the screen door, he opened it playfully as he did a little jig. "I want you to meet my wife, Esther," he said almost apologetically. "She speaks no English, but I'm sure she'll understand your broken Spanish."

I offered her my hand. She took it, but her shyness kept her eyes from connecting with mine.

"When did you get married? How long have you known her?" I fired question after question at him.

"I met her three days ago at a corn festival. We danced the whole night of the celebration while I convinced her to marry me. Later we eloped. We'll live together until my divorce goes through from my first wife."

Later that evening, Alma convinced Mauro that it wouldn't be acceptable to live in sin among our families. He talked Mauro into being taken with Esther to the Galeana springs, where he would baptize them into our church and marry them by the holy priesthood. The spring's water flowed out of a group of hills located northeast, about three miles from the colony. The trees and vegetation were like a sparkling oasis in a grassland valley. It was a designated spot for baptisms.

Still in wet clothes, the two cleansed sinners stood before Alma, where he confirmed them as new members into our sputtering organization. The chilly September breeze gave the couple goose bumps. Wrapped in towels for protection from the cold, they held hands as Alma led them in a holy vow. Willingly they entered into a sacred covenant to be husband and wife for all eternity. But, unbeknownst to Esther, as the service progressed, she also was told she had to live the holy principle of plural marriage. Esther was clueless that she would be making covenants to minister to her husband by helping influence other women to enter into their anticipated family kingdom. To her horror, she learned Mauro was instructed to gather women unto himself so that he would complete a quorum of seven wives, thus assuring their entrance into heaven. Esther's shocked look alarmed Alma. Paralyzed with fear, she had only cooperated to be married, but somehow she had been inadvertently caught up in a new church.

Later she told me she thanked God she was on a secluded ranch where Mauro's dreams of grandeur would not be feasible. With her Catholic morals, the mere *thought* of him taking another wife shook her to her very core.

THE NEWLYWEDS MOVED into a small room connected to my house. One evening Mauro invited me to enjoy a cup of coffee with them. I'd been taught Joseph Smith's Word of Wisdom all my life: righteous saints were never to let caffeinated coffee or tea even touch their lips. We were taught that those hot drinks were stimulants and not conducive to one's health. But at his insistence I gave in, feeling guilty as Esther handed me a cup. I had taken just a swallow or two when in barged Verlan, unannounced. Verlan smelled the aroma, looked at the cup in my hands, and asked, "Irene, what are you drinking?"

"Coffee," I answered guiltily.

"Irene, you know better than that! You're supposed to be setting an example for these new converts, and you know it's contrary to my wishes. Now just why are you drinking that coffee?"

Mauro cut in, trying to defend me. "It's okay, Verlan. I insisted she drink it, so it's my fault!"

Verlan ignored Mauro. "Irene, *why* are you drinking that?"

My mind clicked frantically, trying to find a good excuse as

I set the now-drained cup on the table. "Do you really want to know?" I asked, trying not to laugh. "I'm drinking coffee so I can stay awake tonight—to read the Bible!"

THE OPPORTUNITY FOR ANOTHER PARTY of sorts came along a short time later.

Señor Monroy, a retired government dignitary from the state of Guerrero, Mexico, was not a member of the church, but he was planning to build his home in the colony. Verlan wanted to cultivate this man's friendship, allowing him to get to know our family, so he invited him to come to our home. When Señor Monroy arrived, just as Verlan was leaving to go back to work in Las Vegas, Verlan left strict instructions for me to give him the "royal treatment."

I promised Verlan that I'd see to it that he enjoyed himself and leave with a good impression. Since we'd had very few visitors over the years, I was overjoyed at the opportunity to entertain. Naturally, though, I was embarrassed that our humble circumstances made it impossible to serve him in the manner to which he was accustomed.

When I told Verlan I was looking forward to entertaining, I hadn't expected to actually be the entertainment!

Our guest spoke no English, and every time I opened my mouth, I murdered the Spanish language. Whenever I spoke he'd get a big kick out of trying to decipher what I had actually said.

Trying to salvage my dignity, I had invited Lucy over for supper because she spoke Spanish fluently and interpreted for me when necessary. Our neighbor, Mauro, just happened to drop by, so we invited him to stay and help entertain our illustrious guest.

When the conversation died down, I was embarrassed by the silence, so I decided to tell Señor Monroy about my latest goof-up.

Using my hands for emphasis, I talked in halting Spanish, asking
Lucy to fill in a word every now and then. I told my captive audience how I'd made a big mistake the day before. An elderly convert, Brother Ray, was paying me to prepare his meals. I washed
and ironed his clothes also. He'd brought over two identical pair
of tan work pants to be mended. He had torn the new pair in
the knee and asked me to cut the leg off the old pair to mend the
new one. With all my responsibilities and my four small children
underfoot, I was rushed as usual, trying to do more than I had
time for. I hurriedly cut a leg off one of the pants, and when I
grabbed the other pair I realized—to my horror—I'd cut the leg
off the new pair. I knew Brother Ray would be angry, but what
else could I do? I just sewed the leg back on, let the cuff out an
inch or so, patched the tear, and handed them back to him.

Our guest got such a kick out of my story so I decided to add
a punch line. I tried to say, "I would rather wash for the old man
five times than to mend his pants once." My Spanish version
was "*Yo prefiero darle cinco lavados al viejo que remendar sus pantalones
una vez.*"

Lucy and Mauro looked horrified! But Señor Monroy almost
fell off his chair as he doubled over laughing, tears streaming
down his cheeks.

I got upset but wondered, *Why are they all being so rude?* I
repeated my statement, and, trying to clarify it further, I added,
"Well, it's easier and a lot more fun."

Lucy flailed her arms as she begged me, between howls of
laughter, to keep my mouth shut!

When Mauro came up for air, he smartly held his arms above
his head with his fingers in a holding position. Between peals of
laughter he mimicked me, asking, "Can I hold it for you?"

Now I was mad! "What the hell did I say?"

He repeated it one more time in Spanish as the three of them

cracked up all over again. "You said"—he laughed even harder—
"you said…you'd rather…give the old man five *enemas*…than
mend his pants once! That it's easier and a lot more fun!"

I ducked my head in embarrassment. Although I was purple
with humiliation, I couldn't help but join in the laughter.

With tears streaming down his face, Señor Monroy tried to
console me. He swore my story was the funniest thing he'd ever
heard.

Reluctantly, the very next evening I again served supper to
Señor Monroy, with Lucy's help. After serving them, I served
myself a small plate of homemade cottage cheese with tomatoes
and a few string beans from our garden. Then I joined my guests
at the table, instructing Lucy to do all the talking.

Señor Monroy knew how terrible I felt from the night before,
so he tried coaxing me into talking to him. He asked why I
wasn't eating the same food I'd served them. I told him I was
dieting. Then trying to be polite and keep the conversation
going, he asked, "If you're dieting, where do you weigh yourself
around here?"

He was raising his spoon of soup to his lips, looking me in the
eye, waiting for my answer. I blurted out in my terrible Spanish, "Oh, that's easy. I just run over to my girl friend's house and
jump on her scale."

He burst out laughing so hard he blew soup right off the
spoon. He couldn't stop laughing and finally excused himself
from the table, exclaiming, "*Que precioso, que precioso* (How precious, how precious)."

I wished I hadn't brought Lucy over to translate when I realized what I'd said. She spoke between bursts of laughter. "You
said you run over to your girl friend's house and jump on her
nipple—*pezon*—to weigh yourself."

Later as Señor Monroy was departing, he assured me that this had been the most entertaining trip he'd ever had. He cautioned me to be sure *not* to learn perfect Spanish, for I'd always be a conversation piece in any crowd.

LONELY, DEJECTED FLOREN was completely devastated. Like Verlan, he had found himself an American wife when he found Anna, but she had left him. So, when Mauro arrived back at the ranch with Esther, Floren lost no time in interrogating him, asking if he had any suggestions as to where he could find himself a wife. Mauro informed him that Esther had an older sister, Yolanda. He thought it might be an excellent idea if Floren proposed to Yolanda. It would give Mauro more security if Esther's sister would marry Floren and move to the colony.

I was shocked at how fast things went. In less than a week, Floren returned with Yolanda. He set up house in another one-room, cement-floor adobe shack and Yolanda became pregnant shortly thereafter. She and Esther were inseparable. When Yolanda was five months pregnant, I heard her wailing a block away. Her howls of despair could be heard by every person on the ranch.

I hurried outside, wondering what was wrong. Was she hurt? Cut? Bleeding to death? I ran toward my wooden gate to meet her. She was so distraught, weak from crying, that she nearly fainted in my arms.

"What's wrong?" I demanded.

Between her tearful sobs, she gasped, forcing her words out, "He blew out my candles! He said I can't be Catholic and still be married to him." Out of breath, she leaned her exhausted body on mine as I led her into my house. I gave her a glass of water, hoping she would be able to calm down. Floren had followed behind her, hearing my negative advice as he entered my kitchen. (I had told her to leave. She certainly was not here for the religion, so why suffer?)

"You have no right to take sides with her," he cut in. "I told her she could *never* light those damn candles in my home!"

"You'll be sorry," Yolanda threatened between tears. "I'm leaving tomorrow."

I wondered again how a man thought he could take all a woman's rights away. Wasn't a woman able to make choices and think for herself? How could anyone rip her sacred rituals from her, especially when she was so devout in worshipping God in the only manner she knew? How callous and heartless!

Brokenhearted, Yolanda left on the bus the following morning. She returned to Villa Ahumada, where she lived with her mother and gave birth to Floren's son, Jesus, a name commonly used in Mexico. But they called him Chui. She never came back; it was always her sister Esther who took the bus to visit her.

CHAPTER NINE

A convert in his late teens, Karl Wachs, was reeled into the colony, hook, line, and sinker, consumed with a passion to be numbered among the saints. He arrived in our new Zion from Utah with a few changes of clothes plus a stash of rare early Mormon books packed in the trunk of his car. Ervil took the young zealot under his wing. Though disappointed in his puny frame and small stature, Ervil figured he would look beyond the boy's frailties, at least long enough to get possession of the coveted books. Ervil was especially interested in the volumes of the *Journal of Discourses*. It contained sermons by all the early Mormon presidents and prophets.

Ervil's thirst for knowledge became insatiable. His inflating ego grew with each sermon he read. His visions of grandeur rose to greater heights as he consumed the early Mormon dogma, teachings that were an embarrassment to the contemporary LDS Church and had been conveniently discarded by them. When Ervil read about the "Danites"—avenging angels of God who took oaths to cut down sinners who opposed their leaders—he could hardly contain his ecstasy.

He read that Joseph Smith had introduced polygamy as an absolute requirement for exaltation. The revelation was recorded July 12, 1843, and is now in the Doctrine and Covenants, section 132.

Joseph's brother Hyrum went to Joseph's wife, Emma, to share the newly revealed doctrine. She read it with disgust and burned it in the fireplace.

Joseph Smith claimed to be hesitant to pursue the "command of God" and proceed with plural marriage until an angel of the Lord had come to him three times. An angel did, and the last time the angel appeared with a drawn sword, threatening that if he did not enter into plural marriage that he and his people would be destroyed. The new prophet eventually married more than thirty women, including many who were wives of other men.

The young Mormon prophet convinced his followers that other than Jesus Christ he was the greatest man to ever walk the earth.

On one occasion he spoke of "blood atonement," declaring that the apostle Peter once told him that he himself had hanged Judas; and apostle Heber C. Kimball claimed that others had kicked out his bowels.

Ervil soon learned from these discourses that people could be blood atoned for many reasons.

The first offense was for leaving the church. Heber C. Kimball stated, "If men turn traitors to God and his servants, their blood will surely be shed or else they would be damned" (*Journal of Discourses,* 4:375).

For adultery and immorality, Brigham Young confirmed in the February 18, 1857, issue of *Deseret News,*

All mankind love themselves, and let these principles be known by an individual, and he would be glad to have his blood shed. That would be loving themselves, even unto an eternal exaltation.... Will you love that man or woman well enough to shed their blood? I could refer to you plenty of instances where men have been righteously slain, in order to atone for their sins.... I have known a great many men who left this church for whom there is no chance whatever for exaltation, but if their blood had been spilled, it would have been better for them. The wickedness and ignorance of the nations forbids this principle's being in full force, but the time will come when the law of God will be in full force.

This is loving our neighbor as ourselves; if he needs help, help him; and if he wants salvation and it is necessary to spill his blood on the earth in order that he may be saved, spill it. Any of you who understand the principles of eternity, if you have sinned a sin requiring the shedding of blood, except the sin unto death, would not be satisfied nor rest until your blood should be spilled, that you might gain the salvation that you desire. That is the way to love mankind.

For covenant breakers, Jedediah M. Grant explained in the July 27, 1854, issue of *Deseret News*,

What disposition ought the people of God to make of covenant breakers.... What does the Apostle say? He says they are worthy of death.... It is their right to baptize a sinner to save him, and it is also their right to kill a sinner to save him, when he commits those crimes that can only be atoned for by shedding his blood.... We would not kill a man, of course, unless we killed him to save him...the more spirit of God I had, the more I should strive to save your soul by spilling your blood, when you had committed sin that could not be remitted by baptism.

For stealing, president Joseph Smith said, "... I want the elders to make honorable proclamation abroad concerning what the feelings of the first presidency is, for stealing has never been tolerated by them. I despise a thief above ground" (*Times and Seasons* 4:183–84).

Brigham Young held the same view about stealing, "I should be perfectly willing to see thieves have their throats cut....If you want to know what to do with a thief that you may find stealing, I say kill him on the spot, and never suffer him to commit another iniquity" (*History of the Church* 7:597).

For taking the name of the Lord in vain, Brigham Young said, "I tell you the time is coming when...the penalty [for taking the Lord's name in vain] will be affixed and immediately be executed on the spot" (*Journal of Hosea Stout* 2:71).

For not receiving the gospel, Brigham Young stated, "The time is coming when justice will be laid to the line and righteousness to the plummet; when we shall ask, 'Are you for God?' and if you are not heartily on the Lord's side, you will be hewn down" (*Journal of Discourses* 3:226).

Regarding marrying a black person, on August 22, 1895, George Q. Cannon said that the prophet Joseph Smith taught this doctrine: "...The seed of Cain could not receive the Priesthood...and that any white man who mingled his seed with that of Cain should be killed, and thus prevent any of the seed of Cain's coming into possession of the priesthood." Wilford Woodruff, later president of the LDS Church, recorded in his journal a speech Brigham Young gave January 16, 1852. He stated, "And if any man mingle his seed with Cain, the only way he could get rid of it or have salvation would be to come forward and have his head cut off and spill his blood upon the ground; it would also take the life of his children."

For apostasy, Brigham Young threatened, "I say, rather than that apostates should flourish here, I will unsheathe my bowie knife and conquer or die" (*Journal of Discourses* 1:83).

Liars, too, were to be blood atoned. According to Brigham Young, "I . . . warned those who lied and stole and followed Israel that they would have their heads cut off, for that was the law of God and it should be executed" (*Manuscript History of Brigham Young,* 500).

For counterfeiting, Brigham Young said, "I swore by the eternal gods that if men in our midst would not stop this cursed work of stealing and counterfeiting their throats should be cut" (ibid.).

After reading the violent accounts, Ervil believed he had been shown how to implement full control of his flock. He claimed that God had unequivocally given him the knowledge of the civil law through the Bible and the Doctrine and Covenants. He started preaching the death penalty for adultery, stealing, marriage to an African American, for not receiving the gospel, using the name of the Lord in vain, lying, for those who dishonor their fathers, those who worship false gods, and for apostasy. He claimed to be God's avenger. He had found a license to kill in the name of God.

Possessed by this hidden knowledge that he now knew how to *control* the saints, he would weed out the wicked, thus preparing for a perfect society that would be prepared to meet the Savior.

Ervil was ecstatic because he knew the Mormon Church and all its splinter groups would eventually have to bow down to the new kingdom, or the wrath of God would subdue them. Ervil would soon implement regimentation and build up an army for God.

Joel announced that his own position was like unto Moses; he alone had access to speak to God. Ervil was next in line because he held the office of Second Grand Head or Patriarch.

With this appointment to second in command, Ervil felt a new sense of worthiness, and his charismatic demeanor took on a new intensity. At every opportunity, Ervil reminded his listeners how the LeBarons had been despised by those who knew them. Filled with increased arrogance and feelings of superiority, he would say, "Mark my words. My brothers and I will eventually rule the world."

NEW CONVERTS TO THE CHURCH of the Firstborn experienced the shock of their lives upon their arrival at the ranch. The dry, barren landscape, the mud huts, poverty and isolation, made them question whether they'd made the right decision. Their only hope was the promise that the prophet Joel would lead them into the millennium. Their security lay in the fact that Joel told them many times during Sunday's lengthy meetings that he knew the beginning from the end. He spoke with authority: "No one will stand between me and Jesus Christ, for I will be the last prophet before the Second Coming of the Lord."

The future might have been bright, but for "Firstborners," the present looked pretty bleak. Since the only land to build on belonged to the LeBaron brothers, the brothers divided the upper east land into lots and sold them to the saints. Once their new homesteads were established, however, the converts realized they had no way to support their families, let alone the great cause. The disgruntled men were forced to leave their loved ones in Mexico and return to the States to work. This put great stress and burdens on the new believers, and Joel spent hours trying to console them.

"I'm the One Mighty and Strong," he told his flock. "I will set the house of God in order. It should take no more than forty years before the final winding-up scene."

They calculated that from 1955 to 1995 Joel would prepare a people so that Christ would come and dwell in their midst. His followers clung to Joel's every word.

"I am the promised seed of Joseph Smith by which all the nations will be blessed. I hold the scepter, which gives me authority to usher in the millennium. I will redeem Israel."

These powerful messages renewed their spirits, buoying them with hope. Each felt compelled to continue on when they realized the burden of the kingdom was on their shoulders. Joel convinced them that the end was so near; their sacrifices would be justified if they would just hang tight and trust in their prophet.

They felt a sense of relief when Joel announced to his congregation, "I've been given a promise by my grandfather, my father, and by Jesus Christ himself, that I will not fail."

Convinced that they had an infallible prophet who would take them into the presence of God, they surrendered their complaints. They would do whatever was necessary, go wherever their prophet led, so that they might be prepared to be caught up in the clouds to meet Christ.

Ervil also felt validated preaching to the saints. He made sure they understood what was required of them. His long hours of speaking caused him to lose his voice at times. When he felt threatened, thinking he was coming down with pneumonia, again, he would retire to his throne—the bed.

CHAPTER TEN

An important event that gave a great boost to the new church and preceded its final organization was the arrival of the French missionaries.

As a student at Pasadena City College, Bill Tucker received multiple awards and graduated early. He also learned French. He planned to attend UCLA to obtain a PhD but decided to postpone his education. Like all young Mormon men, he would do his duty to the LDS Church and fulfill a mission in France. He used his almost perfect French diligently to convert new members. He was soon recognized by the French mission president, Milton Christiansen, who appointed Bill to be his counselor, which was an honor. Bill's fervor was contagious. He spurred his fellow companions on, and soon they transformed their mission field, becoming more successful than ever before.

Bill, a devout seeker of truth, studied the scriptures painstakingly. They led him back to fundamentalist teachings. He became aware that the LDS had given up saving principles such as United Order (a sort of communal property arrangement made between the church and its members) and plural marriage. He began holding study meetings early in the mornings with other missionaries, where they discussed early Mormon principles. Three district presidents, Bruce Wakeham, Stephen Silver, and Dan Jordan, questioned the changes in the LDS Church and, as a result, found themselves being converted to original Mormonism.

In 1958, David Shore, a friend of Bill Tucker who had completed his two-year mission in France, promised Bill that he would search among the fundamentalists for the One Mighty and Strong. He happened upon a pamphlet in a bookstore in Salt Lake City, titled *Priesthood Expounded.* It was written by the LeBarons and laid claim to Joel's true priesthood authority. Shore mailed the pamphlet, along with other fundamentalist literature, to Bill in France. Using knowledge that the LDS Church considered forbidden, Bill continued influencing other missionaries. Word leaked out about Bill's disobedience to the church's rules. He was called in before President Milton Christiansen, who expressed surprise when Bill admitted that some missionaries were interested in little-known Mormon history.

David O. McKay, the prophet of the Mormon Church, was notified immediately. It was determined that a few church officials, who were about to meet in London for a temple dedication, would make a thorough investigation and correct the situation.

During the questioning, the leaders were already against Bill, believing he was the culprit. They thought he'd used "hypnotic powers" to deceive the others. They believed it was perhaps too late to save Bill Tucker—he had fallen from grace.

The brethren urged the others being investigated to stay in the mission field and complete their two-year mission. They warned them that if they didn't comply, they'd bring disgrace on the church and their entire families.

When pressured to state whether they believed David O. McKay was a prophet of God, all the missionaries involved replied no, and nine missionaries were excommunicated.

Marilyn Lamborn, a college graduate, and Fay Fulk had

absorbed every truth Bill had revealed to them. Caught up in the excitement of their new knowledge, both women decided to accompany the other missionaries back to the United States. The now-excommunicated group boarded a Greek liner, the TSS *New York,* and sailed from Le Havre to New York. They were euphoric. Dedicated to their new ideals and anchored in their faith, they pursued their quest to find the One Mighty and Strong.

Stephen Silver wrote in his journal, "As I finish this account, we have been to sea five days. I am determined to go to Mexico. All of our studies have led us there. God's authority is still on this earth, for it was promised to remain. We shall find it."

Once they arrived in New York, Bill Tucker, Dan Jordan, Neil Poulson, and Bruce Wakeham left directly for Colonia LeBaron with a promise that they would contact the others when they were certain they had found the true priesthood and prophet who was to come forth and lead the righteous into the millennium.

How well I remember seeing the four young missionaries waiting just beyond my wooden gate, shielding themselves from our barking dog. I was surprised to see Americans on the ranch, but I walked out to the gate, introduced myself, and invited them into our adobe house.

When Charlotte, Lucy, and I learned the visitors were missionaries from France who had come to investigate Joel's claims, we stood in awe over these four handsome, intelligent young men, driven to find the truth. We listened for two days as they related their stories of success in France as missionaries, their search for truth, and their powerful convictions. They soon had spiritual testimonies of the validity of Joel's claims. My head spun with a giddiness that I'd never experienced before. Just the thought of intelligent, educated men joining our sputtering church seemed to be a miracle from God.

Two days later, after the four missionaries left for the States,

Marilyn Lamborn and Stephen Silver arrived in Mexico by bus. Lost in the middle of the night, they experienced another miracle when a Mr. Romney saw them hitchhiking and gave them a ride to the ranch.

Not sure they were in the right place and because it was four o'clock in the morning, they settled under a large tree, waiting for someone to stir within the three small adobe dwellings.

Charlotte arose about seven. It was her day to wash her clothes, so she went out to pump water to fill a large tin tub in which she would do her laundry.

When Marilyn and Stephen saw her approaching, they shook themselves off, brushed their wrinkled clothing, and then introduced themselves. Stephen, a blond intellectual, looking the part with his horn-rimmed glasses, explained why they had come to Mexico.

Marilyn, a tall blonde, very sure of herself, followed Charlotte into the house. Soon they learned that Charlotte was Verlan's first wife, I was the second, and Lucy was the third. Our visitors seemed intrigued by our polygamous lifestyle, and it was obvious that I would soon be giving birth.

We spent all day visiting, then Charlotte invited them to sleep in her house. Lucy and I retired to our nearby three-room house.

During the night, I went into labor. My pains were too close to send to Spencerville for Aunt Sylvia, a midwife, so Lucy summoned a new convert, who had recently arrived from Short Creek, to deliver my baby.

The next day when I failed to join them for breakfast, Marilyn and Stephen wondered where I was. They were shocked when Charlotte informed them that I had given birth in the night to a baby boy. Their biggest concern was that no doctor had attended me. They couldn't understand in this day and age why a woman would not be under the supervision of a physician. But all went well and I decided to name my baby after Stephen, preferring the spelling "Steven."

The next day, when Ervil heard that the two French missionaries had arrived, and, learning that one was a female, he made a quick move. He spent the next afternoon with Marilyn, offering himself to her as a potential husband. He said Bill had shown him a picture of her a few days earlier. In that moment, God revealed to him that Marilyn was to be his wife. Marilyn was confused. She wondered if this was a test from God. She wanted to do God's will, but Ervil, though handsome, did not appeal to her.

Still Ervil was relentless in his quest. During their conversation, Ervil flattered Marilyn, promising her heavenly rewards. He told her how urgently he needed such an intelligent English-speaking woman as herself. He explained that his two Mexican wives were not converted to his religion and expressed his dissatisfaction with both women. He promised that if Marilyn married him, she would become an elect lady in God's eyes. Not letting her get a word in, he bragged about his intelligence and his gift of being an orator and "the most knowledgeable man in Mormondom." However, nothing he said impressed Marilyn. She felt that she should marry Bill Tucker..

WHEN THE FRENCH MISSIONARIES GATHERED for conference, the members all believed that their conversion had been accomplished by the mighty hand of God. Their presence greatly animated everyone.

Just after Marilyn's wedding on October 19, 1958, she and Bill headed for California, hoping to convert her sister, Carol, and brother-in-law, Earl Jensen. Ervil had appointed Bill to be mission president over the western states.

Bill and Marilyn decided not to inform her parents of their

marriage, or of their baptism into the Church of the Firstborn until later.

Carol was skeptical when the two arrived at their home in Sacramento. She'd heard from her parents in Utah that the LDS leaders had branded Bill as the "devil's agent." Both Carol and her husband, Earl, blamed Bill for Marilyn's excommunication from the Mormon Church that they so wholly revered. Her severance from what they believed to be the one and only true church upon the face of the earth caused Marilyn's family great sorrow. To them, her excommunication was worse than a death.

Before Marilyn had returned home from France, a couple of their church members had warned the Lamborns to not allow their daughter back into their home. They feared Satan had control over her. Her parents refused the advice. After all, she was their flesh and blood and they loved her.

Carol, an upper-class Mormon, had heard what a devil Bill was. When he and Marilyn arrived, she scoped Bill out. He was dressed in a pin-striped suit with a dingy white shirt. She was surprised at how short he was, but she thought he had a splendid smile and "eyes that gleamed." She asked herself, "Is this the kind of smile Satan would have?"

Earl and Bill separated themselves from the two sisters, retiring to a quiet office where they discussed religion and examined the scriptures for several days.

Bill won Earl's respect. In the days that followed, Carol could see the change coming over Earl. He was definitely leaning toward the LeBarons' priesthood claims. Realizing that it was a spiritual life-or-death situation, Earl could not take a chance on being deceived. His future salvation depended on it. Therefore, Earl invited Bill and a couple of companions to join him and other Mormon scholars to discuss the topic of priesthood.

Earl felt that the Mormon scholars remained silent because

they were unable to refute Joel's doctrine. Earl, who had once held so much respect for his LDS Mormon leaders, felt let down by them. The debate, according to Earl, turned out to be an embarrassment for the LDS.

Unable to rest until he found the truth, Earl went to Salt Lake City. There he met with several members of the Quorum of the Twelve. Disappointed, he became convinced that they did not have the answers that he was seeking.

He drove back to Chihuahua, Mexico, to meet with the new prophet. There he entered the waters of baptism, being baptized by Joel LeBaron, the prophet himself. In Sunday meeting, the few of us who heard Earl's heart-wrenching conversion were jubilant.

We had to smile when Earl admitted how he had previously thought that Bill was an agent of the devil and how he had been determined to confront Bill and intellectually destroy him and his satanic doctrine. His conversion reassured us that God was gathering up his elect, especially when someone of Earl's caliber was converted. When Earl informed us of his involvement in the FBI and the CIA, we knew for sure that God had given us one of his brightest minds.

Upon his return home, Earl was very patient with Carol, informing her that he was not pushing her to join the new church. He wanted her to follow her own conscience, but he was moving to the new Zion.

Carol must have felt tormented, vacillating between the two faiths. She thought that if she abandoned the Mormon Church, it would probably kill her aging parents. Nevertheless, she received her own testimony of the truthfulness of Joel's work, even accepting the law of plural marriage. Later, she became instrumental in helping to court Earl's additional wives.

In the spring of 1959, Carol decided to attend the semiannual conference in Colonia LeBaron. I'll never forget how stately she looked with her bleached blonde hair twisted and coifed and piled upon her head. I smiled when I saw what looked like a chopstick pushed through it. Her silk dress looked divine. I knew that her expensive high heels would soon be ruined from walking on the gravel roads. To me she looked like a fairy-tale princess. Most of us were dressed in secondhand, ill-fitting clothing, as were our Mexican members. Carol looked out of place among the impoverished crowd. Her stoic face and teary eyes gave evidence of the disappointment and humiliation she tried to conceal. I could tell she thought this was all beneath her. The only hope she had of surviving among the impoverished LeBarons was the knowledge that she'd have her family and sister, Marilyn, to comfort her.

As always, immediately after the first session of conference, Ervil stepped down from his place behind the podium. He cut through the small crowd. He then invited Carol to follow him outside. He wanted to teach her the beauties and the benefits of the new church. His long-winded sermon was tiresome, but as he exhibited his knowledge and enthusiasm, it only reinforced her already existing conversion.

The new converts, along with several other missionaries, left their lovely homes behind in the States. Earl built Carol an impressive, two-story home with a full basement. Joel tried to persuade him to build a smaller adobe home with a tin roof, similar to those of the other settlers. Joel wanted equality among the saints. He felt it was unwise to build such a sprawling new home, stuccoed white, with red clay tiles on the roof.

I heard bickering among the disappointed members as they referred to the grand palace that was under construction. A couple of the poorest Mexican members were upset by such an action. However, the construction of the new home did provide some of the impoverished peasants with plenty of work, which silenced their complaints, even though Alma, Ervil, and Joel had preached many a sermon on equality. We were told that we Americans had come to Mexico to be "nursing fathers and mothers to the Lamanites [Mexicans]." Joel's vision was for us to assimilate ourselves among them, living closer to their economic level.

While the Jensen home was being built, Earl joined Ervil, Dan Jordan, and Bill Tucker on a mission to the States. The four men complied with the scriptures and traveled with "neither purse, nor scrip" (Luke 10:4), but Earl soon returned to finish building his home.

Even I was jealous when Earl had the first flushing toilet in the colony. I also resented that he had the only generator. I'd been led to believe that we were all going to live the "United Order" where one saint would not possess that which was above another.

I shared a Maytag wringer washer with my other two sister wives, Charlotte and Lucy. The gas motor failed on many occasions. While we waited for Verlan to bring a needed part back from the U.S., we pulled out the washboard and scrubbed our clothing until our fingers were red and raw.

Alma grew vegetables in a community garden with the help of his three older boys. Also, he summoned about a dozen youngsters or so, male and female, mostly Mexicans, to weed, water, and hoe the garden. Once or twice a week, he'd deliver vegetables throughout the colony.

Seeing the need for a store in the colony, Earl built a fifteen-by-thirty-foot adobe room and appointed Maudie (Lucinda's daughter), who was his first plural wife, to run the small business. It was a boon to the colony. Most women, like us, Verlan's three wives, had no vehicle, so the new store was more than convenient. We no longer had to catch a bus and travel the forty miles to Casas Grandes. (People had preferred to go there instead of the twelve miles south to Buenaventura because Casas offered cheaper prices and a great variety of products.)

CHAPTER ELEVEN

Fay Falk returned from France to her mother's home in North Carolina. She worked for a few weeks, awaiting word from Bill Tucker about Mexico. When he never wrote, she became impatient and hitchhiked by herself to El Paso, Texas. She arrived by bus at the LeBaron colony with a small suitcase and forty dollars.

I bonded with Fay the moment I saw her. Tall, brunette, and vibrant, she had a voice that rang with excitement when she spoke. She pitched in, cooking, cleaning, and changing babies. I loved her bubbly personality. She was so positive and full of life.

When I inquired why she had traveled so lightly to Zion, she laughed, a little embarrassed. "I didn't bring much because I thought I would come to Zion and have to make a new wardrobe. I had envisioned you all in eighteen hundred–style dresses." She and I were wearing jeans, and we both cracked up laughing at the absurdity of her imaginings.

Doggedly, Ervil whisked Fay away out of my presence one afternoon so he could attempt to brainwash her. He was forthright in his convictions. "I've had a revelation from God that you are to be my wife." His pronouncement didn't faze her at all.

"Sorry," she replied. "It's been revealed to me that I should marry Bill Tucker."

Fay had qualms about her situation because before she arrived Bill had already married Marilyn. Fay felt bad because Bill had never written to her as he had promised. Bill had never officially asked her to marry him, although she hoped he would. She wondered where she stood with him.

A short while later, Marilyn and Bill arrived in Zion. And not long after, Fay went to the springs and was baptized. Then she was sealed to Bill for all eternity, becoming his second wife. Her excitement was short lived. She felt totally rejected when Bill informed her the following morning that he and Marilyn had to leave for the States. After one blissful night, her dreams were dashed—no honeymoon and no time to make plans for the future. She was completely crushed when Bill left her with me. As a second wife, I understood her dilemma. We both felt like intruders in our husband's lives.

In theory, plural marriage sounded like a piece of cake, but in reality it was a glimpse of hell.

I'll never forget when pretty blonde, blue-eyed Rhonita Stubbs moved to the colony from Short Creek, Arizona. Bill asked her to marry him and she accepted his proposal.

Verlan surprised me about five o'clock one evening. He rushed into my kitchen, out of breath, and said that if I wanted to attend Bill and Rhonita's wedding, we had to leave right then. We had no time to lose. I took less than five minutes to change my dress and comb my hair into a ponytail.

The wedding was held at the baptismal springs in Galeana, a place we all considered sacred. This was the same spot where, some weeks before, Marilyn had been dunked in the baptismal water, then soaking wet she had married Bill on the bank of the stream.

Verlan found a place to park. Then, as always, he lit out ahead of me, taking long strides, making it impossible for me to keep up with him. I complained, so he waited a minute for me. He held my hand as we hurried around a small hill. About twenty church members stood reverently at attention in our view. From afar we could hear heartbroken cries coming from Fay, who stood beside Bill waiting to give Rhonita to her husband in matrimony. We hurried to take our places close to the couple.

I'd never expected such despair from Fay. Her futile cries tore at the women's hearts, while I sensed the disgust and judgment from the men. Bill looked tacitly at Fay, hoping she'd stop making such a scene. Her torrents of tears gushed forth, blinding her. I could tell she was in total anguish.

Joel the prophet, realizing that Fay's cries would have to be tolerated, commenced reciting the priesthood vows: "Do you," he asked Fay, "take sister Rhonita by the right hand and give her unto your husband to be his lawful wedded wife?"

Her answer was drowned out by deep, guttural sobs that startled the guests. But not even that could stop the ceremony, as she unwillingly complied.

Throughout the next few weeks, I remember attending church with Fay. She tried so hard to impress Bill. She looked radiant, all smiles as she sat in her pew. Bill spoke almost every Sunday. She would keep her focus on him, hoping he would make eye contact. But he made sure he never did. My heart ached to see Fay so brokenhearted. She accosted him on the road on several occasions, but he would not give her a second of his time. She wanted to be obedient. She tried sharing him with other women, but her heart could not tolerate it.

Fay could not control her jealousy. She repeatedly fell apart, and he repeatedly insisted that she get a hold of herself. When she persisted in her rants of jealousy, he told her to leave his home. He demanded a divorce.

Eventually, wanting to reform and hoping God would give her strength, Fay entered into plural marriage again. The lucky guy was Mauro Gutierrez, one of our first converts, and a beloved friend. Though married to three other women, including my niece Joan, Mauro flipped over Fay. He lived in poverty—though he did his best to support his families with what he earned in his welding and mechanic shop—and he had nothing to offer her—except love. She felt it was sufficient, so she joined him in the mountains to live with his other wives in the small town of Las Varas.

WHEN I BECAME GRAVELY ILL with typhoid fever, I spent two weeks in the Casas hospital. I was back home again, but too sick to care for myself. For the first two days, my sister wife Lucy took my four children to her home to tend while I recuperated a block away in another two-room adobe house.

The July heat was stifling. We had neither air-conditioning nor electricity. While recovering, I was so weak that I could not even stand up. I'd been sick for a week before I was taken to the hospital, and I'd lost so much weight, I was too frail to walk. I needed constant care.

Sixteen-year-old Gaye Stubbs, Rhonita's sister, was appointed to give me sips of water and feed me Jell-O and fruit juices. Too weak to make it to the outhouse, I used a small enamel pot which I usually kept under my bed, but it had been temporarily left on my doorstep.

Verlan had come home from Las Vegas, leaving his pressing work long enough to check on me. He couldn't sit by my bedside continually because his other two wives also needed him.

Gaye was attentive. I appreciated so much her willingness to nurse me back to health. She had fallen in love with Joel and intended to marry him as his third wife. Her sister Jeannine had secretly married him as a second wife. And Joel was doing his best to keep his marriage to Jeannine and his courtship with Gaye a secret from his first wife, Magdalena.

In spite of the sweltering heat, my body started chilling. My teeth chattered. I felt as though I was freezing. Gaye went into the kitchen to heat up some spearmint tea, hoping to warm me. When she returned with a cup of tea in hand, I motioned for her to set it on my nightstand. She excitedly said, "I see Joel coming down the street. Do you want me to invite him in to see you?"

"Sure," I replied weakly. "I need him to come and pray for me." I figured maybe a prophet's prayers would heal me.

Gaye opened the screen door in the kitchen, calling out to Joel, who evidently had other plans.

"Come in and pray for Irene," she pleaded, hoping she would get a chance to flirt with him.

Joel was unaware that I had returned home. He had heard that I was hospitalized, but he had no idea I was still so ill. He entered and sat at the foot of my bed. I sipped tea as my chills subsided. Feeling warm, I had Gaye remove the blanket, so my body was covered with just a sheet.

We were unaware that Magdalena had seen Joel enter my house. She knew Gaye was tending me, so she had suspiciously watched Joel's every move. Jealousy caused her to think that he had gone into my house to see Gaye. She flew in like a frustrated hen trying to defend her chicks, shocking all of us by smacking Joel in the face, then lunging forward to grab Gaye. Joel caught Magdalena's arm in time to restrain her. Magdalena's accusing hysterical screams frightened Gaye, who looked to Joel for protection. Though she could not understand Spanish, she could tell by Magdalena's demeanor that she was out to get her! Magdalena wrenched herself from Joel's grasp, flailing her arms, and lit into Gaye. Joel pulled her away, commanding her to stop and yelling in Spanish, "Are you trying to send Irene back to the hospital?!"

Pushing her toward the door, he demanded that she leave my home. "You know Irene's sick. I want you to go now."

Too frustrated to think, Magdalena charged at Gaye again, who ran out my bedroom screen door as though the house was on fire.

Then, to everyone's astonishment, Magdalena began beating on me, falsely accusing me of helping Joel court Gaye. Joel sprang forward to stop the assault, yelling orders for her to leave at once. She continued her tirade as Joel held her arm tightly with one hand and removed his leather belt from his Levi's with the other. Once he had freed the belt, he held it at eye level, threatening to use it on her unless she obeyed.

Infuriated, she tore out of his grasp and again began hitting me as I cried helplessly. Joel was furious when she continued pounding on me. In anger, he swung his belt, lashing out for all he was worth at his enraged wife. He acted so fast that he didn't realize he had used the wrong end of the belt. Magdalena dodged and the belt buckle hit my left thigh. I whimpered, writhing in pain. The buckle broke from the belt and flew across the bed onto the floor.

When Joel realized that he had accidentally hit me, all hell broke loose. He grabbed Magdalena, forcing her out my screen door onto my cement step. Still out of control and completely devastated by Joel's actions, Magdalena retaliated. She saw the enamel pot half full of my diarrhea that Gaye had left on the step, intending to empty it later in the outhouse. Magdalena gleefully threw it through the screen door all over Joel's Levi's and onto my rug, even splashing it onto the side of my bed. Without hesitation Joel grabbed Magdalena with one hand and whipped her with his belt all the way out to the side of the road. She cried and begged him to stop. He told her he would quit once she was off my property. Once out of my yard and realizing she had lost the fight, Magdalena bawled all the way home. Forgetting to pray for me, Joel ran across the street to the irrigation ditch where he pulled up a handful of weeds and, dipping them in the water, tried to wash the excrement from his putrid-smelling jeans.

Gaye kept an eye on me while Joel went to look for Verlan. I was distraught, still traumatized from the lash of the belt. When Gaye removed the sheet to check on my thigh, I could see the concern on her face. The belt buckle had cut into my flesh, drawing blood.

Verlan returned me to the hospital for four more days. In my deteriorated condition and after losing fifty-three pounds, I had somehow forgotten how to walk. I couldn't seem to control my legs. Others had to hold me up and then help me for a week or so before I could get around on my own.

My sickness taught me something my parents hadn't—to use the wisdom of doctors. Neither I nor my siblings had ever received immunizations. My parents believed relying on vaccinations meant they weren't placing us in God's care. After my severe bout with typhoid fever, I made sure that every one of my children was vaccinated. I wanted to spare them the harrowing experience I had endured.

A PORTLY, GRAYING SIXTY-YEAR-OLD joined the Church of the Firstborn. He had previously been affiliated with the fundamentalists in Short Creek, Arizona. His two wives were dedicated women who tried to demonstrate through their actions that they loved plural marriage and one another.

This newcomer was a strict disciplinarian, whose explosive

temper made his wives comply with his every whim. He had served on a mission for the Mormon Church but became convinced the LDS Mormons wrongly had given up plural marriage, a law he felt was essential for his salvation.

He married his first wife shortly after the two returned from their missions. Desiring to marry another woman, and to avoid persecution, he decided to divorce the first one. Soon, his first wife found herself being the plural wife. She had to hide from her immediate family and friends when she became pregnant. If it were discovered that the three of them were living polygamy, they could be arrested.

He had become acquainted with a fundamentalist from Roy Johnson's splinter group in Arizona, so he and his two wives moved to Short Creek, but before long he became discouraged with the group's control over him.

Joel invited this man to come to Mexico and investigate his claim to be the One Mighty and Strong. Accompanied by a dozen fundamentalist believers, they arrived at Colonia LeBaron and spent fifteen to sixteen hours a day discussing the Mormon scriptures. By the end of their discussion, Joel had made believers out of every visitor. Impressed by Joel's answers and ability to expound the scriptures, every man swore allegiance to their new prophet. I was shocked that this brother moved his large family to Mexico so soon. Four of his sixteen children decided to stay with the Short Creek group, but soon two of his daughters were married to the prophet Joel.

This brother was determined to build up God's kingdom. He felt that he had come across an unknown law that God allowed—if kept secret. So, when a childless couple from Holland moved to Zion, immediately the brother from Short Creek went to them, offering his services. He spent endless hours convincing them of his plan. He put them under oath to not reveal the "unknown law" to anyone else because he knew there would be repercussions.

Once the Dutchman was convinced he would be blessed with children, he reluctantly loaned his wife to the brother until he had impregnated her. After years of barrenness, the couple was jubilant, celebrating her conception while everyone else thought she had miraculously conceived with her husband. Then, to everyone's disappointment, the baby died shortly after birth.

Soon, another "miracle" happened. The woman became pregnant again. It was then that "Brother Stud" began to brag to other members, revealing that he was the father of the unborn child. The members were appalled, wondering how he could possibly impregnate another man's wife...and with his permission?

Due to the fact that Brother Stud was a father-in-law to the prophet, the sin was minimized. He was asked to "lay off" and not interrupt the couple's lives again. He temporarily complied, but continued claiming he was in love with the woman and she would be his in eternity and the Dutchman would be their slave eternally.

We all became privy to what Brother Stud called the "law of the eunuch" when he approached another childless couple, offering his services. That woman became so irate, she turned him in to the prophet. However, Brother Stud still claimed if a man was sterile, he could appoint another man to step up and do the job. To the disappointment of us women, he was never excommunicated...just tolerated.

CHAPTER TWELVE

Ervil had been so occupied helping build Joel's kingdom that he had neglected his own. Seeing Joel and Verlan marrying more wives, he felt compelled to get with the program before they left him in the dust.

Ervil's longtime friend Nephi Marston (son of Joe Marston who had been a convert of Ben's for a short while) heard about Joel incorporating a new church. On the first trip to the new colony and after eighteen consecutive hours with Ervil, he was 100 percent converted to their new doctrine. He now believed that Joel was the prophet who had come to set the house of God in order. No one else he knew had made such claims except Joel's brother Ben, a few years earlier.

He remembered whenever Ben met people for the first time, he would greet them with a random and bizarre introduction. Shaking hands he would state, "You're in the same category as George Washington," or "You're in the same category as John the Baptist." He would then look them in the eye and ask, "Do you understand?" He wouldn't let go of their hand until they said yes, even though most of them probably had no idea what Ben was talking about. Nephi had wondered if maybe Ben was labeling them all according to their worthiness. He was glad his family had given up their belief in Ben.

Nephi was now married to redheaded Anna Mae, and they had five beautiful children, one who had recently passed. Anna Mae was infuriated by Nephi's conversion and his insistence on attending conferences in Mexico with the LeBarons. She threatened to leave him if he even thought of taking her and the children there.

After the conference in April, Ervil invited himself to return with Nephi to the States and stay at his home while he preached the gospel among the Mormons. Nephi voiced his concerns, telling him that Anna Mae would never move to the new Zion. "She tries to control everything I do. We fight so much. Ever since I've joined this church, she has fought me tooth and nail. Sometimes I wonder if our marriage will last."

"I'm positive that if I preach to your wife, I can persuade her to join the church," Ervil assured Nephi.

Nephi still thought it was a bad idea and told Ervil so. "My wife has warned me to never let a LeBaron in our home. I'm afraid if you show up with me, she will leave me for sure. She wants nothing to do with the LeBarons."

Ervil's big grin seemed to convince Nephi that he could handle the situation. Both men left feeling optimistic about their new challenge.

Less than a month later, Ervil returned to Colonia LeBaron with Nephi, Anna Mae, and their four children. With him also was Nephi's younger sister, Joy, whom Ervil had also converted. He had convinced her that she would benefit by marrying him, a true servant of God, so she did.

Ervil thought it was a perfect setup, ordained by God himself. Joy and her seven-year-old daughter from a previous marriage would live with Anna Mae. This living arrangement would prevent Delfina and Mary Lou from suspecting anything. Ervil wanted to keep the "things of God" to himself for a while, especially since Delfina was still weak minded. She hadn't made a full recovery from her last emotional breakdown. At the moment, he preferred not to deal with his two unbelieving Mexican wives.

Mary Lou often expressed her jealousy toward Delfina, but Ervil couldn't understand how an emotionally cracked woman could be such a threat. He could only imagine what Mary Lou, with her flighty temper would do when she discovered he had finally been awarded a prized, pretty, Caucasian American wife. The fact that Ervil had explained to her through the Book of Mormon that she would never be "delightsome" in his eyes, but their half-breed children would be, only fueled her resentment.

Nephi had purchased a small house in Colonia LeBaron; upon his family's arrival, faithful Nephi spent the day unloading a six-by-eight-foot trailer of Joy's and Anna Mae's belongings. Though tired, he never complained. He felt slighted that Anna Mae seemed to avoid him that night by refusing his advances. He wanted to strengthen their bond. It seemed the past year of their marriage suffered because of their opposing religious views. Nephi wanted validation, especially since he would be leaving early in the morning. He felt overwhelmed with a new burden on his shoulder. Not only did he have to sacrifice being separated from his newly converted wife and children, but he had to support two households. The thought of being on his own in the States, with no one to come home to, saddened him. When Anna Mae rejected him, he turned over to get some sleep, praying to God to comfort his heart.

After Nephi left for the States, Ervil spent most of the day and late into the night with Anna Mae and Joy. Delfina threw a tantrum, sending her second daughter, Sara Jane, over to retrieve her father, demanding that she not return without him. Ervil would invariably lie to Delfina and Mary Lou, saying that he was spending the night with the other one. Somehow he would end up in Joy's bed.

In less than a week, Joy's feelings for Ervil were completely over. She would not be privy to Ervil's lies to his other two wives, or his flirtatious antics toward her sister-in-law Anna Mae. Not only did she feel devalued, but she realized that she had been conned into a marriage of convenience (for Ervil, of course). She was furious, not only at Ervil, but at religion itself. Joy packed her essential belongings into her gray Volkswagen, and drove out of Zion with her daughter.

When I initially learned that Joy had left, I was surprised. She had just shared with me how she had been a single mother for five years and had been smitten by Ervil. None of us had any idea why she had left so secretly and abruptly. I thought her suspicions about Anna Mae were completely unfounded, but then I learned she had cried to others, accusing Ervil of betraying her brother.

I mourned for Joy as I cleaned my kitchen. In her short life, she had experienced two LeBaron prophets, first Ben and now Joel, both of whom claimed to be the One Mighty and Strong. I hoped that her leaving Ervil and the church would not interfere with her brother Nephi and Ervil's lifelong relationship. Nephi was such a well-meaning servant. He had shown his love and respect by sharing his home with Ervil and his sister, and he had expressed his loyalty to Ervil on many occasions. In my presence he once proclaimed, "The sun rises and sets on that man." I hoped he wouldn't be hoodwinked by Ervil's unscrupulous tactics.

JOY WAS RIGHT. From the moment Ervil's lustful eyes had peered into Anna Mae's, he knew he'd have to figure out a way to marry her. Despite the fact that she was already married to Nephi, here was Ervil's chance to have another American wife now that Joy was gone. Sure, he understood, along with every other Mormon, that marriage was for all eternity, but he wanted her now. Not even God was going to stop him.

He knew he'd be punished, even demoted or excommunicated, if he took another man's wife, for people would cry "adultery." Everyone knew the Doctrine and Covenants said that after a woman had been married "... if she be with another man, she will be destroyed." According to Mormon scriptures, there was no way a woman could divorce a man. Once she had taken her vows, they were binding throughout this life and in the life to come. No one dared challenge the doctrine. After all, it had been revealed by Joseph Smith himself.

Ervil had to conceive a plan that would be justifiable and appease the people.

Alone in turmoil, with burning passion for Anna Mae consuming him, Ervil decided to ask the Lord to solve his problem. The vision came; it was as plain as night and day. The Lord told him in no uncertain terms that if a woman had made a mistake, marrying the wrong man, she would not be held accountable if she divorced him. No wonder Nephi and Anna Mae had marriage problems. It was obvious that Anna Mae should have married Ervil in the first place. The fact that she was married legally to Nephi was now no concern to him.

MY NEW FRIEND BETTY TIPPETTS, who had recently moved down from Salt Lake City, barged into my freshly mopped kitchen with all the decorum of a herd of stampeding buffalo. I could feel her rage.

"What's the matter?" I asked.

She led me into my bedroom where we could have privacy in case any of Verlan's other wives had seen her arrival. Betty was still panting, and she looked so angry I could almost see smoke coming out of her nostrils.

"Irene," she said, "I cannot follow Ervil another minute." Defiance and disgust marred her otherwise attractive features. She breathed deeply, trying to regain her composure. "I'm gonna tell you something, just because we're best friends, but you can't tell anyone. It would put my life in jeopardy." She pushed a wisp of hair out of her eyes and looked toward the ceiling as if she were hoping to find the right words printed there.

"I walked across the road to Anna Mae's house to check on her, you know, just to see how she was surviving without Joy and Nephi. When I entered, she wasn't in the kitchen, so I followed the sound of her laughter into her bedroom. I opened the door..." Betty shuddered and burst into tears.

"Irene, I saw it with my own eyes. Ervil was having sex with her. He stopped pumping," she said sarcastically, "when he saw me. I've never been so appalled or let down in my whole life. Our patriarch, second in command...the one who threatens our lives for lesser things than adultery. He's a traitor to Nephi! A damn, f____ing traitor! My husband and I have disrupted our whole lives...given up a good job, everything! Here we've come to Zion to await Christ's return...and now this!" Tears seeped through her long fingers as she covered her face with her hand.

I went absolutely numb. I wanted to run into Verlan's arms for reassurance, hoping beyond hope it wasn't true, but Verlan and Betty's husband, Harold, were away from the colony, both working in the States to support their families. After vowing me to secrecy, Betty rushed toward home, concerned for her small children that she'd left alone. I felt like throwing up, and I wasn't even pregnant.

Ervil met Betty on the road in front of her cinder block home as she was returning. He walked over to her sheepishly, offering her his hand, but Betty refused. "Aw, c'mon," Ervil scolded her. "You thought you saw something illegal. Well, it's not!"

"I know what I saw," Betty replied bitterly.

Ervil grinned cunningly. "Yes, I know, but sometimes things aren't the way you see them." He grabbed Betty's upper arm, his usual method of showing his superior strength with every woman in town. He held on to her as though she was a child who needed to be reprimanded. "Too begin with, I want you to understand that I have been married to Anna Mae for three days. You can ask Dan if you want; he performed our marriage."

Burning with anger and disgust, Betty said, "Sure, you marry another man's wife as soon as he leaves town."

"Now, now, let's keep the spirit of the Lord. She was never meant to be married to Nephi in the first place. Why do you think they've had so many marriage problems?"

Betty blew up. "We all have problems! So shall we all get divorced as soon as our husbands leave town?" She continued her tirade. "What right do you have to steal Nephi's wife from right under his nose?"

"Well," he continued, still rationalizing, "Anna Mae was born into this world for greater things. She made a mistake when she married Nephi. The Lord knew that in the preexistence, she belonged to me. In fact, for over a year, Nephi couldn't convert her or even get her to attend a conference. The first time she laid eyes on me, she knew we were soul mates." He boasted further. "When I preached the gospel to her, she believed every word I said. She is far more valiant than Nephi. In fact, he's a pathetic excuse of a man. He allowed Anna Mae to wrap him around her finger. He's no man! Do you think he is worthy to be her husband?"

Fuming, Betty cut in. "Who gave you the right to give her a divorce? She is married legally to Nephi."

"Ah! It makes no difference...because as patriarch, I have authority over all marriages here on earth."

Betty felt crushed. She couldn't tolerate such egotistical garbage. "Please, Ervil, leave me alone. I cannot deal with this," she said as she pulled away.

"Well, just do me a favor and don't tell anyone what you saw earlier, okay? Can you do that much for me?"

"I already told Irene," she shot back. "I had to tell somebody."

Thinking he had settled things with Betty, he made a beeline to my home. He tried to hug me when he entered, but I turned away. "I can't believe you, Ervil! You've just got to be the big chief, don't you? Always doing what you want when you want. You continually step on everyone else's toes on your way to the top. I loathe you for ruining Nephi's life. You know he buried his five-year-old daughter not too long ago." Then raging, I emphasized, "And now...you *steal* his wife."

"C'mon, Irene, wake up! Can't you see what caliber of men we have down here? Most are worthless freeloaders; they're unworthy of having even one wife."

"Nephi's not in that class. He's been your friend for years. He's the one who's been sacrificing his money to help you support Delfina and Mary Lou. You are a traitor, that's what you are," I cried, breaking down.

"Let's not have any tears," he begged. "I love it when you fight with me. Nothing disappoints me more than a passive woman who never uses her brain." Returning to his justification, he said, "For your information, Dan married me to Anna Mae. She is legally mine before the Lord."

"What about Nephi?" I yelled.

"Don't get so bent out of shape. I'll make it up to him." He laughed, smirking. "When he comes home, I'll give him two wives for the one he's lost." His eyes danced with mischief. "I've already lined up two seventeen-year-old Mexican girls who I know will be willing to marry him as soon as he returns. Remember," he said, heading for the door, "the Lord giveth and the Lord taketh away."

Nephi had been absent for two weeks when, through my living room window, I noticed his car drive by. I hurriedly left the house, hoping to get to Anna Mae's before all hell broke loose. There I greeted Nephi as his kids ran outside joyfully to meet him. He took his small daughter Ramona and swung her into the air, then hugged the two older boys. "Now open the trunk and bring all the groceries in," he told them.

I entered the rock house just seconds before Nephi. He followed, walking toward Anna Mae with open arms. But, she pushed him away, preventing him from planting a kiss. I could see the hurt in his eyes. "Is that any way for a wife to treat her husband?"

"I'm not your wife," she snorted self-righteously and began putting away the groceries that the children had stacked on the kitchen table.

Nephi walked quietly back outside, looking as dejected as a dog that had been kicked in the rump. I followed him as his boys entered the house with a few remaining things from the car. "Come on, Irene." Nephi's voice cracked as he spoke. "I'll give you a ride home."

Nephi and I shared a special connection. I'd admired him since the first day I met him. When we were both seated in the car, he turned and looked me straight in the eye. "Tell me what's going on. What does Anna Mae mean, she is not my wife?"

I couldn't hold back my tears as I responded. "Ervil married *your* wife while you were gone."

He stopped the car in my front yard, then jumping out, he leaned his convulsing body against the car door for support and wept like a child. I wondered if Anna Mae could hear his loud, pitiful, sobs from a block away.

An hour later, Ervil found Nephi and made his offer. "Don't feel so bad. All that woman ever did was give you hell." He laughed, trying to make light of the situation.

Nephi, numbed by the betrayal, listened to Ervil's latest instructions from the Lord. "God has lined up two girls for you, Dalila and Oralia." He beamed, no doubt hoping his enthusiasm would rub off on Nephi. "God is giving you a double blessing—two wives at once. Here's your chance to do something great." He continued with his flattery. "You can help bring forth white and delightsome children for the Kingdom of God."

Nephi, docile and complacent, seemed to smother his inner rage and despair. Unbelievably, he accepted Ervil's words as from the Lord, determined to move on. If he rejected Ervil, he would be giving up his children and his newly converted father, Joe. He was bound by his beliefs to accept his leader without further questioning.

Pregnant Mary Lou was not as complacent or understanding. When word reached her that Ervil had married Anna Mae without even consulting her *or* Nephi, she flew into a violent rage, striking out at Ervil in despair.

No one saw the confrontation between the two, but several frightened neighbors listened to Mary Lou's screams. It was evident that Mary Lou was receiving the whipping of her life, but no one went to her rescue. They knew better than to cross Ervil. Besides, no one wanted to interfere with another man's kingdom.

Ervil beat his wife so severely that he asked a neighbor and his wife to look after Mary Lou until she recovered. Two weeks later, she was still bruised. His fists and his belt had left their imprints on her body, reminding her that complete obedience was required.

Surprisingly, Delfina handled the news about Anna Mae better this time. She did not lose her mind, but she sank into a deep depression that made it nearly impossible for her to tend her children. Ervil, unable and unwilling to tolerate weakness, felt justified in spending all his time with Anna Mae while others consoled Delfina.

Ervil presented the new doctrine he'd received about divorces to the believers, revealing that he now had authority over *every* person on earth. To say people were disturbed and dismayed would be a massive understatement. We all knew the implications of Ervil's words: since the laws of God superseded the laws of the land, Ervil had full control.

In a women's meeting, he informed us that *nobody* had the right to enter into marriage without his consent. Ervil made it his mission to enlighten the group, and his profound teachings seemed to be accepted by the women.

During this private meeting, we learned of our new rights as women. He explained how God was going to free certain women who had wrongfully married inferior souls. Using the example of his and Anna Mae's marriage, he minimized what we mistakenly labeled as sin. "If any of you are serious, I mean absolutely sure, about wanting out of your marriage, I'll release you, and you'll be free to marry anyone you choose—with my approval, of course."

ERVIL GLOATED IN HIS ROLE as a true servant of God. Now that new converts willingly appropriated monies apart from tithing, he was able for the first time in his life to dress like a professional. Back when I first met him in 1953, he looked like a typical country bumpkin, clad in a well-used white-going-on-gray shirt with sleeves rolled up to cover the fact that they barely passed his elbows. His Levi's were five inches too short and split in the crotch. It was an embarrassment because he wore no undershorts. Baling wire served as shoelaces. He totally ignored the discomfort that came from wearing no socks, compounded by the holes in his shoes. I'll never forget that scene. He was just a strikingly good-looking guy who reminded me of those pictures you see of Abraham Lincoln. He had long legs and big raw-boned hands.

Now, with the help of a couple of converts he shopped for and bought expensive clothing, feeding his already-out-of-control ego. Ervil began running around in sixty dollar shoes and thirty-five dollar shirts. He also acquired a late-model, four-door Impala with a shiny tan interior and gold exterior. Ervil claimed that God had revealed that he should obtain the vehicle because it would be more impressive to potential converts. First-born members dubbed Ervil's yellow car "the Golden Calf."

He was sure his new image would attract flocks of new converts. He had the good looks, plus he was armed with a few alarming scriptures that he would use to warn the people to flee to Mexico before the day of the final destruction.

One day Ervil received a specific revelation aimed at one man: Darren (not his real name, changed to protect the guilty) had been chosen by God to do Ervil's bidding and support him. His unspeakable joy overrode the fact that his finances were next to nil, and his wife was already suffering from neglect. But Darren believed that he would be rewarded a hundredfold for being obedient, so he accompanied Ervil to the Lamb Chevrolet dealership in San Diego. After Ervil completed the test drive, Darren signed the papers and the pleased patriarch drove his new possession out of the car lot.

Ervil had purposely chosen a gold-colored car. It reminded him of one of the heavenly treasures he'd eventually be receiving. He imagined himself driving down the streets of gold.

When prophet Joel heard the news, he was not at all happy. He felt Ervil needed to remain humble. It seemed to him that Ervil had forgotten the motto of one man not possessing that which is above another.

Ervil's earlier obsession had been to gather wives for his eternal kingdom. Now it appeared that his focus had changed to amassing monetary wealth.

Ervil had just given Delfina's and his fifteen-year-old daughter, Sara Jane, to Dan Jordan for his third wife. Dan was known throughout the church as Ervil's right-hand man because he always obeyed Ervil without question. Ervil chose him to accompany him on a mission to gain converts. Though other men were outraged, Ervil could hardly wait to drive his "golden calf" into the mission field, thereby, he thought, creating an image of credibility and importance.

At the inception of the church, Ervil had taught that missionary work was to be done according to the scriptures—with "neither purse, nor scrip." In this way the missionaries would test unbelievers; those who fed and cared for the missionaries would be targeted as potential converts. Ervil's use of his flashy car stood in direct contradiction to both his own words and the word of God.

WHEN ONE OF THE NEW CONVERTS, Lewis Ray, wanted to return to Moab, Utah, he invited Ervil to accompany him. He knew that Ervil's charisma and knowledge of the Mormon scriptures could persuade his children, Thelma and Vern Ray, to leave the LDS Church. Lewis was correct. Ervil convinced Vern in almost no time to join the church, and Vern and his wife and eight children moved to Mexico a short time later.

Ervil felt that he was fulfilling his calling by making such spectacular conversions. He always felt God's approval when receiving his daily promptings, and he was confident that no one else on earth was as capable of such an undertaking.

Ervil felt led to remain in Utah when Vern and his father returned to Mexico. He had convinced Vern's sister, Thelma, to join the church, but her husband, Bud Chynoweth, was a hard nut to crack. He quietly opposed his wife. He loved the Mormon Church and their lifestyle. He had worked for years to establish and maintain their standard of living, and he had no intention of uprooting his family and moving to a foreign country. Busybody Thelma worked incessantly to convince Bud to make the move, pointing out that since her two older sons had moved out and lived on their own, they no longer needed their large home.

Lorna, Thelma's teenage daughter, a tall brunette pursuing a career as a model, immediately attracted Ervil's attention. However, to Ervil's dismay, her busy schedule kept her away from home quite a bit.

Thelma sat like a sponge at Ervil's feet every chance she got, hungrily absorbing his every word. She was falling in love with the gospel as fast as Ervil was falling in love with her daughter, Lorna, who ignored him. She told her parents in no uncertain terms that she would be happy when he departed. As she and a girl friend were leaving the house, Lorna mumbled to her mother, "Ever since this man arrived, you've neglected everything but him. I'm going out."

Having won Thelma's deep love and admiration, Ervil made his move. In Bud's absence, he whispered to Thelma a command he'd received from God: "God loves you so much that he has elected you to do his bidding."

Thelma was overjoyed. Not only had Ervil baptized her, but she was now a strategic instrument in the plans of God. She listened intently as Ervil searched for the proper words to explain how God was going to mightily use her and her daughter, Lorna, in his kingdom.

In fact, Ervil said, Lorna had been chosen before the foundation of the world to be here at this particular time. Thelma sighed with excitement, drinking in the heavenly news. She believed Ervil's warning that Babylon was about to be destroyed, that she and her family must go to Mexico if they wanted to be spared, and now, that she had been called to be a servant. But she was knocked momentarily off her perch when Ervil explained her first assignment.

"God wants you to persuade Lorna to quit her modeling. It will take her to hell if she does it another day."

Thelma was stunned. She knew her daughter would be crushed. At a loss for words, she remained silent.

Seeing the concern on her face, Ervil lowered his voice and continued his brainwashing: "This is our little secret. God wants you to act fast. You must encourage her to marry me."

Thelma knew she couldn't stand in God's way, so, believing in Ervil's authority and heavenly revelations, she complied.

I'll never forget when Verlan relayed some of the details of Lorna's marriage and added, "She and Ervil spent their honeymoon in my small trailer house in Las Vegas. Ervil suggested I leave for a week to give him time alone with his new bride, so I did. She is so classy; I'm worried that Mexico will be too drastic a change for her."

On Lorna's arrival in Colonia LeBaron, one of the members offered a private room in his home where Lorna could live until Ervil provided better quarters.

Bud and Thelma hadn't relocated to Mexico yet, but Thelma

came faithfully to the April and October conferences to meet with the saints and to visit her daughter. She made the trip several other times as well, bringing Lorna tuna, peanut butter, mayonnaise, raisins, and other treats the rest of us couldn't afford. However, Lorna wasn't happy, and everyone knew she was miserable. She confided in a friend that she hated this life. She was disappointed that her father and older brothers had been conned into joining the new cult—Thelma had convinced Bud, against his better judgment, to follow her in the new quest. The grandeur of being a holy man's plural wife provided no comfort. Her frequent fights with Ervil began to wear him down. Her disobedience was causing him to classify her with Delfina and Mary Lou. He knew if she continued in her rebellion, he would have to take her down a couple of notches. He'd hate to have to whip another wife into submission, as he'd been forced to do with Mary Lou.

Six months pregnant, Lorna seemed to sink into a deep depression, which worried Thelma. She hated to leave her daughter in Mexico, but she found it necessary to return to her own duties. She and Bud were trying to sell their home. They would soon make the move to Mexico.

ON ANOTHER MISSION TRIP to Salt Lake City, Dan and Ervil were befriended by a middle-aged woman named Lorna Kirkendall. She opened her home to the two missionaries, giving them permission to use it as their headquarters. She took comfort in serving two holy men, whom she was sure God had called forth to do such a great work before the final days.

Linda Johnson, a young, plump, masculine-looking, short-haired accountant in her early twenties, frequently visited Lorna.

Knowing they would not be in Salt Lake City for long, Ervil saw that he had to act fast. He felt it important to have this young woman married to him to help fill his quota of wives for the kingdom. He was *not* attracted to her. Nevertheless, he knew she would be a tool in furthering his goals. Besides, she could support herself because she was an accomplished accountant. With Lorna Kirkendall's strong influence and Dan and Ervil's indoctrination, the three convinced Linda to be Ervil's sixth wife.

Unbeknownst to Linda's family or friends, Dan Jordan secretly performed the wedding ceremony in Lorna's living room. Lorna was privileged to be a witness because of her input and valuable help. She felt fortunate to have been included.

With only one more wife needed to fill his quota of seven, Ervil could hardly contain his joy. Not only would he become a god, but he'd be given a world of his own where he could rule and have total control forever.

AS I MENTIONED EARLIER, Ervil had never done much around the ranch. But when he returned from Salt Lake, he took laziness to a whole new level. He said to everyone that God had revealed that he was to labor only in spiritual matters. He decided that the best way to command everyone's attention and explain his inability to work was to retire to a sick bed. From the time he began his rule, he pinned a square piece from an old wool sweater beneath his T-shirt, covering his chest. He believed it kept him warm, preventing his recurring bouts with pneumonia. The strong odor of Vicks that was plastered on the wool piece almost overpowered his visitors.

Fathering, so to speak, his dozen or so children wore on his nerves. He claimed he needed solitude away from the constant bickering of his wives and demanding needs of his children.

Anna Mae, who owned the best home, gleefully shielded Ervil from the public and his other wives. She guarded the bedroom door, making sure no one entered without invitation. If a matter was of great urgency or importance, then it was acknowledged, but mostly only by appointment.

Anna Mae was adamant about keeping Ervil's rules. She put forth every effort to fulfill his demands. No one was to speak in Ervil's presence louder than a whisper. He felt by someone's being vocal, it showed disrespect for him. So he made his children speak softly; he felt they should be "seen" and not "heard."

Always propped upon three or four large pillows, Ervil took delight in each captive visitor. He preferred to receive callers one at a time. That way he would have less to distract him from the spiritual impressions and revelations he was constantly receiving. He also felt more in control with just one other person in the room; one individual was less likely to contradict or try to discredit him.

Often content to stay in bed most of the time, he sent messages with Delfina's and Anna Mae's children to ask several other women in town to bring him hot meals. The women were peeved, to say the least, but what could they do. The Lord wanted Ervil to have the best, and he could not perform physically or mentally if he wasn't properly nourished. He needed to maintain his strength, but his duty to his wives kept him drained.

CHAPTER THIRTEEN

It had been revealed to the prophet Joel to form a new gathering place for the saints in the Sierra Madre Mountains, so Verlan's families along with several other LeBaron followers moved there. While living in the mountains, I was gradually drafted into midwifery. At first I delivered just my nieces and nephews. Then I assisted friends and other women in the group.

The closest I came to receiving formal training was from two young interns. After arriving at the government hospital, they heard I was a midwife and occasionally asked me to assist them. As a result, I spent several nights receiving priceless knowledge and experience.

I enjoyed helping the poor in Mexico and I had the honor of having three babies named after me. I miraculously made it through many difficult deliveries. I never charged for my services; the recompense I got was the satisfaction of knowing I'd helped someone in need, thus alleviating some economic burdens for my wonderful friends.

One day while washing breakfast dishes, I could see through my kitchen window my neighbor Roseanne running toward my house, her pace indicating that something was wrong. I dried my hands on my apron, scurried to the back porch, and confronted her.

"What's the matter? Is someone hurt?"

"No, my sister wife, Lidia, is having her baby. Come quick! She already wants to push."

I hollered back to Lucy, asking her to keep everything under control while I went to deliver the baby. Lidia was my neighbor who lived directly behind my house, about thirty yards up on the hill.

I followed Roseanne's quick strides, running as fast as I could, trying to keep up with her. I'd been informed that Lidia was alone, that their husband had gone that morning to a nearby town to work. Although she was in labor, I heard no moans or screams as I entered her one-room adobe house, stepping down about six inches onto the tamped-dirt floor. Lidia shook her head when she saw me and said, "I was afraid you'd never make it."

She was lying on the bed in her bra and panties. From the looks of things, I wasn't too sure that this woman was as far advanced in labor as Roseanne had claimed. Every other Mexican woman I'd delivered had screamed and carried on from the pains as though they were in the clutches of death.

"I wanna push," Lidia warned me.

"Just hang on a minute."

Roseanne held a gray enamel wash bowl filled with hot water and Lysol for me to disinfect my hands. Then she helped position Lidia on the plastic that covered the bed.

Taking my place beside the travailing woman, I gave instructions to Roseanne.

"Hold her legs open so that I can examine her."

I could feel the baby's head. I pinched the bulging water bag with my fingernails, breaking her water. Lidia pushed, holding on to both Roseanne's and my hands. Just two hard pushes and the head was crowning. I prayed to God that I could get the baby out without any complications.

Lidia never made a sound. She just took a deep breath and on the very next push, thrust the baby's head out. I was shocked to see the baby's large shoulders. I tried turning the baby's shoulders with my fingers as Lidia pushed several more times. To my great relief, the baby plopped out onto the bed.

As soon as it was out, Lidia said, *"¡Bueno, lista para otro!"* which means "Good, I'm ready for another one!"

It's a good thing she was able to handle the pains of child-bearing because she eventually gave birth to nineteen children, including one set of twins.

I asked Roseanne to fetch my baby scales, and when I weighed the newborn the scale read a hefty 10.8 pounds! That was only the third baby that I'd delivered by myself. It was also the *only* time that I ever witnessed a woman maintaining her silence during birth.

I sent Roseanne out with a shovel to bury the afterbirth, then left her to care for Lidia. After having to be so responsible and expecting the worst, I hurried home, where I had a good cry. I could never let anyone know how inexperienced I was. After all the emotional stress, I vowed to deliver babies only in emergency situations, where I was the only hope.

On another occasion, Dan Jordan's truck came to a screeching halt in front of my house. "Hurry," he ordered. "Linda Stanley's having a baby and says she's hemorrhaging! She's hysterical!"

I was sick with anxiety. I knew almost nothing about complications, but I quickly gathered up my delivery supplies. Dan rushed me over to her house. Linda and her husband, Chuck, new converts to the church, had moved to the mountains hoping that the prophet Joel would give them a piece of land for their eternal inheritance.

I found Linda on her bed crying. "Help me, Irene. I'm scared. I'm just over eight months along. I don't want to give birth before it's time."

"What happened?" I asked. "What do you think started your labor?"

She shook her head, embarrassed. "A huge pig pushed open my kitchen door and sauntered right on in. I kicked the damn thing as hard as I could, and my water broke. Now I've discovered a little blood."

Upon examining her, I found to my relief that it was just a big boil on her bottom that had burst. That was the blood that had spotted her bed. I couldn't help laughing. I looked up at her and asked, "Hey, Linda, is it a 'boil' or a 'goil'?"

But her labor had started, so I stayed with her throughout the night, timing her contractions until the baby came. It was the most difficult birth I'd attended, but fortunately we made it. She gave birth to a baby girl. I loved Linda, and this experience drew us even closer together.

CHAPTER FOURTEEN

Ervil's determination to find American women for wives intensified, and no woman—no matter how young or how married—was safe from his advances.

Earl and Carol Jensen had four children. Earl was at this point away from home for an extended period of time, trying to earn a living in the States. This gave Ervil the opportunity to sweet-talk Carol. She deeply admired Ervil. His good looks, intelligence, and charisma seemed to cast a spell on her. She'd cater to his every need as he spent hours in her home preaching. Ervil explained how important his position here on earth was and how God was going to use him mightily. His only drawback was that he needed three faithful, united wives. Brigham Young said a man would never go astray as long as he had three praying wives. Ervil informed Carol that Anna Mae was his worthy wife, but he could not count his other five in the equation. Their rebellion had disqualified them. "I need another submissive wife, a wife who will obey me implicitly."

Carol, who seemed to understand the magnitude of his calling, wholeheartedly agreed—that is until Ervil dropped the bomb. "God revealed, with great urgency, that your daughter

Kristina has been preordained before the world began to be one of my three special wives."

This almost shattered Carol's faith in him as a prophet. She sputtered in disbelief. "Ervil, it can't be the word of the Lord. Kristina's only fourteen."

"I know, I know. Just keep calm. It's difficult for you to understand the ways of God. If it weren't for direct revelation, I wouldn't have believed it either. But, remember, the Bible says, 'It's not our way, but his way.'"

Too baffled for words, Carol listened as Ervil ranted on. "Her age is significant. She has truly been chosen at age fourteen. Just like the mother of Christ. Did you know that Mary was only fourteen when she gave birth to the Savior of the world?"

Carol was stunned, and she felt vulnerable as tears fell. Ervil put his arms around her and said, "This is where you come in, Carol. God has chosen you to convince Kristina to marry me." He hugged her tight, then let go as if everything were all settled. "I'm sure," Ervil continued, "that if you can convey the magnitude of the whole situation to her, she'll understand and go for it. Explain to her how she is not only chosen, but she gets the privilege to marry the second most important man on the face of the earth."

Carol was confused and upset, still not quite sure she believed Ervil. Why, she thought to herself, her daughter hadn't even begun to menstruate.

Ervil flashed his conniving smile. "May I have the pleasure of seeing Kristina today?"

"No," Carol answered decisively. "I'll have to speak to her first and win her over, then when Earl returns he must be convinced and give his approval. But, I need to tell you," she said apologetically, "Kristina has never liked you."

"Well," he said, grinning, "sacrifice brings forth the blessings of heaven. Just make her understand that all this silly stuff about love isn't from the Lord. Love is just a decision."

Soon after that, believing that Joel was a true prophet and that Ervil was the patriarch, Earl became convinced the marriage was God's will. He gave his consent by performing Kristina's marriage to Ervil. She became his seventh wife.

At the next women's meeting there sat little innocent Kristina by Anna Mae's side. She looked small in comparison to Anna Mae's portly size-twenty-two body. No one dared question her presence, although the women wondered among themselves. They had understood that their meetings were for married women only.

Shortly after Kristina's wedding, a secret leaked out among the saints: Joel himself had married a fourteen-year-old. Needing another wife to help fill his required quota, he asked a faithful follower, Harold, if he could have the man's tender virgin daughter. Harold was honored. He felt so special in knowing his sweet daughter would be married to the long-awaited holy messenger. Shy, submissive Claudine fulfilled her father's wishes.

VERLAN ALLOWED ME to accompany him to Las Vegas, where we stayed for two weeks. During that time, Ervil preyed upon another young innocent beauty. He used the same tactics on her that he had used to con his seventh wife, Kristina. Fifteen-year-old Debbie had been separated from her family in California at Ervil's insistence. He had told her father and mother that the Lord had warned him that if they allowed Debbie to return to the States after a conference she would become a "first-class whore."

The shocked parents were devastated that he could think such a thing of their darling daughter. They knew she was sweet, submissive, and obedient. What did God know that they didn't?

Not wanting to refute the patriarch, they reluctantly complied, leaving Debbie in Mexico at a trusted friend's house.

Then Ervil made his move. He spent whatever time he could with Debbie. She hated him, telling her best friend, Franny, that he gave her the creeps. "How can a thirty-seven-year-old man try to impose himself on me?" Debbie was adamant. She tried to avoid Ervil, but he doggedly pursued her, using Anna Mae to invite her over to eat and play Monopoly. She used fudge, which was a rarity, as an enticement.

Big-hipped, jovial Anna Mae had completely flipped over Ervil. She looked at him not only as her husband and lover, but as her savior as well. With great determination and excitement, she would plead with Debbie, revealing the coveted position that the Lord himself was offering her. She could obtain a great heavenly title if she'd just give in and marry Ervil. Anna Mae explained how Debbie would complete his quorum of three *united* wives. Pressured, Debbie was warned that if she refused she would suspend God's whole plan. In fact, without her, the Kingdom of God would be put on hold. Distraught Debbie longed to return to California to her parents. The religious cult frightened her.

One sunny day, Debbie was outside helping with the wash. The wringer was broken, so her blouse was soaked from wringing wet clothes by hand. Unexpectedly, Anna Mae appeared from around the corner of the house, out of breath from her three-block walk. Debbie cringed when she saw her, knowing she would once again be the victim of Anna Mae's bullying and coercive tactics.

Anna Mae's bright smile softened Debbie's nervousness. She continued rinsing her laundry as Anna Mae spoke. "You've got to come with me right now," she informed Debbie.

"I can't. I'm too busy."

"No, it's urgent. Ervil sent me to get you."

Though perturbed and feeling imposed upon, Debbie obediently accompanied Anna Mae back to her house. She had no idea she was being led like a lamb to the slaughter. During their walk, Anna Mae praised her, affirming her unusual beauty and confidence, trying to impress upon her supple mind how God was going to use her for a mighty purpose. Debbie's heart sank further with each step she took.

"I'm willing to do what God wants as long as he doesn't want me to marry Ervil."

"Ervil's not that bad," Anna Mae said defensively. She opened her screen door, allowing Debbie to enter first. Debbie's heart skipped a beat. She knew she was trapped when Ervil and Dan rose from the sofa.

Debbie, too frozen with fear, didn't have the courage to reject Ervil's embrace.

"You pretty little thing! God loves obedience. And he's the one who has called you here today!" Debbie looked around frantically for a way to escape what she knew was coming.

Ervil saw her eyes darting around the room and took her face in his hands.

"I've asked Brother Dan to carry out God's plans today," he said. "You see, Debbie, God made known to me quite some time ago that you are to join my family. You have been singled out and chosen above anyone else to be one of my three united wives. I need three special wives to advance the kingdom. Only Anna Mae, Kristina, and now you will qualify."

Tears of anger, shock, and disappointment streamed down Debbie's pretty face. "I don't want to marry you," she yelled out in despair. "I don't love you. Why don't you get the point?"

"Ah, but you don't need to love me. We're not out to fulfill our own wishes and desires. Don't you want to please the Lord?" he asked, concerned. "I'm surprised myself, Debbie, that God asked both of us to obey him in this matter. I sent for you because God told me this morning that he wanted me to marry you right now."

Shaken, Debbie managed to say, "Please don't make me do it!"

Anna Mae put her arms around the girl's trembling body, but her words held no comfort as she spoke. "Debbie, just marry Ervil. You don't need to worry. God is not expecting you to have sex with him until you feel like it."

Horrified and utterly confused, and without her parents to protect her, Debbie realized she had no other recourse than to comply. Embarrassed to be seen in her wet blouse, however, she grasped for a last straw. "Look at me! I look terrible! I can't get married looking like this."

But Dan ignored her comments. He began the ceremony anyway, hoping she would calm down. "Do you, Sister Anna Mae, take Debbie by the right hand and give her to your husband to be his lawful and wedded wife for time and all eternity?"

Anna Mae exuded excitement and joy. She not only gave her consent willingly, she was overjoyed that she'd been used by God to snare Debbie into Ervil's fold. She assuaged her guilt by thinking about her future glory.

Debbie didn't grasp a word of the ceremony. She blocked out Dan's voice, feeling nervous and praying to God that she wouldn't faint. Her sweaty, small hand seemed lost in Ervil's huge grasp. Dan's words crushed her, and she knew she was trapped forever.

"I now pronounce you husband and wife with the right to come forth on the morning of the first resurrection." With those words, Dan finished speaking.

Ervil bent down and forced a kiss on Debbie's unresponsive lips as she turned her head away from him. Her abhorrence intensified at the stench of his breath. She wanted to die. The grave held more appeal than eternal life with Ervil. If he was her heavenly prize, she hoped there would be no resurrection.

★   ★   ★

WITHIN THE YEAR, Ervil set his sights on yet another potential wife. Tall, willowy Rosemary seemed distanced from her husband, Ralph Barlow, from the day they arrived in Zion. When she told me they no longer shared a marital bed, I realized why she acted so aloof whenever he was around. She was the one woman I knew who was relieved when her husband was out of her sight. She also told me that from the very beginning of her marriage she had known Ralph was not a leader. She despised his quiet, docile demeanor, judging him to be weak. The two never really communicated on any sort of deep level, yet their marriage had produced five children. As I observed the Barlow kids, I saw evidence of emotional neglect, apparently due to Rosemary's inability to decide that divorcing Ralph would be justified. Her answer soon came in a women's meeting.

When Ervil explained to the group of women about men not measuring up, being less than useful in the Kingdom of God, Rosemary felt Ervil was speaking directly to her. She felt compelled to ask for a divorce. Her sights were set on the kingdom, and she needed a qualified, godly man to help prepare her for Christ's imminent return. She was drawn, not only to Ervil's profound counsel, but to Ervil himself. Soon she became extremely interested in Ervil's teachings. She asked him to come to her house, where she'd feed him a good meal. There he could give her "personalized" instruction, helping her to better understand the "civil law." Soon, I noticed Ervil sneaking over to Rosemary's at all hours, day and night. When I confronted her about it, quoting the Bible verse that tells us "to shun the very appearance of evil," she secretly confessed that she had been sealed to Ervil for all eternity.

When Ralph returned from Utah to visit his wife and children, he was completely devastated when Rosemary informed him that she had married Ervil. My heart went out to Ralph because Rosemary was all he had. He shed tears of agony to me the night before his final departure. Fearing Ervil's death threats, and afraid his body would be used for compost, he never returned.

CHAPTER FIFTEEN

Brother Thomas Hardman from southern Utah—unmarried, in his sixties—arrived at the colony after his miraculous conversion. Years earlier, he felt he had received a promise from God that he would one day be acquainted with the One Mighty and Strong. When Joel identified himself, Hardman's prayers were answered. He filled up his dilapidated motor home with gas and headed to Mexico to be among the chosen few.

Once he was set up in the colony, he invited the townspeople and their children over for hotcakes. He'd cook up a storm, feeding all who straggled in. Members sat outside on several folding chairs or on the tailgates of their trucks while they ate. The kids in town loved him. He'd watch for them to come by and then invite them inside for candies.

Soon after gaining trust from the saints, he began to prey upon several children. He promised two eight-year-old girls—one of Earl Jensen's young daughters and one of mine—sweets if they'd wash his dishes. Within a few weeks, Hardman invited the innocent girls to lie down to take a nap, offering them more candy. Sandwiched between the two small girls, he put his hands in their panties, fondling them simultaneously. His bathrobe conveniently open, revealing his nakedness, frightened them. The girls broke away, running for home as fast as they could go.

As usual, Earl was not in town. His job in the States kept him away, typically two weeks at a time. When he returned home, his daughter reported the incident. Earl went ballistic. He would not tolerate a man molesting his daughter. Infuriated, and with his .45 in hand, he jumped into his car and raced off to Brother Hardman's motor home. The moment he pulled up, he bounded out of his idling vehicle and kicked open the metal door. "Mr. Bathrobe" sprang to his feet, but before he made it to the door, Earl forced his way in. With his .45 cocked and aimed right between the offender's eyes, Earl didn't wait for any explanations. "I'll give you until five o'clock tonight to leave town," he threatened angrily.

Fearful and guilty, pulling tight his bathrobe to cover himself, the man stuttered, "Okay! Okay! I'll–I'll leave. I–I promise."

Earl settled that problem in a hurry. He could barely endure patriarchs and prophets, let alone a pedophile!

Though Earl believed that Joel was a prophet, he nevertheless wondered about him. He had willingly accepted Joel as his spiritual leader, hoping that soon he and his family would be taken into the clouds to meet Christ at his Second Coming. He believed Joel's revelation "that my people might be prepared to be caught unto the clouds while fire and brimstone are rained upon the face of the whole earth to the utter destruction of the wicked and ungodly."

Never having had a conversation with God himself and learning that Joel had, Earl held him in high esteem. His only gripe had been Joel's lack of control over the new church. Joel seemed to let Ervil have full rein, and Earl resented it. He began to question the leadership, especially when Joel did not reprimand or punish Ervil for some of his blunders. He wondered if Joel was a prophet or a puppet. Earl wanted clarification.

Joel soon convinced Earl that God would assure their success. So, during the church conference on April 3, 1966, Joel formally organized the church. Joel held the office of first grand head prophet, Ervil that of patriarch, and Alma that of the presiding bishop. Joel, Earl Jensen, and John Butchereit were the first presidency. Then, twelve men became the Quorum of Twelve apostles, and twelve others the High Council. Enthusiasm surged through the church and Joel's leadership was fully acclaimed.

CHAPTER SIXTEEN

Joel's Church of the Firstborn tried to practice the Mormon version of the United Order. The idea behind it was to create equality of income, eliminate poverty, help make the group more self-sufficient, and prepare the community for the millennium. Eventually people who joined the church would consecrate all their property to the United Order. The order would then deed back a "stewardship," which gave control of that part of the property to the member who had given it. Then, at the end of the year, any excess the member or family produced from that property was voluntarily returned to the order. On a more practical level, living the United Order meant that for a while we shared all things in common.

Upon learning about our economic system, several Mexicans converted. The sting of their constant poverty encouraged them to believe in the new social system. Wages in Mexico were only eight pesos (one American dollar) a day. The small number of American converts could hardly comprehend subsisting on such meager wages, but we were glad to welcome all new converts. Four of these men were long-lost brothers of Mauro Gutierrez, whom he had convinced to follow him in this new religious adventure.

Joel had designated Alma as bishop over the economics of the church, in fact, theoretically over the whole world. Bishop Alma wrote vouchers each week, giving every family an equal amount of money. Alma had arranged for the vouchers to be redeemed in Casas Grandes at a large mercantile. The owner of the Madrigal de la Luz felt very fortunate to oblige. He anticipated making a windfall. When Alma explained that the church would pay the bill monthly, he agreed, undoubtedly thinking his dealings with Americans would be to his advantage. However, there were no businesses in the colony; therefore most of the Mexican converts worked the land of the LeBarons. It had been anticipated that the church tithes would supply enough to pay the bills, but it didn't take long for the store owner in Casas Grandes to see that he had been duped.

While the Mexican converts enjoyed the economic benefits of living in the colony, they became incensed when they discovered they were not allowed to marry any Caucasian women, but their own daughters were being coerced into marrying the gringos.

To address the contention and unrest, Ervil held separate meetings for the Spanish-speaking members in which he read from the Book of Mormon principles he felt they could not refute. For example, he showed them 1 Nephi 12:23: "And it came to pass that I beheld, after they had dwindled in unbelief they became a dark, and loathsome, and a filthy people, full of idleness and all manner of abominations."

Brother Paisano, a new convert from Puebla near Mexico City, threw such a fit when Ervil read that verse that it riled up the whole Spanish-speaking group. Ervil did not want a riot on his hands. He listened to the opposing voices. Many expressed their anger; they said they resented that Ervil was treating them unfairly, as though they were second-class citizens. They felt threatened in their own land.

Another man also made a fuss. "You LeBaron brothers—you have all married our native women, but what about us? It's not right! You said we'd all be treated equally in Zion. No one is to have that which is above another."

(Indeed Verlan later married two Mexican women, Brother Paisano's daughter Beverly and Fernando Castro's daughter Esther, who became his fourth and fifth wives.)

Ervil continued his sermonizing, and eventually the men were forced to accept the fact that their women would be used by God to further his plan to produce "white and delightsome" children for the Kingdom of God.

Eventually Ervil quieted the commotion by asking Brother Paisano to remain for a private conversation with him after the meeting was adjourned.

Two days later, I was surprised when Ervil invited me to a private wedding. He explained how he'd conceded on this special occasion by allowing Brother Paisano to marry a white sixteen-year-old girl.

Furious, I protested. "How can you change your mind about the Lamanites' not marrying our people?"

"Ahhh . . . you don't understand. This is the lesser of two evils. Sometimes God changes his mind for the good of the people."

At the wedding, Eileen clung to her father's hand for support. She was embarrassed that she stood six inches taller than her soon-to-be-husband. Her mother and I sat nearby listening to Ervil rattle on and on in Spanish. Paisano's first wife, Julia, was home sobbing, on the verge of a breakdown.

Ervil began his long sermon. Invariably he expounded the scriptures boisterously, claiming that every word he spoke came from God. Eileen blushed as he praised her, sometimes in English because her Spanish was so minimal. He enlightened her, explaining how she had been chosen to marry among the Lamanites. He smiled with satisfaction. "We'll become, as 1 Nephi 21:23 says, nursing fathers and mothers to them." He laughed and then crudely joked, "Soon you'll fulfill that literally when you have a child." Eileen turned beet red, and, ashamed for Ervil, I wanted to crawl under the rug.

Both Eileen's father and mother looked so very sad. Her mother whispered to me, looking for reassurance I think, "She doesn't understand much Spanish. I hope she'll be okay." Nodding toward the groom, she asked, "He's at least in his mid-forties, isn't he?"

"Yes, and his first wife has eight children," I whispered back to her.

A few days later, from my yard I could see Brother Paisano yelling angrily at the top of his lungs. I walked over to him, wondering why he was causing all that commotion. As I approached I looked toward where he was gesturing wildly. Eileen was playing baseball on a vacant lot with a group of teenagers. Frightened by Brother Paisano's anger, the kids stopped the game. Eileen had barely made it to second base.

"What's the problem?" I asked.

He shook his finger in my face, raging, "You tell my wife to get home immediately. She has no right to be playing with her friends. She is a married woman now, and I want respect!"

I immediately came to her defense. Though my Spanish wasn't perfect, I knew he would understand. "She's young. You can't impose those kinds of restrictions on an immature girl like that."

He cut me off as Eileen approached us, frightened by his agitated demeanor. "What does he want?" she asked tearfully.

He grabbed her by her arm, forcing her back to the one-room adobe hut he'd borrowed for her to live in.

Her shame at being led like a child plus her ignorance of what she'd actually gotten herself into broke my heart. I thought how fortunate Eileen was that she couldn't understand a word of his ranting.

A few weeks later I asked my friend Linda if she knew how Eileen was doing. "Oh, her parents got her out of the situation. They rescued her and fled back to the States."

I wanted to jump for joy. I couldn't voice it, but I wished my parents would have rescued me.

CHAPTER SEVENTEEN

S hortly after the missionaries arrived from France, they established a private school named after Alma Dayer LeBaron. Stephen Silver became the administrator. No building was available, so classes were held in the church, which was actually a large ranch-style home built by Bruce Wakeham. The Caucasians who attended the school soon learned to speak Spanish fluently, and the Mexican students were delighted to learn English.

As in any school, the students complained regularly about the strict teachers and rules. However, the administrators eased up at least a little bit and allowed the students to hold dances on the weekend.

Of course, even by 1960s standards, these dances were old-fashioned. The Twist, the Hand Jive, and the Stroll were nowhere to be seen. For that matter, neither were the Charleston, the Lindy Hop, or the Fox-trot. No, a person had to look back a century or two to find the steps permitted at our school's dances: the Virginia Reel, the Scottish Polka, and the John Paul Jones. Previously, all waltzes had been banned as part of a hands-off policy that was issued to prevent promiscuity. Finally, one waltz was tolerated as the final dance of the night, but God help the man who danced too close to a woman. Chaperones strictly enforced the "twelve inches of light between couples" rule, and those who broke it were asked to sit down and forfeit the final dance.

Dances weren't the only entertainment, however. I'll never forget when Stephen challenged the students to see who could bring the most dead flies to school. Flies were a plague that year, a plague that could never be controlled. Residents placed cardboard squares of red poison resembling sugar inside and outside every home. The children would collect the dead flies in a glass quart jar, hoping to win by filling it up.

I couldn't help but laugh when I saw the jars of dead insects lined up against the wall. We'd been taught that we were a "peculiar people," and I guess the flies proved it beyond any doubt!

I wasn't the only one to notice our church's peculiarities.

One Sunday, when my daughter Donna was eight, she and I walked the two blocks home together after the meeting. I asked her to share her Sunday lesson with me so I would be aware of what they were teaching her. She excitedly related the account of Joseph, who was sold by his brothers into slavery in Egypt. I listened as we made our way home, and she wound up her story as we walked into the house. I'll never forget how Donna hesitated a minute. Then she asked, "Mama, why do we have so many weirdos in the church?"

I couldn't refrain from laughing. I'd asked myself that same question many times, but not wanting to give credence to her opinion, I responded, "They're not weirdos. Why do you say that?"

"Because they are, Mom," she stated emphatically. "Can't you tell?"

Sorely tempted to agree with her, I turned, with a smile on my face, and began to put a few things together for lunch. I'd seen Verlan in church briefly, and he told me to plan on him for the noon meal. I served hot beans and rice to my children, then Donna washed the dishes and wiped the table while I set places for Verlan and me.

Rushed as usual, Verlan entered and barely kissed me. "Sorry I never made it over to see you yesterday, but I was just too busy. What's new?" he asked, hoping I wouldn't reprimand him or waste his time on trivial matters.

"Not much," I said. Then I decided to share Donna's observations with him, thinking how interesting it was that an eight-year-old had such insight.

When I completed my story, Verlan looked riled, and the tone of his voice as he spoke to me reflected the look on his face. "There's no way she would think that up on her own! If that's what's in her head, then you must have put it there."

I silently took the tongue lashing, thinking how every adult in that community lived in denial. But oh, what truths come out of the mouths of babes.

CHAPTER EIGHTEEN

As an extension of the United Order, Ervil announced one day that there would be no more meals in individual homes. Every woman was to give her food money to him. The groceries would be purchased in bulk and then equally distributed. Making sure we knew this idea was about becoming godlier and increasing our faith, he impressed upon our minds the importance of having everything in common.

"It is not given that one man should possess that which is above another," he said.

Even though I knew he was quoting from Doctrine and Covenants, I thought he was twisting the verse to say what he wanted it to, and I could hardly stand the thought of what this new regulation would mean. As a mother I could easily imagine the drudgery of getting all my children ready to leave the house, walking them to a community kitchen to feed them, getting them settled, feeding them, and then waiting for all to finish before we went back home. And all of this three times a day! It was not to my—or any woman's—advantage.

When I expressed my views, Ervil retorted rudely, "You have no choice. Every family will participate. Those who are selfish, who keep food hidden to eat privately in their homes, will be punished. By Monday, all your food supplies should be taken to Delfina's house. While she is away, I'll donate her house to be used for the good of the saints. I want to form a committee to run the kitchen." He flashed his charming smile. "They say if you want to get anything done, ask the busiest person you know to do it. Therefore, I am designating Irene to be the manager over the whole operation."

I was not pleased. "It's impossible," I said. "I have four children under the age of six. If I work all day preparing meals, I'll be away from my babies with no one to tend them."

"Well," he replied, grinning, "we'll set up a nursery where your children will be taken care of and taught the gospel."

Ervil's words caused an uproar, and he tried to quiet the women down. "Yes, everyone's children will belong to the community. Doris," he said, pointing at her, "you will be the supervisor over the nursery. Appoint other women to help you. But don't get me involved. I have too many responsibilities as it is."

I knew he had put Doris in charge because he could trust his niece to implicitly carry out his orders.

Before the meeting was over, Ervil had effectively severed us from our children, allowing them back into our care only at bedtime. Adding insult to injury, he said, "I want to raise all these children up like calves in a stall, as it says in Malachi."

With no other option but to obey, I put my shoulder to the wheel. At five o'clock the next morning I awoke and got myself dressed, leaving my nursing baby and the other two children sleeping with Donna, while I rushed two blocks away to Delfina's house, the newly designated community compound to prepare breakfast for the entire community.

I was furious to be under Ervil's control. Verlan was away working in the States and couldn't defend Charlotte, Lucy, and me. Dealing with my two sister wives was overwhelming enough without having to carry out Ervil's latest scheme.

My letter shocked Verlan, and he wrote back the same day, requesting that I not act irrationally.

Go to Joel. I am sure he is keeping an eye on Ervil. As far as the community being united, it will be a good experience. Ervil mentioned to me before I left that he wanted to set up kibbutzes like they have in Israel. Be patient. He is only trying to do what's best for our people. Keep going, at least until I return. Maybe by then we can figure something else out.

I appreciated his prompt reply, but it did little to calm my anxiety and anger over having to spend my days preparing food for a hundred-plus people.

Our meager menu of beans, rice, whole wheat bread, and cracked cereal lacked nutritional balance. We literally had no fruits, vegetables, or milk for our growing children. I had hoped that with communal money, I could change that by buying produce and dairy products in bulk.

However, my plans came to naught and then I discovered Ervil was dipping into the funds that had been designated for the communal kitchen. When I confronted him, he tried to justify his actions, inferring that it was no big deal. He was just trying to buy extra fruits and goodies to keep in his home to sustain his health.

I blew up. "We *all* need extra! Most of the women are pregnant. The little ones are growing and need all the nutritious food they can get. These people deserve the same treatment as you do. What's good for the goose is good for the gander. I thought you promised we would all be equal."

He laughed at my feistiness. "How can our people ever be taken into the presence of God if they are not willing to sacrifice?" Turning serious, almost threatening, he said, "Don't you breathe a word about how I run things around here. It's nobody's business, because God's put me in charge. If people start murmuring, we'll find ourselves in the exact position the Israelites were in. It was their complaining and murmuring that kept them from entering the Promised Land. Let's nip this in the bud and make sure we don't do likewise."

Forced to be on my feet cooking and cleaning for twelve to fourteen hours a day caused painful, pulsating varicose veins in my legs. I mourned for my babies in child care. When my breasts were bursting with milk, I was allowed to leave other women in charge long enough to go to the nursery and breast-feed my four-month-old son.

One afternoon I heard wails of despair from the adjacent room. Realizing it was my three-year-old Andre, I kept the baby latched onto my breast and walked to the other room.

Doris met me at the door and questioned my right to barge into her territory. Andre was squirming on a small chair, his tiny face as red as a beet and his eyes so swollen he could hardly see. I could tell immediately as he tried to keep his eyes shut that something was irritating them. I tried to scoop him into my arms for comfort, but Doris grabbed him in a show of authority, trying to stop me. "He's been a naughty boy and he's receiving his punishment," she said.

"What did you do to my child?" I demanded, forcing him away from her.

"Well, he's a bawl baby, crying all day because he thinks he needs his blanket, and I wouldn't give it to him."

"What's he got in his eyes?" I demanded.

"Well, he wouldn't stop sucking his thumb when I told him to, so I dipped it into a can of jalapeños. The spoiled little brat rubbed the stuff into his eyes."

I grabbed my son, holding him and my baby in my arms for protection. I saw his blanket on the crib, grabbed it, and stormed out of the room. Hell or no hell, I did not put my babies back under someone else's care.

When Ervil asked around the kitchen that afternoon as to my whereabouts, he was very upset that I had not returned to work. He came to my house to persuade me to go back to the kitchen. I gave him a definite no and he knew I meant it.

Not wanting other women to follow my rebellion, he reassigned me to other duties. "I'll allow another woman to run the cafeteria. I want you to run the washeteria. Three Maytag wringer washers have been set up outside behind the kitchen. Four teenage boys will be at your disposal. They'll fill the washers and tubs with water from the well. All you have to do is keep track of each family's clothes, and when they're washed, stack them in tubs. The boys will deliver them to their owners. They can hang their own clothes out to dry."

Again I understood that I had no choice but to obey, so I complied, fulfilling my assignment until Verlan's return. At least I could keep my children with me. They could play or sleep in the shade while I worked and the teenage boys and I kept an eye on them. The women were especially thrilled, knowing that someone was keeping up their wash. Many had previously been scrubbing on wooden washboards, so they were very appreciative to have the burden taken from them. Luckily, I did not receive any complaints.

JOEL HAD BEEN DOING missionary work in the States with other leaders for several months. They were dedicating themselves to preaching the gospel among the Mormons before they took the truth to the gentiles because they believed that God's judgments would begin on the house of God.

When he returned, I caught up with Joel in the kitchen soup line, intending to have lunch with his congregation. "Joel," I said, knowing he could hear the displeasure in my voice, "how long do we have to put up with Ervil's crap?"

He nonchalantly replied, "Just until you all get sick and tired of it." I was dumbfounded by his answer! I could tell that he felt this regimentation was unnecessary and if it were up to him, we could stop immediately.

So, the community kitchen soon came to an end.

WOMEN WERE NOT VALUED in the colony. If we had opinions, we learned to keep them to ourselves. We knew our duty was to bear children for our future inheritance in another world. We were told repeatedly not to let a year go by without seeing that a child was born under this holy covenant of plural marriage. We had been intimidated and frightened by the brethren. Birth control was a wicked practice that would take us straight to hell. The average number of children among polygamists is twelve, although many have fourteen to eighteen children. I knew one woman who was used as a righteous example because she gave birth to nineteen children, including one set of twins.

No woman dared mention her dissatisfaction with bearing children. Even if she was emotionally or physically incapable of enduring another pregnancy, she obediently accepted her role without complaining. Her godhood was at stake.

Clearly, childbearing was used as a means of control. No mother with that many children would dare try to leave the group. She understood the rules. The children she birthed automatically belonged to her husband. She'd been told that she could walk out freely anytime, but she would be required to forfeit her children.

I well remember a conversation Verlan had with Joel, in my presence, many years later. Verlan's sixth wife, Susan, had left him on several occasions, taking her three small children with her to be among her brothers in Utah. Having recently convinced Susan to return to him, Verlan asked Joel what advice he could give him to persuade her to stay permanently. His answer stung my senses.

"Just keep her pregnant," Joel sagely advised. "Soon she'll have so many kids she won't be able to leave."

Obviously, I was already bound and shackled, being pregnant with my thirteenth child.

CHAPTER NINETEEN

A huge flatbed truck, carrying a massive generator, eased down the embankment off the gravel highway into the LeBaron colony. Once the portable power plant was unloaded, word traveled fast among the family and church members. I could hardly wait to enjoy electricity in my home! However, I wondered how the colony had come up with the money to purchase the generator. I knew no monies were available from the church; the little tithing that came in was snatched up by Ervil to support his families.

The rumor spread quickly through the colony: the generator had been stolen. I wasted no time in finding Ervil and accosting him. I knew he could tell by the look on my face and my determined steps that I had caught wind of the deal. As I entered unannounced, he asked, "What's the problem this time, Irene? You look upset."

"I want to know the truth!" I blurted out. "Is the light plant stolen?"

"Now, now, don't get upset. Let's just say that the Lord put it in our hands."

His words verified my suspicions. "How can the Lord condone stolen property?"

As always, Ervil laughed, sneering as though he were questioning my intelligence. "You must realize that God allows us to steal from the gentiles." He tried to pat my shoulder patronizingly.

"That's a bunch of poppycock!" I yelled, pulling away. "Don't the scriptures say to love our neighbors as ourselves? Is that loving them? By stealing from them?"

He knit his eyebrows, staring icily at me a second or two, and then he spoke. "Calm down. You don't understand the things of God. In the first place, our neighbors are those who believe like we do. If you'd just read the Bible, you'll understand."

"You're nuts!" I said defensively. "On one hand you teach that stealing is a sin that carries a death penalty. On the other, you try to justify it from the Bible, telling me it's acceptable. That's just crazy!"

"Listen," he said. Then he sighed and looked at the ceiling as though he were trying to find simple enough words to explain to one as ignorant as I apparently was. I knew he was mentally preparing a sermon, and, though I could hardly bear to listen, I swallowed my pride and stood still.

"We're just doing like the Israelites did. Remember when they plundered the gold and silver from the Egyptians? God was behind that, can't you see?"

"No I can't!" I retaliated, all thoughts of submission gone.

"Well, God allowed them to take the jewels from their wicked masters and carry the spoils into the Promised Land. That's all we're doing. We're using the valuable goods of the unbelieving gentiles to build up the Kingdom of God."

Disgusted, I interrupted. "That's just a load of crap, and you know it. I can't take any more." I left in a huff.

It didn't take long for Ervil to realize that the generator caused more problems than it was going to solve. Afraid the church would lose members when the rumor of the theft was confirmed, he quietly sold the generator to some unsuspecting Mexicans.

According to yet another rumor I heard from several people, when Ervil was questioned about the stolen property, he said, "This group is not yet worthy to understand the things of God."

WITH CHURCH MEMBERSHIP GROWING faster than incoming tithes and offerings, Joel felt increasing pressure to provide for his impoverished flock. To deal with the demands, Joel wrote rubber checks, hoping to find a way to cover them before they bounced. Soon he and Alma were dodging their creditors. Because of the influx of members who needed food and housing, they soon owed thousands of dollars, which they were unable to pay.

Verlan told me how appalled he was when he learned that Ervil convinced five followers that he'd received the solution from the Lord to the dilemma. Verlan was so humiliated he made sure I didn't know who the five men were, for fear I'd lose my faith in the church. Ervil told the men they would go to "Sin City" itself, where they'd gamble for money to pay their debtors. They would redeem the LeBaron name and repay the creditors. He promised the riches of the gentiles would fall into their hands. When Ervil ran his "inspiration" by Joel, Joel was pleased, bestowing his blessings to the euphoric group. With some of the church's tithes and their meager savings, the men set out for Las Vegas.

Once in a modest hotel room, the men talked about their new adventure, wondering how the casino owners would react when the church members beat the system. The men prayed before they left the room, begging God to turn the cards in their favor, as he had promised Ervil. Satisfied that the Lord was on their side, they confidently sat down to play blackjack at the Horse Shoe Casino.

Believing they had been given a system inspired by God himself, the men laid down big bets. The hopes of the gamblers were dashed all too soon, however, as several thousand dollars vanished before their disbelieving eyes. They barely had gas money for their trip home. They were crushed, and blamed Satan for cunningly stealing their money.

Their faith shaken, they got into the car to return to the colony. Ervil, never one to pass up an opportunity to preach, spent the entire trip chastising the group, accusing them of lusting after money. He said they had lost the spirit of God because they had diverted their attention away from the very purpose of the trip. The dejected group wondered among themselves what exactly they had done to tick God off. Fervently believing Ervil's whispers were from God, they took responsibility for the foiled mission.

One disgruntled member, who had donated his nest egg, asked Joel why he had allowed them to participate in the failed venture. Joel offered consoling advice: "God wants to give us his treasures. This is just a small setback. The scripture promises us the riches of the gentiles. We will prosper mightily as we build up the kingdom. This is just a test to see where our hearts really are."

Floren, Ervil, and
Verlan as children.

Dayer LeBaron with daughter Lucinda.

Verlan at age sixteen.

Joel and Floren riding horses.

Ervil LeBaron, the infamous cult leader.

Joel claimed to be a prophet and started his Church of the Firstborn of the Fullness of Times.

Floren was with Joel when the church was established.

Nephi Marston was a childhood friend of Ervil's, and they had both followed Ben as a prophet at one time. Ervil stole Nephi's wife Anna Mae and replaced her with two Mexican maidens. Nephi died in a tragic automobile accident with five other church members.

Alma, Ervil, and Delfina with the kids headed to Spencerville for church.

Lucinda was locked up in a two-room adobe house for years.

Joseph, Joan, and Maudie became orphans when their mother, Lucinda, was in a mental hospital.

Joe's truck was used to haul produce to sell in the mountains.

Mauro Gutierrez was the first male Lamanite to convert to the Church of the Firstborn.

Floren, Lucy, and Verlan in 1955.

The LeBaron and Spencer children in Spencerville.

Joel and Ervil on an
LDS mission.

Colonia LeBaron, 1962.

All of the French missionaries.

Joan holding Andre in front
of my adobe house.

Joy Marston, me
and Gaye Stubbs.
Joy Marston (Nephi
Marston's sister) was
Ervil's first Caucasian
wife. Gaye Stubbs
was the prophet Joel's
third wife. When
Joel was courting
her, she took care
of me when I had
typhoid fever.

Joe Marston (Nephi Marston's father) once followed Ben LeBaron as a prophet, along with Alma and Ervil. He later joined Joel's church.

Betty Tippetts was like a sister to me. She caught Ervil in bed with Nephi Marston's wife Anna Mae.

Maud LeBaron.

Ervil's daughter Rebecca with her husband, Victor Chynoweth. Ervil ordered that Rebecca be put to death.

Ervil Morrel LeBaron.

Verlan and me, 1969.

Dan Jordan and Ervil.

Floren, Alma, Verlan, Joel, and Ervil at a church conference.

The remains of the tower, which was burned to lure out the townspeople.

The LeBaron brothers with their mother in Mexico.

CHAPTER TWENTY

My mother-in-law, Maud, owned about fifty acres within the LeBaron spread. Each parcel was fenced and divided up among her family. When she was about sixty-eight, her sons took turns planting crops on her land, using the proceeds to help support her.

One sunny morning while I was visiting Maud, we heard the sounds of a tractor nearby. From her window, she glanced out toward her bare field, surprised that one of her grandsons was plowing her land. "I wonder why he's on my land?" she asked uneasily. "He doesn't have permission to use it. I told Verlan he could plant there this year to help support his wives."

Knowing it would be too great an imposition for her to walk the distance to confront her grandson, I offered to inquire about it. He saw me walking to the barbed wire fence where I awaited his arrival. He kept his eye on the plow until he was almost to the fence, then he lifted the hydraulically controlled plow, allowing him to turn the tractor around. Once the tractor was in neutral, he jumped off and walked toward me. "What's going on, *Tia*?" he asked, addressing me as "aunt." He hadn't turned out as white and delightsome as his two younger siblings. His appearance was more like that of his mother's, short and darker skinned.

"What are you doing?" I inquired. "Your grandmother sent me over to investigate. She wants to know why you're plowing her land."

"Oh, it's not hers anymore. Uncle Ervil said he needed the money, so he sold it to me."

"Well, Grandma knows nothing of this. You'd better check with her before you do any more plowing."

Sure enough, Maud's own son had defrauded her by selling off her property. She never did confront Ervil, but she was sickened and brokenhearted by his betrayal. Despite her feelings, she kept quiet, preferring to bear the shame of her son's actions privately.

BETWEEN THE BIRTHS of her nine children and Ervil's quests to gather new wives, Delfina suffered bouts of severe depression. Regularly, she'd lose touch with reality and often needed to be hospitalized. Her mental weakness infuriated Ervil, so he used it as an excuse to search out new wives. He belittled and defamed her, making sure everyone knew she was a thorn in his flesh and that the devil controlled her.

Though Ervil had written her off, I felt a deep compassion for Delfina. I befriended her, becoming her confidante and helper. Her five small girls had so few clothes that I made it my responsibility to sew dresses for them, using the discarded clothes Verlan brought to Mexico from Vegas. Also, I sewed nylon panties, making six pairs apiece for them. Delfina was so grateful. It did my heart good to finally see her focusing on something other than Ervil. I identified with her. She was separated from her parents and siblings. She had no real marriage and in her poverty was left to fend for herself.

On two separate occasions, she successfully petitioned a Mexican friend in El Valle who owned a clothing store to allow her to sell dresses from house to house on commission. She rode the bus to nearby towns and knocked on doors, selling her goods. Delfina thrived on her accomplishments, and I was tickled to see that she had found a purpose and now wore a couple of pretty new dresses herself.

When he found out, Ervil insisted that Delfina stop her enterprise immediately. He told her she was degrading him by selling on the streets. Obediently, she returned the few remaining dresses to her friend. Again, I witnessed Delfina relinquish reality, sinking deeper into her life of shattered dreams.

At times, though, Delfina held on to what seemed to be a small ray of hope, watching...waiting...for Ervil's return. Though she felt his rejection and his disdain toward her and even her children, she could not even entertain the idea that Ervil had abandoned her, let alone her children.

Her daughter Sylvia Esther married Thomas Liddiard when she was fifteen, becoming his second wife. Another daughter, Sara Jane, was, at fifteen, forced to marry, literally fighting her father as he dragged her to the altar. She was given to Dan Jordan to be another one of his plural wives.

Beautiful Rebecca, the apple of Delfina's eye, had been promised to Victor Chynoweth at the tender age of fourteen. For two years, Ervil dangled her like a carrot before Victor, enticing him to supply Ervil with large sums of money from his lucrative auto dealership in Ogden, Utah. Delfina was brokenhearted seeing her adolescent daughters used as pawns in the game of polygamy.

On the other hand, because of her total loyalty and dedication to her father, tall, sweet, sixteen-year-old Lillian was allowed to marry Victor's brother, Mark Chynoweth, whom she loved.

I couldn't help but admire Ervil's daughter Alicia. She was beautiful, blonde, and determined to keep out of her father's clutches until she found her own path in life. Her father's unscrupulous actions had stripped any vestiges of religious convictions from Alicia's mind. She knew she would fight for freedom whatever the cost. She tried to appease her father—and get out of his way—by asking permission to marry a man she loved. When Ervil denied her request, the couple hastily left for the U.S. to live a life of their own choosing.

CHAPTER TWENTY-ONE

I couldn't help but laugh over an incident Verlan shared with me about the time when he, Joel, and Ervil were proselyting at Harold Blackmore's home in LaVerkin, Utah. Harold was an independent polygamist who was gracious enough to give the men lodging and meals for a couple of days while they preached their claims of superior priesthood.

One morning, Ervil told Harold, "I've got something very confidential to tell you."

Blackmore asked, "Oh? What is it?"

Ervil wanted to get Harold alone to assert his personal authority, so he put his arm around Harold to make him feel special, as he often did with those he tried to manipulate, urging him outside to speak in private. Harold resisted, "Just spill it out for everyone, we're not keeping any secrets here."

Ervil reluctantly complied, taking a serious tone. "An angel appeared to me last night and told me that you should join us— consecrate your life and your possessions to the work of God."

Joel and Verlan were surprised that Ervil was so blunt. Harold asked Ervil, "Was that angel crippled?"

"No," Ervil answered.

"Then why didn't he have enough sense," Harold quipped, "to just come in the next room and tell me himself?"

For once, Ervil had no answer. As for Harold, it was the end of his hospitality.

I found this terribly funny but didn't fully understand why until years later. It illustrates the fatal flaw in religious fundamentalism. It's one thing to claim that God talks to *you*. It's another to claim that God talks to you *for other people*, that *your* revelations apply *to them*. If "God is no respecter of persons," then God can talk to anyone directly, without an intercessor. But Ervil was determined to convince everyone that *his* revelations applied to *them*. (Aspects of my account are cited in another version of the story, *Prophet of Blood*, p. 92.)

Roy Wooley, from Ogden, Utah, was a new convert to Joel's church. He invited Verlan and me to stay at his home while Verlan did missionary work, hoping to convert some of Roy's friends. Verlan had gone to Salt Lake City for two days and left me alone at the Wooleys. Roy, his wife, and four children were seated at the dinner table with me when Dan Jordan and Ervil dropped in. Roy's wife, Evelyn, invited the men to join us for dinner.

Dan and Ervil had barely sat down when Ervil blurted out that the Catholic Knights of Columbus were out to kill them. Dan nodded in agreement. Ervil went on to say that they had been pursued through Mexico and into Ogden. He confidently claimed there was a conspiracy to kill him to thwart the will of God.

Apparently, when they were sleeping at a YMCA, Dan's pistol somehow accidentally had gone off. Both men had jumped to their feet and fled.

The longer Ervil talked, the more skeptical I became. His stories weren't ringing true, and I could see he was exaggerating his importance and being paranoid. I sensed his account was the product of his vivid imagination and his deep longing to be somebody. He claimed that as he was God's anointed, Satan was out to destroy him, making it impossible for him to set up the Kingdom of God.

While we were eating and listening to Ervil's rhetoric, someone rang the doorbell. Both Dan and Ervil leaped up from the table, knocking over plates and Dan's chair. They made no effort to be quiet as they stampeded to the basement to hide. We all knew that whoever was on the other side of the door had heard the scuffle, and the Wooleys looked quite embarrassed even before the two men disappeared down the stairs.

Roy got up to open the door; it was his bishop from the LDS Church. Roy and Evelyn invited him into the living room while the children and I finished dinner. Feeling extremely awkward, Roy searched for words but couldn't come up with an explanation for what the bishop had heard. Finally breaking the uncomfortable silence, Roy admitted to the bishop that he had joined Joel's church, and he requested that his name be stricken from the LDS Church's records.

Dan and Ervil spent the following two days hiding in the Wooleys' basement, even demanding that Evelyn bring their meals downstairs. They still believed the Knights of Columbus or the Masons were trying to kill them.

When Verlan phoned me, he related his plans to continue to preach for a few more days. I knew he had enough family problems, but I felt compelled to inform him that I thought Ervil had lost a few of his marbles. I was embarrassed and disappointed that our new members had witnessed Ervil's paranoia, so I told Verlan I felt Ervil would do more harm than good in the mission field. I thought he should be sent back to Mexico.

After Verlan returned from visiting with Ervil, he was mad

at me for even insinuating that Ervil had any mental problems. Months later, however, he apologized to me. He was beginning to see for himself Ervil's determination and hunger for power. He could see that Ervil had become a law unto himself, and Verlan wondered what would eventually happen. Looking back on their childhood, he recalled how Ervil had always called the shots. He had flaunted his superiority to his siblings, always demanding they be subservient to him. Verlan's hopes for a united church and the fulfillment of their father's dream—that his boys would rule the world and prepare for Christ's return— were slowly and steadily eroding.

WHILE VERLAN WAS EXPERIENCING this disappointment, his brother Ben was bringing unwanted attention to the family name. When the news of Ben reached him, Verlan was humiliated. Here the LeBarons were trying to convince the world of Joel's coveted position as the foretold One Mighty and Strong, yet Ben was undermining the authenticity of Joel's claim by writing a testimony about his own divine authority to my uncle Rulon. On July 5, 1962, Ben attested in a letter:

Dear Brother Allred,

I am the Prophet Mighty and Strong . . . I am King of Kings today . . . I am God, the third; the Holy Ghost; or the third member of the Trinity since Adam went to Mars nearly 300 years ago, leaving Jesus and Joseph Smith and myself in charge. Jesus was killed for saying he was the Son of God. Joseph Smith was killed for inferring that he was one of the Trinity.

I was killed for the same reason—but an angel of God has raised me from the dead and I stand truthful in all things . . .

I will be translated as were Enoch, Moses, and Elijah. I am the

Lord's anointed and hold the scepter of power. Moroni was not as
great as I am, and neither is [LDS President] *McKay...*
  Ervil is King of Israel...
  Take two more wives thus saith the Lord.

Ben T. LeBaron *(*The LeBaron Story, *p. 61)*

Verlan was mortified when the contents of Ben's insane letter circulated throughout "Zion" (Utah). Verlan saw it as just one more blow against the LeBarons, who were already stigmatized. LDS in the Mormon colonies, and even other fundamentalist groups, already thought the LeBarons were wacko. Lucinda was in a mental institution, as Ben had been on several occasions. Alma and Ervil had denounced LDS Mormonism and were known as "apostates." So now people would judge the new church as even stranger due to Ben's letter.

CHAPTER TWENTY-TWO

Moans of dissatisfaction rang through the congregation. Ervil had just announced there would be no Christmas celebration ever again. Instead, we would celebrate Joseph Smith's birthday on December 23. He warned the group that he would not tolerate a Christmas tree or decorations displayed in anyone's home. He spent half an hour informing the less knowledgeable about Christmas being a pagan holiday, and that Jesus' birthday was really on the 6th of April.

After the meeting, several of my friends complained. "Christmas is the best time of year. Everybody has vacations from school and work. People travel across the country to spend time celebrating with their families. We need that, especially with our husbands away working so much of the time." Even more, the women felt appalled that Ervil would discredit Jesus. The whole world celebrated his birth, so why not us?

I thought Ervil had gone too far. We were so poor. The children never had any toys or gifts other than at Christmas, and even then the presents were meager. For Ervil to deny us that one small joy seemed cruel and mean-spirited. Besides, I knew

Verlan would be upset when he heard the news; he absolutely loved Christmas and doing something special for his children.

Seeing our disappointment, Ervil tried to counteract it by excitedly depicting the wonderful birthday party we could have for Joseph Smith, the founder of the Mormon Church. Ervil felt Joseph Smith deserved the glory and praise for restoring the everlasting gospel. We would have a potluck at the church every December 23 and sing praises, giving honor to this great prophet.

Verlan returned home in time for the birthday party. Appalled by Ervil's ridiculous order, Verlan felt that Jesus Christ should be honored, and, besides, he had arrived home with many used toys for the children. He was prepared to celebrate Christmas! So, despite Ervil's order, Verlan observed Christmas in our home. Although we didn't have a tree or any decorations, we celebrated with a feast of popcorn balls, molasses candy, peanuts, oranges, and cinnamon rolls.

Ervil chastised Verlan the following day, but Verlan let him know that he had no right to tell him what he could or couldn't do with his own family.

The wedge between the brothers widened.

ERVIL SEEMED TO HAVE SET his sights on every young female in town. As if fourteen-year-old Kristina and fifteen-year-old Debbie weren't enough to satisfy his sexual cravings, he desired fourteen-year-old Susan Ray, who had promised to marry Verlan. Sneaking behind Verlan's back, Ervil sent Anna Mae to the church's private school to sign Susan out, giving the excuse that Ervil needed a private audience with her, so she had to comply.

Unbeknownst to her parents, Ervil was lying in his bed, with Susan seated in a chair next to him, where he attempted to brainwash her. "It's God's will that you marry me! You can marry my brother Verlan if you want, but the Lord told me to warn you, if you want a greater glory, you must marry me."

Susan had been infatuated with Verlan for six months and had her father's permission to marry as soon as she turned fifteen in October. Ervil knew if he didn't act fast that she would proceed with her plans.

"Why does God say I have to marry you?" she asked, pouting.

Ervil smiled cunningly, hoping to ease the pressure a bit. "You don't *have* to marry me. God is definitely giving you a choice, but . . . like I say, Verlan is the lesser choice. Don't you want to do what God thinks is best for you?"

Innocent Susan found herself unprotected in Ervil's arms, fighting off his advances. Even his bad breath repulsed her. She knew Ervil had crossed the line. She broke away and refused to answer his summons again.

Verlan never gave much validity to others' complaints of Ervil's cunning practices, but when he was the victim, he could ignore his brother no longer. His own flesh and blood was undermining him, sneaking around in an attempt to steal his promised bride. Verlan was furious.

He burst into Ervil's bedroom uninvited and had it out with his brother. After a short time, though, Verlan walked out. He couldn't bear to listen to Ervil's absurdities for another moment. He wondered how Ervil could use God in every other sentence to his own advantage. Once again he questioned Ervil's sanity.

A forgiving man, Verlan returned after his marriage and honeymoon with Susan, hoping to make amends when he ran into Ervil. He offered his hand, but Ervil refused it.

CHAPTER TWENTY-THREE

My niece Jenny Lou, Wesley's daughter, was turning fifteen, and I knew Ervil had brainwashed her into marrying a man twenty-five years her senior just after her birthday.

I loved hanging out with her and the other young teens, and I often invited them to gather in my home to play board games and eat dessert.

Since I knew Jenny Lou would soon leave the teenagers' group and be initiated into the adult community, I decided to give her a surprise birthday party. I sent one of Jenny Lou's friends from house to house, inviting those in her age group to come to my home at seven thirty that night.

Walking back from the small store where I had just bought powdered sugar to make frosting for the birthday cake, I was accosted by Dan, one of Ervil's enforcers.

"I hear you are illegally holding an unauthorized party in your home," he said, puffing out his chest, doing his best to look menacing.

"It's nobody's business who I have in my home. I can have a party if and when I want to!" I retorted hotly, stepping to the side to get away from this inane conversation.

He detained me. "Believe me," he threatened, "if you hold a party in your house, you and everyone who attends will be excommunicated from the church."

"Well," I said determinedly, "I'll take the crowd with me up to Spencerville, and we'll have a party up there, because, again, it's no one's business what I do."

Unwilling to concede, Dan continued. "Ervil sent me to put a stop to this before you find yourself in big trouble."

Starting to cry, I yelled, "This sounds like damn communism to me!"

I sidestepped past him, heading for home, powdered sugar in hand, as he yelled behind me, "Just try being defiant. You'll be run out of town permanently."

So much for birthday parties, I thought. With Verlan gone, I didn't dare defy Ervil.

I tried to understand Ervil's control. He had prohibited us from celebrating Christ's birth, but I couldn't understand why we couldn't celebrate a special day with innocent teenagers. After all, her birthday just may have been Jenny Lou's last day of happiness before she married Ervil's friend, becoming his third wife.

That day my dislike and irritation with this egotistical despot began to turn toward hatred.

CHAPTER TWENTY-FOUR

One day, on a whim, Ervil called the women together to relate God's most recent orders. "Everyone here is responsible to somebody...and for somebody. We are all connected! You *are* your brother's keeper. Do you understand? If you see someone bad-mouthing your leaders, and you do not turn that person in, then you will receive the punishment they deserve." He glared at the group and clarified the command further: "Even if it's your husband, mother, sister, or child. If any of you even think about having an affair, lying, stealing, gossiping, or not keeping my trust, you will be found out. We must all be on the lookout," he cautioned, "to keep sin from raising its wicked head among us."

Shortly after our orders to *tattle* on everyone, I found myself in a dilemma. My friend Jody entered my kitchen bright and early one morning, before my kids were up and dressed. Her swollen, tear-stained face revealed her pain. Putting my arm around my friend for comfort, I asked her, "What is it? Are you having a rough time down here in this foreign country?" I'd heard the despair of several new arrivals from California who said they'd prefer death to having to go on living here in Zion. Jody held on to me as she burst into tears. Embracing her, I asked again, "What's the matter? Let me help you. You'll be all right."

"I can't tell you." She sobbed harder.

"Well, you don't have to if you don't want to. After a few minutes, you'll probably feel better."

"No, you don't understand!" she said more insistently. "I *have* to tell someone so they can report it to Ervil. I don't want to, but I'm forced to. If I don't, I could receive the death penalty."

Out of respect, I kept calm. I thought she was taking her problem too seriously, but I was willing to hear her out. "What could be so bad?"

"We had a friend come over for a visit last night. Darren and I were comforting her because she was having problems in her marriage. At midnight, I went to bed. Later, I was awakened by what I thought was the whimpering of the dog. When I went to investigate, there on the sofa was Darren in the act of making love to this woman." She cried again, relieved that she had been able to spit it out. "I'm afraid Darren will hold it against me if he finds out I'm the one who ratted on him."

"Does he know you saw him?" I asked.

"No, I was so shocked I just quietly went back to bed. Promise me you won't reveal a word to anyone except Ervil. Promise me," she pleaded. "I feel so bad that I have to be the one to tell on my own husband."

I had held on to my faith, believing Joel was God's anointed. Surely Joel could keep Ervil in control, so I pushed my fears aside again. "I don't think you need to worry, Ervil is just full of hot air."

In that instant, a bolt of fear shot through my body. For a fleeting moment, his scare tactics got to me. I thought I knew him well—that he was just big talk, that he exaggerated his threats just to scare us—but...if there was *one* chance in a million that Ervil was serious, then I would be held accountable if I remained silent.

So, at Jody's insistence, I promised her that I would be the bad guy; I'd do her dirty work.

I found Ervil, as usual, shut up in his bedroom, propped up by three feather pillows, under his covers in bed. He always lit up when I was in his presence. He invariably tried to flirt, telling me what a prize I was and how he had lost out by not having me (which I never stopped resenting through the years).

"You've taught us that we are responsible to somebody...and for somebody, haven't you?"

"That's right." He smiled, satisfied that I knew the rules.

I continued. "Someone came crying to me an hour ago. She was weeping because she caught her husband in the act of adultery with someone else's wife."

Ervil threw his bare legs over the side of the bed, planting his large feet on the floor. Then, pulling a blanket around him, he covered his knees as he sat up. "Tell me who it is," he demanded angrily. His face became red with excitement. "You tell me who it is and I *promise* you we will make an example out of him! He will be punished to the fullest extent. I'll have his wife taken away from him and give her to a more worthy man."

With each sentence, he became more incensed, promising to carry out his radical measures. I was relieved that Jody wasn't there to endure his harsh words.

When I realized how severe the punishment might be, and seeing Ervil's determination, I was reluctant to admit the perpetrator's name for fear I'd be an accomplice if the penalty was death. "It's...Darren," I finally confessed, hoping Ervil wouldn't fly into another violent rage.

"Darren?" he asked, dumbfounded.

"Yes, Darren," I repeated.

Ervil stuttered, grasping for words. "Who knows about this?"

"Just Jody and me," I admitted.

Ervil's scowl was replaced by his cunning smile. "I *demand* that both of you keep this under your hat." He paused to be sure I understood. Then, trying to justify his calmness, he said, "You see, Darren is contributing to a great cause." He went on with his rationalizations. "If he faithfully continues to support me by making the payments on my new car, I'll continue to let the Lord use him. After all, he can still find forgiveness. When a sinner sacrifices for a servant of God to the fullest extent, he can someday have his sin blotted out."

AT NOON, ERVIL SHOWED UP for lunch at my house. I knew he had come over to be nice to me and to warn me again to keep our little secret.

Ervil had a strong sense of entitlement. He would regularly go through town, stopping in unannounced, searching for a better meal than he could find at Delfina's. He knew he would eat like a king and receive special treatment because of his position in the church. He felt it was beneath him to eat at his own house, where he would be served only beans and tortillas.

On one particular occasion when he invited himself to a member's home, I was visiting there when he barged in unexpectedly. Ervil seemed to be anywhere except home when mealtime came around. The lady of the house hurriedly set a plate and utensils on the table as her two kids crowded closer together to make room for Ervil. The family was just preparing to pass the plate of food around to one another. Out of respect, the woman offered the platter of sunny-side-up eggs to Ervil first so he could serve himself. To our chagrin, he simply slid all eight eggs onto his plate.

In his usual offensive manner, he handed the empty plate to the astonished woman and pompously insisted, "If you want anyone else to have any eggs, you'd better jump up and cook some more."

I boiled with resentment toward him, and my motherly instinct wanted to apologize for his rude behavior. From the bewilderment on our hostess's face, I knew she was unfamiliar with Ervil's tactless antics. He was always butting in unannounced, acting like a bull in a china shop. He may have thought that his charisma and chiseled good looks made up for his obnoxious behavior, but he was wrong. In fact, I feared that his kingdom would fold if he didn't display better manners and show respect for his recent converts.

WHEN ERVIL WAS CONFRONTED by three uneasy followers concerning the ugly rumors that were circulating about death penalties, he knew the time had come to set things straight once and for all. He called an impromptu meeting that every adult—age fifteen and over—was required to attend, with absolutely no exceptions. The room buzzed with conversation. We took our seats, but the commotion continued as the saints talked among themselves, asking questions and venting their fears.

Ervil appeared bundled in his coat, his wool scarf wrapped tightly around his neck. A hush fell over the room. Scowling, he walked to the podium, coughed, and readjusted his scarf.

He began the meeting by complaining about the inconvenience he was enduring, having been forced to call his unenlightened people together. He grumbled that we had caused him to get out of his sick bed and suffer in the cold just because of a few naysayers. "Mind you," he said, "none of you understand the workings of the almighty God."

We listened without comment to his castigating remarks.

"If you knew the purposes of God, you wouldn't have to impose on me tonight." He smirked as he opened his worn Book of Mormon, thumbing through the pages. He smiled, satisfied, when he located the verse. Certain he was exhibiting superior knowledge, he said to the crowd, "I'm reading to you tonight from 1 Nephi 4:12, yes, that's 1 Nephi 4:12. It says, 'And it came to pass that the Spirit said unto me again: Slay him, for the Lord hath delivered him into thy hands.'" Then he read verse thirteen: "'Behold the Lord slayeth the wicked to bring forth his righteous purposes. It is better that one man should perish than that a nation should dwindle and perish in unbelief.'" He remained quiet a moment, letting his words seep in.

Then, with great emphasis, he said, "See? It's right here, as plain as the nose on your face: 'The Spirit said...Slay him!' Now let's read verse seventeen: 'I knew that the Lord had delivered Laban into my hands.' And verse eighteen: 'I did obey the voice of the Spirit, and took Laban by the hair of the head, and I smote off his head with his own sword.'"

Awestruck, the crowd appeared transfixed.

"I see by your faces that some of you are upset," Ervil said. "But, in case you don't know, Christ said he did *not* come to bring peace. He came to bring the sword!"

MY EIGHTEEN-YEAR-OLD HALF BROTHER Sam was staying with us. He heard Ervil's nonsense about blood atonement and openly rejected his outlandish teachings. Miffed, Ervil informed him, "We'll have a large following soon. The day will come when everyone will be called to make a blood covenant. Actually," he continued to explain, "blood will be sprinkled on the altar when the saints have been sufficiently taught. Once they understand

and have taken vows, they will be forced to obey, or their lives will be taken."

"What will they have to do to be worthy of death?" Sam inquired, though he had no intention of joining up with the LeBarons.

"Well, for instance, those who serve false gods will be sentenced to death. Also, false prophets will be put to death."

Sam interrupted. "How do you know who the false prophets are?"

"Isn't it obvious?" Ervil sneered reproachfully. "The leaders of the polygamist groups who don't come and join our church and take upon them this blood covenant will be cut down!" Ervil spewed out more explanations. "In the Bible, in Numbers 15:32–36, it says a man should be stoned even for gathering wood on the Sabbath. Adultery is another reason."

"Ervil," Sam said defensively, "You're damn scary. You make me afraid to even sneeze around you for fear you'll sentence me to death!"

"You won't have anything to worry about because God gave us a dividing line. All those who uphold the civil law and abide by the Ten Commandments will be called saints, and those who oppose it will automatically be sinners. As long as you toe the line you'll have nothing to lose sleep over."

I challenged him. "Where does Christ come in? The Bible says he paid for my sins when he died on the Cross."

Ervil exploded. "That's a lie! His death did not cover your sins. We have to be responsible for *all* of our own actions. When we break a law, then we must pay. If you'd been reading your scriptures, then you'd know that *mercy* cannot rob *justice*. Every Mormon knows that there are certain crimes that the atonement of Christ will not cover. That's why the sinner himself must pay the debt through the shedding of his own blood! I'm not making this stuff up, so don't be upset. I'll prove it to you by the early Mormon teachings," he said defensively.

"For instance," he grabbed volume three of the *Journal of Discourses* from his black satchel and turned to page 247, quoting Brigham Young: "'There is not a man or woman, who violates the covenants made with their God, that will not be required to pay the debt. The blood of Christ will never wipe that out, your own blood must atone for it.'" Ervil closed his book with authority.

He delighted in his memorization skills, and, always looking for an opportunity to display them, he continued reciting without reaching for his book: "Jedediah M. Grant said in the *Journal of Discourses*, volume four, pages 49 to 50, 'If they are covenant breakers, we need a place designated, where we can shed their blood.' Grant also said, 'It is also their right to kill a sinner to save him, when he commits those crimes that can only be atoned for by shedding his blood. . . . We would not kill a man, of course, unless we killed him to save him. . . . and the more Spirit of God I had, the more I should strive to save your soul by spilling your blood.'"

CHAPTER TWENTY-FIVE

I was taking my turn in Las Vegas with Verlan when we received the news of Mauro Gutierrez's death. He was at a bar in the mountain town of Las Varas, with Ossmen Jones on January 1, 1966. He heard a heated argument outside and walked out to defend a friend. When he interfered, the instigator whipped out a pistol and shot him dead.

Everyone in the mountains admired Mauro. He was happy, friendly, and always eager to perform work in his mechanic shop for the poor Mexicans, whether or not they had money. Everyone knew he had four wives, and they never ceased joking about it. They affectionately referred to him as *El Viudo* (the Widower). Mauro's weekly advertisements by radio were heard far and wide throughout the local towns.

To me, Mauro was like a brother. He brought his families and stayed with me whenever he needed to attend a conference or tend to business in the colony. We often laughed together, staying up late enjoying each other's company. I'm grateful that when I was hospitalized years earlier, suffering from typhoid fever, Mauro donated blood. I'm comforted in knowing that also through marriage Mauro's blood runs through eleven of my grandchildren. I see traces of him in their faces, and I feel satisfied that a part of him lives on. His death was a great loss to me.

His wife Fay was in Colonia LeBaron when the prophet Joel notified her of her husband's tragic death. Fay, with her unwavering belief in Joel, said, "I'm not worried. If you stand as God to the people as you say, then I know that you can bring him back to life."

Joel shook his head and cringed. "Please don't ask that of me. I can't do it."

JOHN BUTCHEREIT, LUCINDA'S EX-HUSBAND, and one of the apostles of the United Apostolic Brethren, arrived in the colony unexpectedly. He was one of Uncle Rulon's right-hand men in Utah, and my uncle had dispatched him and another member, Joe Rostenberg, to persuade the LeBarons to realize the "error of their ways."

Butchereit was quite a student of the scriptures, and the LeBaron family held him in high esteem, especially for marrying their sister Lucinda as a plural wife many years before. They still considered him a brother-in-law.

Verlan accompanied both men to Ozumba, Mexico, to a conference with Brother Margarito Bautista.

Unfortunately for the Allreds, during the long hours of traveling and discussing scriptures, both emissaries were completely converted to Joel's priesthood. They submitted to baptism into the Church of the Firstborn before returning to the U.S. Determined to follow God's anointed, John Butchereit soon moved to Colonia LeBaron, leaving his family behind.

Three blocks west of the colony, Butchereit lived in a small room, by the coop where he raised chickens. One evening, after he had tended his newly hatched chicks, a couple of drunken

Mexicans knocked on his door, demanding that he loan them his truck. When he refused, an altercation followed, and after beating him and riddling his body with bullets, the intruders fled on horseback, leaving him for dead.

The following morning, a worker who helped him with his poultry business discovered his body kneeling over his blood-stained bed, as though he had spent his last moments in prayer.

During their flight, one of the culprits lost a spur, which finally was used for evidence in bringing him to justice.

I was living in Ensenada, Baja California, at the time but was fortunate enough to accompany Verlan to Salt Lake City for John Butchereit's funeral.

I was appalled when an old acquaintance confronted Verlan and me during the viewing. "So, first it was Mauro Gutierrez, and now it's John Butchereit! How many more of your group will be executed?"

Verlan assured the accuser that the LeBarons were not impli-cated in either death. Unfortunately Verlan's words came too late. Rumors spread throughout the fundamentalist groups, and many came to believe that my in-laws were responsible for the deaths of the two men.

LeBarons have been accused—often with good reason—over the years of many radical crimes, but they were definitely not responsible in these cases.

ERVIL'S INABILITY TO SUPPORT his ever-expanding family didn't even faze him. When he put the problem before the Lord he received good news. He claimed that the Lord informed him that his presence as a leader and missionary was of far more importance than the mundane task of taking care of his family. He was to deal strictly in spiritual things. His monetary needs were to be supplied by a few unsuspecting men. The impression he received clearly designated four new followers. The Spirit whispered to Ervil, "None of them have the balls to enter into plural marriage, so they deserve to step up and support you and your faithful wives."

Realizing that the four God had pointed out were slackers, Ervil knew they would need some enticement to come through each month with their funds. So, by virtue of his authority, he promised one of his teenage daughters to each duped devotee.

On different occasions, all four men confided in me that they'd been favored and called by God to fulfill the patriarch's needs. When I was made privy to Ervil's unscrupulous tactics, I accosted him.

As was his manner, he grasped my upper arm tightly, hoping his words of wisdom would sink in as he laughed, blatantly sharing his scheme with me. "Don't worry about my daughters. I wouldn't allow them to marry any of these men."

"Then why did you lie to them?" I yelled, disgusted. "They're all thinking they'll be rewarded by having a plural wife."

He rolled his eyes. "Aw, c'mon, Irene. You know everyone needs hope. That's all I was trying to do. The Bible says with faith all things are possible. I'm just doing my best to shape up a few misfits, hoping that at some future date God will refine them enough so that they can still be used in his kingdom."

EARLY IN MARCH 1966, Linda and Tom Liddiard arrived after dark in Colonia LeBaron. Pregnant with her fifth child, Linda waited in the car for Tom's return. He knocked on Marilyn Tucker's door, inquiring about a place for his family to sleep. Linda's four tired children moved around in the seats, wanting to get out of the car after driving from Salt Lake City.

Out of the darkness appeared a plain, masculine-looking

woman. She approached the car suspiciously, armed with a pistol in her hip holster, making sure Linda saw it. Uneasy, Linda slowly rolled down her window, and the aggressor asked, "Who are you?"

"I'm Linda Liddiard from Utah. Who are you?"

"I'm Linda Johnson, one of Ervil's wives. He sent me over here to check you out." After giving Linda a once-over and looking in the backseat at the children, she left, saying, "We're just being cautious."

Linda was relieved when Tom returned to the car, having secured a place to spend the night.

Immediately after we met, Linda Liddiard and I became best friends and confidantes.

BILL TUCKER, WHOM VERLAN DUBBED as the most brilliant man he'd ever met, became disillusioned. After much fear and unrest and deep soul-searching, Bill quietly gave up his beliefs in Joel and left the colony. Before that, he had convinced Hector Spencer, an LDS Mormon bishop, to join the LeBarons and move to their colony. Hector was jubilant realizing that he had been taught the fullness of the gospel. Bill convinced him that the LeBarons had the *truth* and that Joel stood as God to his people. Therefore, Hector sacrificed everything to join the saints.

After Hector's relocation, he decided to visit Bill. He walked the three blocks to where Bill lived, anxious to communicate with his mentor. On the road, he encountered another member. After brief salutations, Hector shared his joy and commitment, expressing his anticipation in seeing Bill, the eloquent man who had converted him.

The other member shook his head sadly. "Haven't you heard? Bill left the church."

Hector was crestfallen. He felt as though someone had punched out his lights. "Are you sure? I can't believe it. Bill just converted me and now you say he's gone?"

"That's right..."

Bill sent for his families after he found work and settled in California. Shortly after, he was hospitalized with appendicitis. In spite of excellent care, he died a few days later of peritonitis. When the cult learned of his death, rumors ran rampant throughout the church. Everyone sadly shared the tragic news with one another, but... everyone seemed to believe that God had taken Bill's life because he had given up the truth.

Within a few short years, every one of the French missionaries left the Church of the Firstborn. Only Dan Jordan clung to the LeBarons' priesthood claims, but he'd switched his loyalty from Joel to following Ervil, becoming Ervil's right-hand man in Ervil's newly founded Church of the Lambs of God.

When the French missionaries separated themselves from the LeBaron group, I was devastated. Not only were they my friends, but I held them in high esteem. They had attended college and seemed to be self-confident and empowered. It was because of their proselyting that the Church of the Firstborn grew in numbers. Bill Tucker and Bruce Wakeham had tact and finesse, qualities that Ervil and Dan lacked; they had influenced many convents.

ERVIL'S NEW DRESS CODE was strict. Ladies were required to wear sleeves to their wrists if possible, and their elbows had to be covered at all times.

My very first altercation over the new code was with Alma. As we approached each other on the gravel road, my voice rang out.

"How's Brother Alma doing this afternoon?" To my amazement he didn't acknowledge me.

Instead, he stopped directly in front of me, staring me down. "You know better than to have your elbows showing. How many times have you been told that you must keep them covered?"

I couldn't believe this "sin" was even worth mentioning. It actually struck me funny. I laughed as I challenged him. "What's the big deal about me keeping them covered?"

"Well," he said, hoping to educate me, "you may not know it, but a woman's elbow actually turns a man on."

"What the hell's your problem?" I said disgustedly, wanting to give him shock therapy to prove my point. I immediately bent my arm, deliberately showing my *enticing* elbow as I shoved it toward his face. He dodged, pulling away from me. Again, I taunted him. "Does this turn you on, Alma?" He backed farther away, as my sexy elbow danced mockingly in his face. "Tell me . . . does it?"

Alma wouldn't answer. I'm certain my words punctured his authority and his pride. As I walked away I offered a parting shot: "You make me sick."

After my squabble with Alma over my tantalizing elbow, he sent a church elder named Vance to convince me of the error of my ways. Vance followed Alma's instructions to the letter. Although at times he admitted Alma was a little odd, he upheld his authority without question.

Surprised to see Vance, I welcomed him inside. His serious countenance gave me a hint that something was amiss. He spoke firmly as he apologized for having to be the one to chastise me. "Alma asked me to see if I could reason with you." He hesitated, wondering, I'm sure, if I'd rebel against him also. "Irene, you must try to understand Alma. As the bishop, his job is to enforce the rules among our people. He doesn't like rules any more than you do, but due to the wickedness among us, we need to be strict. Look at it this way. What if you were invited to a birthday party, and the *only* requirement to attend was to comply with their rules and wear a pink bow in your hair? Wouldn't you conform in order to go?"

"No, Vance," I said, trying not to laugh. "I would stay home from the party."

"C'mon, Irene, don't be so obstinate! What would it hurt for you to wear the pink bow in order to associate with your friends?"

"Sorry, Vance. I just wouldn't associate with someone who would impose something so ridiculous."

He bristled at my impudence. "Boy, you are defiant! Well," he said as he rose to his feet, preparing to leave, "I'll tell you one thing for sure. If you were *my* wife, I'd force you to wear the pink bow in your hair." He turned and opened the door.

"Vance," I said, knowing I had one over on him, "if *I* were *your* wife...I would...shave...my...head!"

The next day, my best friend, Linda Liddiard, and I had a hearty laugh when I told her about the ridiculous incident. "Girl, you are downright spunky!" she said. "It's about time somebody protested those crazy rules."

Laughing, I interrupted her, "I can see Alma now, meeting me in the road with his demands, shaking his finger, pointing at my head. 'Where is your pink bow?'" I giggled. "Imagine him stomping his foot as usual, yelling at me. I can hear him now." By now my sides ached from laughing so hard. "Can't you see him demanding one final time that I show him my pink bow? I'd put my hands on my hips—just to annoy him—and say, 'Alma, I just happen to be wearing the bow in my hair.' He'd sputter as he yelled, 'You're lying. It's not in your hair; I don't see your bow.'

Then I'd flash him"—I pointed to my crotch—"and run away, saying, 'I'm just obeying your orders.'"

Linda was laughing so hard she could barely talk. She gasped for breath and said, "And then you'd tell him, 'You never said in which hair!'"

I'LL NEVER FORGET THE DAY Vonda White arrived in Colonia LeBaron. She was a Mormon from Stockton, California. She stood out because of her shapely frame and her short, dark hair. When she was converted to the priesthood of the LeBarons, she quietly left her husband and fled to Mexico with their two children. The next time I saw Ervil, he told me to keep quiet and not tell anyone that Vonda was in the colony. He informed me she had been married to a Vietnamese, a heathen who had never understood the gospel. Vonda was afraid her husband would try to find her and take away the children. So, Vonda hid out in an undisclosed home with a promise from Ervil that he would protect her.

A couple of weeks later, I saw a distraught Asian man, about thirty, sadly walking through the streets of the colony, crying and asking every person he encountered if they had seen his wife, Vonda. When she realized he would not leave until he found her, she decided to confront him. I saw them together talking, but I was told later that he had left, dejected, and without his children.

Ervil first used Vonda as a pawn. He'd converted a navy man from California who already had a wife and a couple of children. Ervil felt this man needed stability in the new church and a reason to stay in Zion.

To my surprise, Ervil accompanied Vonda and her future husband to my house, where I witnessed Ervil perform their marriage ceremony. He sealed Vonda to the newcomer for time and all eternity.

Ervil felt confident that the man would follow in his footsteps and gather many wives. He also felt certain that this man would cough up money every month to help him support his numerous wives and children.

I never did learn the particulars, but that marriage soon failed. When Ervil heard of the breakup, he immediately received a revelation that Vonda was to be his tenth wife. She acquiesced without hesitation, feeling special that she was found worthy to enter Ervil's harem.

She later joined Linda Johnson in San Diego, where the two lived on welfare until Linda found an accounting job. Vonda tended Linda's and her children while Linda worked to support them.

Vonda idolized Ervil, considering him a genius and her savior. She was loyal to Ervil's every whim. Not only was she willing to die for him, but eventually he would convince her to kill for him.

CHAPTER TWENTY-SIX

One Friday evening, Nephi dropped by the Big Brown House in Ensenada, Baja California, where I was caring for twenty-six of Verlan's children while Charlotte and Lucy worked in the States to help support the family. Verlan had built the Big Brown House to accommodate his growing family. Nephi had driven eleven hours from Las Vegas and was thoroughly worn out, but he was determined to still drive the remaining three hours to Los Molinos, the Baja California colony where we would later move.

He was going down to get a friend, Herman Roper, and his family, then return to Vegas by Monday in time for work.

One of Nephi's wives, Dalila, was traveling with him. She was nine months pregnant and completely exhausted from the long trip. She was holding her one-year-old daughter, Maria, who clung to her.

Nephi wanted me to accompany them to Los Molinos in case Dalila suddenly went into labor, but I just couldn't leave with all my pressing responsibilities. When they insisted I let my twelve-year-old daughter, Donna, go along to help them with little Maria. But an internal and insistent foreboding seemed to warn me, *don't let Donna go.* I usually gave in, doing almost everyone a favor no matter how burdened down I was. But my feeling was so strong that I refused, knowing I couldn't spare her anyway. They said good-bye, promising they'd drop by on their way back to visit a little longer before going back to Vegas.

Monday morning, I was outside washing clothes in our run-down Maytag. The wringer was broken, so I was sopping wet all down my front from wringing out clothes by hand. I looked up to see a friend's car flying over the dirt road west of our house, trailing dust as it entered our yard and screeched to a halt. It was DeWayne Hafen and I just knew he had bad news. I hurried up to him just as he jumped out of his car in the driveway.

"Is it Verlan?" I asked. "Is Verlan dead?"

"No, but come quick. I need you! There's been an accident. It happened last night. It's Nephi and the Ropers!"

My heart dropped. I thanked God that I had listened to my heart and not allowed my precious Donna to accompany them to Los Molinos as Nephi had requested. I quickly slipped into clean and dry clothes and grabbed a hairbrush to do my hair on the way. I left Donna and Charlotte's oldest daughter, Rhea, in charge of the other twenty-four kids until I returned.

DeWayne said he didn't know a thing about the details other than that little George Roper was in the hospital. Nephi's other wife, Oralia, had called DeWayne from Las Vegas, asking him to pick me up. He had driven down from San Diego to Ensenada just to have me go with him to find out what had happened because I spoke Spanish. We decided to go to the mortuary first, thinking we might get more information there than at the hospital.

I told Mr. Gonzalez, the undertaker, why I was there. He led us down a dimly lit hall, where we walked between stacked coffins of various colors and sizes, into a smelly, dank room. I was shocked when he flipped on the light. There, on the cold cement slabs, lay several uncovered naked bodies.

I saw little George first. The undertaker informed us that his body had just arrived from the hospital. I could see that he had been operated on from the stitches in the gash that went across his forehead and all the way behind his left ear.

Dalila's face was unrecognizable. The only way I knew it was she was by her dark skin, long black hair, and the incision on her abdomen where they'd taken her baby trying to save it. Sadly, the operation had failed, and the baby lay lifeless on the cold slab beside her.

To our utter dismay we realized that the next table held more of our friends. Rhoda Roper, who was fifteen, and her mother, Cora, were both badly disfigured. As I identified them, Mr. Gonzalez tore wide strips of adhesive tape from the roll, placed the tape on their upper arms, and wrote their names there.

We were completely devastated. Five dead! I turned to Mr. Gonzalez. "Can you imagine? Five of our people killed!"

"I'm sorry to tell you this, Señora, but there are two other bodies that may be your friends also."

He led us to a large cement sink that was partially filled with water. There in the water was a half-submerged, slumped-over corpse. Mr. Gonzalez pulled back the corpse's head by the hair as both DeWayne and I took a quick glance. We grimaced, but we were relieved to see it was a total stranger.

He then led us into still another room. There, beside stacked caskets, lay a corpse on a stretcher covered with a gray blanket. He unhooked the belt that held the body in place, and pulled back the corner of the blanket to give us a view. For the first time, I started to cry. There lay my friend Nephi. He had a gash in his forehead, and his caved-in chest bore the marks of the steering wheel that had snuffed out his life on impact.

DeWayne put his arm around my shoulders, comforting me, as I said, "Let's get out of here. This is too much for me."

I knew I had to gain my composure. I'd have to call down to Sonora, Mexico, to tell Nephi's father, then call Salt Lake City to notify his mother and two sisters.

I asked Mr. Gonzalez why they hadn't dressed the bodies. "Oh, you have to bring clothes for all of them. We don't furnish that."

I promised to return as soon as possible. I wanted to make sure that they were all dressed before relatives arrived to see their naked bodies.

I took Verlan's only other suit, a white shirt, and his shorts to the morgue for Nephi to be dressed in. I used my children's clothes for little George and the newborn baby. But having no money other than my weekly allowance, I had to ask for clothes from two other families in our group for the women to be buried in.

We learned that nine people had been crowded into the small car traveling at high speed when they slammed into a stalled flatbed truck, loaded with produce, that had no taillights or even reflectors on it.

At the hospital we found Herman Roper, a graying man in his fifties, who was still in a coma. His black-and-blue face was swollen beyond recognition. I felt relieved that he was still unconscious. I dreaded for him to wake up and find out his wife and two children were dead. His two younger daughters, Bevalyn and Theo, miraculously had survived, as had Dalila's little daughter Maria.

Later, I took Herman's daughter Yavona, who had arrived from Utah, to the hospital with me, where she saw her father for the first time since the accident. The nurses told us he'd come out of his coma, and we tiptoed into his room dreading to tell him about his family. I didn't have the heart to break such devastating news to him, so I had prepared Yavona to relay the information.

He was unable to see either of us because of the bandages that covered his swollen eyes, but he heard our footsteps and called out, "Who is it?"

"It's me, Daddy, Yavona," Yavona responded in a barely audible whisper.

"Tell me the truth," Herman demanded. "Is Mama dead?"

Yavona looked at me questioningly. I nodded for her to go ahead, motioning to her to break the bad news gently, but she choked up.

"She is dead, isn't she?" Herman asked again.

Tears slid down Yavona's cheeks. She shook her head, letting me know that I'd have to tell him.

"I'm sorry, Herman...really sorry." My voice faltered. "Cora *is* dead."

"Where are Rhoda and George? Are they dead too?"

"Yes, Herman, but Bevalyn and Theo survived, and so did Nephi's daughter Maria." It was agony for me to deliver even that much of the bad news. When I could no longer bear to see him so banged up and helpless, I left the room.

Relatives and friends began arriving long before I'd taken care of all the details of planning the funeral. Exhausted and six months pregnant, I stayed up working throughout the night. I cooked beans, rice, and fresh loaves of bread to feed the crowd at my house before and after the funeral.

The kids had done great with the housework and tending babies. Donna and Rhea had done their best, but, even so, I scrubbed dirty fingerprints off walls and door frames, mopped floors, and ironed clothes for us all to wear to the funeral.

How we survived this sad ordeal I'll never know. Six people all lost at once and buried in Ensenada.

* * *

A COUPLE OF MONTHS after Nephi's accident, my brother Douglas and my mother arrived from Montana with Douglas's ten children. It had been five years since I had seen them.

Mother couldn't suppress her feelings of disappointment. The ragged furniture, the cold bare cement floor, and the chaotic noise from Verlan's numerous children brought forth her sadness. Her judgmental eyes acknowledged my poverty and evident unfulfillment. I talked incessantly trying to redirect her focus on to me. How badly I needed her acceptance. She could see where my choices in life had taken me. She had warned me sufficiently before I had made the plunge into plural marriage and I was nauseous from anxiety. I panicked as I resolved to not give way to my feelings of guilt and rejection. Because of all the commotion, Mother suggested I accompany her outside, away from the excited children who overwhelmed her as they crowded around her. I led her out the door into the yard; her pace deliberate and weak as she hung on to my arm for security. Though she was only fifty-eight, seeing how Mother had aged tugged at my heart.

"I wanted to talk privately to you," she began. "The terrible rumors I have been hearing have caused me to fear. I try not to believe them, but they say where there's smoke, there's fire. Our relatives still wonder if the LeBarons killed John Butchereit and Mauro Gutierrez."

Angrily, I cut in. "It's a lie, Mother! Our group had absolutely nothing to do with their deaths. Both men were shot by Mexican outsiders, and I'm tired of the malicious accusations."

Tears filled Mother's eyes as she steadied herself holding on to my arm. "I wish I had proof," she said.

"Well, it's true," I assured her. "You've got to believe me."

I detected the reluctance in her voice again.

"Are you going to tell me that the Ropers and Nephi Marston were not murdered by Ervil either?"

Her unfounded claims riled me. "I can't believe you would even suggest they were murdered," I snapped. "They were killed in a car accident! Nephi, who was driving, rammed into a big truck loaded with produce. It had no taillights. Because of the blackness of the night, it was undetectable. Believe me, Mother, I was the one who identified all six bodies at the morgue. Some were almost unrecognizable."

Her body language told me she didn't believe a word I said.

"Do you think I'm lying, Mother?" I cried. I wondered, had our bonds stretched so thinly, they'd finally been severed? I moaned loudly in despair as my cries fell on Mother's deaf ears.

She patted my arm, "Honey, how can I believe it? Mauro . . . then John Butchereit . . . then you tell me six more died in such a short time? It sounds impossible. Look at the odds."

Through my despairing tears, I insisted that Mother accompany me to a junkyard two blocks away where the demolished car had been deposited.

On our walk, Mother voiced her objections. "How do I know the car we are going to see is theirs?" she asked.

"You've got to believe me, that's all. I saw it many times. It was in my yard two days before the accident. Nephi stopped by, hoping I'd let Donna go with them to Los Molinos to help his pregnant wife and tend her year-old daughter, Maria."

I prayed every step I took that I'd somehow be able to convince Mother that their deaths had been an accident. If I couldn't, I felt it was an affront to my own character.

We entered the sagging chain-link gate where the wrecking yard was almost full to capacity with rows of demolished car bodies. It felt eerie, just like a graveyard, as I contemplated, imagining the deaths of many who had died in the broken wrecked cars.

I easily found the car. The roof was completely squashed down upon the broken bloody stained seats.

"See, Mom." I pointed. "The car was forced under the rear of the truck and flattened. Some must have died instantly."

Mother shook her head, sickened, as she shifted her eyes from the gory sight. She sighed. "I just wish I had proof that this was their car. Was everyone in the vehicle killed?"

"No, Nephi's toddler, Maria, and two small Roper girls, Theo and Bevalyn, survived."

I bent down beside the front passenger seat. The car door had been completely torn from its hinges, no longer on the wreckage. Peering under the broken seat frame, I hoped to find a paper or anything with a name on it so I could convince my mother that the car we were inspecting was really Nephi's. I spied a plastic baby bottle that was lodged under the seat. Using force and exertion, I finally loosened it enough to free it. The empty milk-stained bottle had writing on it. In red nail polish was the name "Maria." I burst into tears...tears of joy. Now maybe Mother would believe me. She didn't confess whether or not she disbelieved the rumors, but in my heart I knew I held the proof in my hands.

CHAPTER TWENTY-SEVEN

Ervil summoned all the married women to yet another private meeting. He insisted that we swear under oath that not one word of what was spoken in the meeting would be repeated to anyone. He smirked as he said, "That means not even your husbands. Do you understand?" He stared at each of us in turn. "Do you?" he repeated, insinuating dire consequences.

I remember so well his first sermon to us about the shortcomings of our husbands. "There are women here under the sound of my voice whose husbands are spineless." He looked disgusted. "Some even allow you women to run their lives. Some of these worthless men will *never*"—he shouted the word for emphasis— "be able to exalt you in the celestial kingdom. Your only hope is finding a godly man whose life has been completely dedicated to the Lord." He snickered, pointing his finger at the small group. "I'm going to prophesy." He shook his finger, then continued. "Pretty soon a few of you women will find your husbands pushing up carrots in the garden."

Horrified by his words, I knew then what Ervil's intentions were. I'd suspected it all along, based on hints he conveniently dropped every now and then. Now, I could see he intended to kill those less-fortunate souls who did not measure up to his pre-posterous standard.

When Ervil saw the shock on the women's faces and heard their distressed sighs, he laughed, apparently thinking he was expressing concern for them. "When your wimp of a husband is removed from your path, you'll be given to a man who you rightfully belong to."

Again swearing us to secrecy, he intimated to us what the consequences would be if we broke his trust. After his not-too-subtle threat, he attempted to be kind and loving as he dismissed the meeting.

Vows or no vows, I went directly to Joel's home. I felt close to him and I knew I could trust him. When I entered, he could see by my demeanor that I was upset.

"What's up?" he asked.

Knowing his wife Magdalena knew no English, I smiled at her in recognition. Then I just sputtered out my fears. "Joel, I've just come from the women's meeting. We were all sworn to secrecy by Ervil, which is a crock of bull! He had all fifteen of us swear allegiance to him."

"Oh, I think he means well," Joel said, trying to ease my concerns. "He just has no tact at times."

"Joel, it's worse than that! He told us that real soon a few spine-less husbands would be 'pushing up carrots in the garden.'"

Joel couldn't help but laugh. "That's so ridiculous. C'mon, Irene, you know he has to be just joking around. I'm sure he doesn't mean it."

I shot back in anger, "Joel, he said it with *blood*...in... his...voice!"

"Don't get all riled up. I'm sure there's really nothing to it," he said lovingly. "But if you're worried, I'll keep an eye on him."

*   *   *

WITNESSING ERVIL'S TIRADES in the women's meetings raised my concerns. Ervil vowed that very soon God would obliterate all false prophets from the face of the earth. They'd be struck down with God's own hand for their wicked participation in stealing the tithes that rightfully belonged in the house of the Lord.

"Every polygamist group is under a curse. All are guilty of robbing God's money. It must be stopped. In the scriptures, God tells us plainly that his vengeance would begin upon his own house. Who has had the truth? What house is he talking about? We know God is speaking specifically to the Mormon Church. They had the truth. They were recognized as a chosen people— until they disqualified themselves. Now listen carefully so you'll understand this. The Church of Jesus Christ received the fullness of the everlasting gospel, but in 1890, when President Wilford Woodruff signed a manifesto, he brought damnation upon God's saints."

Ervil's boisterous voice thundered above the crowd. "When Woodruff signed that satanic document abolishing the sacred law of plural marriage, he signed the death warrant of God's chosen people. That despicable act caused the church to fall from the grace of God. The once true restored church separated itself from our Lord and Savior. That's why it is out of order."

He pounded the podium after each word to emphasize his point. "Do...you...understand...? That's why God spoke to our prophet Joel. He instructed him to organize the Church of the Firstborn of the Fullness of Times so he'd have a vehicle by which to live every aspect of the gospel. We were the fortunate ones! Just think how blessed we are to be God's only church on the face of the earth, the only one recognized by him.

"The ultimate test of a prophet is found in Deuteronomy 18:20–22: 'But the prophet who presumes to speak a word in my name, which I have not commanded him to speak, or who speaks in the name of other gods, that prophet shall die. And if you say in your heart, how shall we know the word which the Lord has not spoken?—When a prophet speaks in the name of the Lord, if the thing does not happen or come to pass, that is the thing which the Lord has not spoken; the prophet has spoken it presumptuously; you shall not be afraid of him.'

"God has not changed. It's the same thing today. It's best that false prophets be annihilated so they won't be a hindrance to God's perfect plan."

I cringed. Fear surged through me as he spoke. I *knew* that he intended to eliminate all who would oppose him. I silently cried, hoping my premonition would not come to pass. It flashed through my mind that his number one target would be my uncle Rulon Allred, who was the leader of the largest fundamentalist polygamist group in Utah. I mourned throughout the long shocking sermon, trying to block out the impending threats of this egotistical man.

My uncle, whom I loved dearly, had always been a father fig-ure to me. After my mother's divorce, Uncle Rulon had filled my father's place in my heart. He was a stately, kind man whom everyone honored with deep respect. His spirit of servitude was hailed by everyone who knew him, a gentle chiropractor who selflessly gave up his own time away from his seven wives to deliver hundreds of babies to polygamous families. He was a model saint known for his leadership in the fundamentalist movement. Many saints followed him, striving to create the same order that existed in his plural families. He was affection-ate and respectful to all his wives who accompanied him to reli-gious gatherings. Not only was he esteemed as a perfect saint, but many even revered him as a potential god.

It was he who had made arrangements for me to marry Verlan when I was sixteen. At that time he exacted a promise from me that once I was married I would never look back with regret.

Ervil hadn't mentioned names in the meeting, but, just because Uncle Rulon had such a large following, I wondered if Ervil would go after him first. With Verlan and Joel away from the flock doing missionary work, Ervil had full reign over all of us.

CHAPTER TWENTY-EIGHT

Verlan returned a month later boiling mad. He told me that he was going to *insist* that Ervil be stopped. "It looks like he has begun his campaign of terror. You know he sent Dan Jordan personally to see your uncle Rulon and gave him an ultimatum: he is to accept and follow the revelation given to him by Joel and move his several thousand followers to Mexico, or suffer the consequences. The tithing money your uncle is receiving from his followers is to be sent directly to Ervil. Your uncle ordered Dan Jordan to leave his office and never return after delivering the threat."

Verlan shook his head sadly. "I can't imagine what Ervil is thinking."

I cut in. "I told both you and Joel several times, and neither of you would listen. He's a law unto himself. He answers to no one, not even Joel. His damn power has gone to his head."

"I know," Verlan said, finally agreeing with me. "I never believed he would go this far. He sent the same warning to the Kingstons and the group at Short Creek, plus every faction that believes in Mormonism." He shook his head again. "It's a huge embarrassment. How can we ever convert people to the work of the Lord? Ervil is destroying people's faith faster than we can convert them.

"Joel doesn't know how to handle him. It's a sticky situation, but one that must be solved immediately." Sadness enveloped me. I feared that when my uncle cut off all association with the LeBarons I would be included. I was partly in my situation because I wanted to honor and please Uncle Rulon. To lose his love would be devastating.

I'D CRITICIZED JOEL on many occasions. He'd been told time and time again about Ervil's unscrupulous tactics, but he refused to deal with his brother. Now I was beginning to question Joel's leadership. I told Verlan that Ervil had intimated repeatedly that even Joel would "go down."

Several converts resented Ervil and feared for their lives, especially when he explained blood atonement. I felt Joel ignored signs of danger because he didn't have the heart to confront Ervil. He worried about breaking their brotherly bonds, especially when Ervil was the one who had convinced Joel's followers that Joel was God's prophet. I wondered if the Church of the Firstborn would continue to thrive if Ervil refused to work in harmony.

Verlan finally realized Ervil's disdain when I told him that Ervil insisted I was living in spiritual adultery. He claimed that in the preexistence I'd made a pledge to be his wife, not Verlan's.

Joel, too, finally reached a saturation point. Unwilling to put up with Ervil's threats, false revelations, ruthlessness, lies, and wife stealing, he prepared to release him from his coveted position as patriarch.

At home in the LeBaron Colony, Joel sent someone to notify both Ervil and Verlan that he needed to see them. Shortly after

Ervil and Verlan arrived, the three brothers retired to a bedroom for a private conversation.

Ervil couldn't contain his curiosity. "What's up?" he asked Joel, wondering why he had been summoned.

Without hesitation, Joel said, "I'm releasing you from your office as patriarch."

Ervil was surprised but thought Joel was just joking. When he saw the stern faces of both his brothers, however, he knew differently. He buried his head in his hands and wept unashamedly. His two brothers joined in, mingling their tears with his. They knew the great disappointment he felt.

When Ervil could speak, he contritely admitted to Joel that it was actually a relief to him, that the patriarchal office had been nothing but a burden to him. Joel and Verlan, realizing Ervil was completely shattered, embraced him warmly, hoping the action would not disunite them.

Verlan came to bed and, with frustration in his voice, told me about the meeting with Joel and Ervil.

"Was he angry at Joel?" I asked.

"No, he knew it was coming, but it wounded his pride. You and I both know that Ervil needs to feel important. He's been stripped of his power and control. I've never seen him so devastated. Joel and I cried with him."

In a conference two days later, on November 22, 1969, Ervil's release was announced to Joel's followers. Joel spoke kindly of Ervil in the conference, thanking him for the great job he had done. He expressed his love for him, stating how he hoped the two would serve together in the near future.

Then Ervil rose to speak. His tears flowed freely as he acknowledged his dismissal with regret. I don't think there was a dry eye in the audience. We all felt his overwhelming sadness. Knowing the magnitude of his position, we mourned his loss as though it were a death, because we all knew what it meant to him.

Nevertheless, after the meeting, many of the saints were over-joyed. They felt Ervil had it coming. Many had been imposed upon, pushed around, and intimidated by his overpowering per-sonality. They sighed a breath of relief, glad to see their prophet Joel taking control over his flock again.

During that conference Verlan was ordained as the president of the church with Siegfried Widmar and Bruce Wakeham as his counselors. And he was soon thereafter ordained the patriarch, the second grand head of priesthood, replacing Ervil.

The intensity of the situation weighed heavily on Joel. Ver-lan also felt terrible when he was given the office of patriarch. He knew how much it meant to Ervil, and to be stripped of such an exalted office was simply a catastrophe. However, Verlan believed God was in control and he'd have to carry on despite Ervil's removal.

Now we hoped a new phase of progress and harmony would begin. But we didn't realize that behind Ervil's facade of humil-ity and acceptance laid resentments of volcanic proportions. Neither Joel nor Verlan had any inclination to believe that their brother was planning to retaliate.

Instead of harmonizing with Joel and the church leaders, Ervil began to recruit Joel's converts. Dan Jordan was soon fully back-ing him.

MANY OF US RECALLED the history of Ervil's religious activities. First he was a missionary for the Mormon LDS Church, then he followed his brother Ben. At that time, Alma had helped Ervil distribute an article that Ervil had written for Ben. It read in part,

Let it be known to every nation, tongue, and people unto whom these words come, that God the eternal Father, by the power of the Holy Ghost, has given us a sure knowledge, that our brother, Benjamin Teasdale LeBaron is...the Prophet unto whom all the nations of the earth must listen to in order to establish world peace and that by his word the kingdom of God will be established upon the earth. We declare this solemnly in the name of Jesus Christ and do not lie, God being our witness. This we prophesy by the power of the Holy Ghost and in the name of Jesus Christ.

Later, in Uncle Rulon's organization, Ervil was baptized by Margarito Bautista and given priesthood.

Then he used the scripture in the Doctrine and Covenants' section eighty-five to prove his point when he decided his brother Joel was God's anointed servant, the One Mighty and Strong. He also declared that their father had conferred the same blessing on Joel that had been conferred on Joseph Smith.

Ervil explained that one holding this office would never lead the people astray because the priesthood, which constitutes the highest office, is called the Right of the Firstborn, which means the right to stand in the stead of the Firstborn in his absence, the Firstborn being Christ. In other words, this is the authority over all things pertaining to the Kingdom of God on earth.

While Ervil upheld Joel in the authority of the first and highest office, he himself was pleased to hold the second office of patriarch.

It's true, Ervil helped write the pamphlet *Priesthood Expounded* to prove Joel's claim. He was the spiritual engine that drove the church in its infancy. Joel and Ervil seemed to be in harmony throughout most of those years as they worked diligently to establish the new church. But now he was singing a different tune.

I'd always felt that something sinister lay beneath Ervil's fervent quest for glory. Obsessed with his lust for power, he seemed to separate himself from Joel, and, while speaking to other members, not only did he disparage Joel, he denied the doctrinal claims they both had professed to believe.

Priesthood Expounded, speaking of the first grand head, states,

Only one man on the earth at a time is given the office that Moses held. The Lord in all ages has promised by oath and covenant to sustain the man acting in that office. The man acting as mouthpiece to the whole human family, who stands as God to the people, will not lead them astray (32).

The second office is described: "This grand self-perpetuating Patriarchal office rightfully holds the keys of all the spiritual blessings...to act in concert with, yet subordinate, to the office Moses held" (15).

In reference to the One Mighty and Strong mentioned in section eighty-five of the Doctrine and Covenants, Ervil completely denied that Joel was to stand as God to the people as he had previously claimed.

He continued to deride, ridicule, and discredit Joel, hoping to undermine his position. Being obsessed with his own importance, he lashed out continually at church members, spewing words of hate toward his brother, threatening to blood atone him. So, Ervil, filled with disappointment, hatred, and bitterness over being dethroned, devised plans to completely undermine Joel and take over the Church of the Firstborn.

First, determined to catapult himself to the top of the heap, he made the ridiculous claim that he had received the patriarchal office from his father eight years prior to Joel's receiving the first grand head office. He twisted and denounced the very scriptures that he'd formerly presented to the world. Ervil began his campaign of terror, not only in his writings, but in almost every conversation with Joel's flock.

I was sickened when he spent an hour with me, insisting that I comprehend the civil law. He warned that as soon as the people were sufficiently taught the law, they'd be executed if they broke any part of it. Shocked, I asked, "What law?"

He scoffed at my seeming ignorance. "All those who break the Sabbath, those who refuse to live the United Order, liars, those who commit adultery, those who will not pay tithing, and"—he smiled cunningly—"all those who uphold false prophets."

I winced because in my heart I knew he was referring to Joel, Verlan, all the fundamentalist groups, and the LDS Mormons. I wondered, Is anyone safe? He spewed out his flattery, insisting I was an elect lady. Then he shared a recent revelation that only he and I were supposed to be privy to. "God wants you to be a military leader in my army of women. With your determination and intelligence," he gushed, "you can accomplish anything."

I declined, hoping I wasn't marked for death by my refusal. Shaken, I hurried home to my children.

CHAPTER TWENTY-NINE

S oon Ervil tried to convince Earl Jensen's third wife, Lawreve, to abandon Earl and marry him. The Lord had spoken to him when he noticed her long golden hair, her smile, and her confident demeanor that so impressed him. On the one hand, he demanded obedience from all, yet he hated a woman's docile spirit. Lawreve was a challenge to any man, tall, lanky, beautiful, and very devoted to Earl.

In Earl's absence from Colonia LeBaron Ervil went to his house on the pretext of preaching the gospel. He greeted the first two wives, Carol and Maudie, as they worked, caring for all their children. He asked for privacy with Lawreve in Earl's office, where he spent hours convincing her that she absolutely had to leave Earl and marry him. He repeatedly told her that she was committing spiritual adultery by continuing her marital duties with her undeserving husband. Ervil prodded, begged, and threatened Lawreve day after day, hour after hour, until he had her completely under his control. Ervil claimed that every command, wish, suggestion, threat, and warning came directly from God to him.

Lawreve was exhausted and completely depressed after each

agonizing session. Ervil would turn on his hypnotic powers full throttle, reiterating his usual line, telling her that it hurt him as much as it did her. And that he also ached for Earl, but that God sees the clear picture. He explained that she had made eternal covenants with him before the foundations of this world. He told her it was God's will, not his, and that God wanted obedience from them both. But Lawreve was not convinced. However, she went to California for a while and Ervil went to Los Molinos.

As president of the church, Verlan felt it necessary to confront Ervil in Los Molinos. He did not want to ruffle his feathers, but the recent scandal had to be squelched. Ervil, the "great lawgiver" was brazenly breaking his own rules again. Through coercion, he was trying to convince Lawreve to marry him, but no one had forgiven Ervil for his earlier indiscretion when he had secretly stolen Nephi Marston's wife Anna Mae, and Ralph Barlow's wife Rosemary.

Now Verlan's responsibility was to confront his brother, making sure he waited the requisite six months. Joel himself had come up with the rule after Ervil had stolen Anna Mae. He wanted to make sure that no one would marry someone else's wife without sufficient time for both to agree to the divorce. Six months seemed ample time for a possible reconciliation. Verlan tactfully stated that Ervil would not be allowed to marry Earl's wife unless he kept the rule.

Verlan had never crossed Ervil before. He knew him well enough to know that doing so would cause nothing but trouble. Ervil, being four years Verlan's senior, had always asserted control over him, and his recent demotion as patriarch was definitely a thorn in Ervil's flesh.

Ervil tried to defend his position, stating that he was exempt from the law because he was living on a celestial level, and only those who had sex on their minds had to wait. He basically told

Verlan to mind his own business, that no one was going to dictate how he'd live his life.

"Well, if you're going to be hardheaded and have your own way, then I have no recourse but to excommunicate you from the church," said Verlan. It was at that time that Ervil began to plot Verlan's death.

Ervil, still trying to convince Lawreve to marry him, told her that his brother Joel had received the same confirmation from God, that she should leave Earl and marry him. He claimed God had made a special visit to Joel to make sure that Lawreve acted immediately according to Ervil's wishes.

Tearfully distraught, and very skeptical, Lawreve had to know for herself, so she contacted the prophet himself.

Joel blew up, emphatically stating that Ervil was lying. He had no idea that Ervil was trying to steal another man's wife again. Joel demanded that Lawreve contact her husband and return to her home at once. Earl retrieved his wife and insisted that she avoid Ervil at all costs.

Earl naturally began to investigate all of Ervil's antics, trying to establish a sense of harmony among all concerned. But when Ervil received the news about Earl's investigation, he again went to God. Supposedly the Lord, in his supreme wisdom, revealed how to settle the problem.

Ervil ordered two eighteen-year-old members to hunt Earl down and execute him. The frightened teens, fearing for their own lives if they declined, asked Ervil how to go about it. Ervil smiled menacingly. "God's speaking to me now. He's ordered you boys to use hot lead and cold steel."

"You mean we'll have to shoot him?" they asked, now nearly paralyzed with fear.

"Exactly," he ordered. "Go now, and don't return until the job is done."

But the boys, more frightened of killing than of Ervil's consequences if they did not do the wicked deed, fled to Las Vegas to
find work and concealment. Luckily for Ervil, that order to kill
was not known until much later.

DETERMINED TO DESTROY the one who had threatened him
with excommunication, Ervil rationalized that the Bible was the
word of God, and he scanned its pages almost daily. He sought,
then used the word of the Lord to justify his ruthless tactics. He
read in Deuteronomy,

> If your brother, the son of your mother, or your son, or your
> daughter, or the wife of your bosom, or your friend who is like
> your own soul should lure you secretly, let us go serve other gods
> which you have not known…you shall not consent to him or
> listen to him, neither shall your eyes pity him, neither shall you
> spare, neither shall you hide him. But ye shall surely kill him.
> Your hand shall be first upon him to put him to death. (13:6–9)

Now that Verlan had taken over the office of patriarch and the
presidency of the Church of the Firstborn, Ervil was convinced
that this passage in Deuteronomy applied to Verlan, because by
not bowing down to God and continuing to follow Joel's teachings surely Verlan was following a false god.

So, on various occasions, Ervil made it known on no uncertain terms that as soon as the Lord gave the go-ahead the sword
of justice would cut down both Verlan and Joel.

NEOMI ZARATE CAME to Los Molinos from southern Mexico
with her parents and siblings. She arrived in a large truck with

sixty other new converts who came expecting to be counted among those awaiting Christ's return. Neomi's husband had stayed behind in Mexico City, but he intended to join her at a later date.

Neomi pleaded with me to give her work. She offered to clean house, wash clothes, or do anything that might provide her an income to support her three children. Trying to survive with my own thirteen children was a feat in itself, but I hired her on the condition that I could pay her with wheat, beans, and produce that I had acquired from nearby farms. I was pleased to have her work for me, and I gave her the task of doing my ironing.

When I'd met Neomi on the day she arrived, her infectious smile cheered us all. Now, I noticed she was silent and somber. When I asked if she was doing all right or if she was sad because she was away from her husband, she burst into tears. "Ervil has convinced my parents that my husband is not worthy of me. He is Catholic; therefore, they feel he can't exalt me."

I comforted her, suggesting that soon her husband would join her or maybe send money for her to return to him. She cried all the harder. "My parents believe Ervil is a prophet of God. They want me to follow his counsel."

"What's that?" I inquired.

She could barely get the words out. "Ervil wants me to marry Bud Chynoweth. I told him I was already married and that I love my husband. Ervil said he had already released me from my vows and that I belong to Bud for all eternity."

I watched the tears stream down her face as she tried to iron a shirt. "Don't listen to Ervil," I said. "Listen to yourself. It's your life. Do what's in your heart. Don't let him talk you into doing anything that's against your own conscience."

While she continued to iron, I went directly to Joel and told him of Ervil's intentions for Neomi to be taken from her absent husband and become Bud's second wife.

Joel emphatically told me, "No way is Ervil going to perform that marriage! I want you to give him a personal message from me, if I don't see him. You tell Ervil that he is *not* to marry that girl to Bud. If she divorces her present husband, she still has six months before anyone else can marry her." (My experience here was also used in *Prophet of Blood*, p. 174.)

I hurried home to join Neomi so Ervil would not discover that I had gone over his head to Joel.

Just then, we both heard a car drive up. From her position, Neomi could see through the window. "It's Ervil," she said fearfully.

Ervil didn't bother to knock. When he saw Neomi in tears, he immediately suspected she had revealed her fate to me. His iciness ticked me off, especially when he ignored my presence in my own home, speaking only to Neomi. "Come with me!" he demanded.

Shaking nervously, Neomi handed me the shirt she was ironing and started to walk away.

In her defense I challenged Ervil. "She's working for me right now, so you'll have to talk to her some other time."

Ervil's face flushed with anger. He grabbed her arm. "She's going with me now." Then he changed his approach and tried to cajole me into accepting his authority. His fake smile disgusted me. "This young lady is going to marry Bud because he needs a plural wife. You know he's too intimidated to court these Lamanite women, so I found one for him."

I cut in angrily, "You know darn well she is another man's wife."

He waved dismissively. "Her marriage was a farce. When a woman is not sealed under the holy covenant by the true priesthood, then the union is not valid."

"Look at her," I scolded. "She's in tears. She told me she doesn't want to marry someone else. She loves her husband!"

Neomi stood quietly. She didn't understand a word of English, but she knew we were engaged in a heated argument.

So to assert a higher authority, I delivered Joel's message to Ervil. Of course, Ervil completely ignored Joel's six-month policy; he wanted to perform the marriage of Neomi to Bud that same day!

Ervil held Neomi's arm tightly and led her out to his car despite my protests. Once she was seated in the passenger seat, he closed her door and came around to his side. He opened the car door, leaning on it momentarily as he spoke. "Just mind your own business. I have told you repeatedly not to interfere with my doings." He squeezed his long body into the driver's seat, started the car, and drove away.

I was sickened by the situation. Not only was Neomi being coerced into marrying Bud, but the two wouldn't be able to communicate; they didn't even know each other's language.

That's when I realized that Ervil had become a law unto himself and would do whatever he pleased.

CHAPTER THIRTY

Venomous reports quickly circulated throughout Zion. Ervil became the ambassador of hate. He vilified Joel, stating that he was a fallen prophet. His disparaging remarks were intended to persuade other members to join his camp.

To destroy Joel's credibility, Ervil asked unsuspecting members for large sums of money. He conned them by stating that Joel had personally asked him to procure loans that Joel would promptly repay. Those duped were not only shocked, but greatly offended when they asked Joel why he hadn't returned their money as promised. Joel was sickened by Ervil's deceitful manipulation. He wondered how Ervil could possibly treat him, his elder brother, in such a despicable manner.

Ervil's right-hand man, Dan Jordan, joined in spreading Ervil's ridiculous claims of priesthood and of being the true prophet. Several people reported that Ervil had made statements that any man who opposed him would be blood atoned.

Finally on August 8, 1971, during our general conference, it was announced that both Ervil and Dan were excommunicated from the Church of the Firstborn.

Ervil's excommunication meant nothing to him; he didn't even attend the court. Instead he retaliated by incorporating a church of his own, the Lambs of God. In Ervil's struggle, he gained the support of three families: the Chynoweths, the Rioses, and the Jordans. Two of the Chynoweth brothers, Mark and Duane, became Ervil's commandos, while the third brother, Victor, financed the group. Their mother, Thelma, who worshipped the ground Ervil walked on, was their matriarch. Ervil felt Thelma's and Lorna's ingrained worldly views might disrupt his plans, and, fearing Thelma would discontinue supporting her daughter financially if she knew of his latest scheme, he concealed his intentions to marry Teresa and Yolanda Rios, who became his eleventh and twelfth wives. The sisters were both in their early teens, dark Lamanite maidens who had joined the work, moving to the colony from Puebla, Mexico. Ervil wasn't well acquainted with either of the girls, but he knew they were both sisters to Nephi Marston's wife Dalila (one of those he had given to Nephi to replace Anna Mae). Ervil had convinced their father that it would be an honor to have LeBaron blood circulating through his grandchildren's veins. If both girls were as obedient and determined as their brother Raul, they could be useful after all.

The two Rios boys, Raul and Gamaliel, became Ervil's bodyguards. Ramona and Eddie Marston, Ervil's stepchildren from Anna Mae, became his soldiers, willing to kill when Ervil gave the orders. Ervil compensated Dan Jordan, still Ervil's right-hand man, by giving him two of his daughters and two stepdaughters as wives.

These families worked together to write and distribute pamphlets. One pamphlet, titled *Priesthood Revealed*, claimed that Ervil was God's top representative and that our people were failing to recognize him as the patriarch of the kingdom.

Without delay, Ervil decided to throw his weight around and show Joel's group who was really the boss.

One Sunday, shortly after the Church of the Firstborn had begun its service in Baja California, in walked Dan Jordan, the Rios family, and the Chynoweths with their three teenage children.

Rena Chynoweth sat down at the piano, authoritatively pounding out a familiar hymn. Her mother, Thelma, raised her hand and, with a smirk, led the group in singing, even though someone from our church had been preaching at the pulpit.

We were never so shocked...and frightened. Even though it was happening right in front of us, we could hardly believe Ervil's followers would walk in unannounced and take over the congregation.

Intimidated, everyone in the meeting rushed out, exiting without expressing an objection to the hostile takeover.

Dan followed the crowd outside and raised his arm, revealing a previously hidden handgun. I couldn't believe Dan's transformation. Once, he had honored and loved Joel, believing and teaching that he was the One Mighty and Strong. He had revered him as the prophet who would save the world. Then he had become Ervil's right-hand man, and now they both worked overtime to persuade Joel's converts to denounce Joel and join Ervil's team. With Ervil's effective powers of persuasion, a few had abandoned Joel's church to follow the charismatic imposter. Their frequent use of force left no doubt as to the identity of Ervil's new soldiers.

Back at the church that Sunday, the disappointed worshippers gathered outside the small building, where Ervil soon appeared. He became very agitated, boisterously reprimanding our group for worshipping in *his* building.

When Joel heard about the takeover of the church building, he extended his token of peace by inviting Ervil's group to share the church, taking alternate hours. Joel was always one to turn the other cheek. Some members were angry that Joel didn't fight for our rights, but Joel was never antagonistic or confrontational.

He felt Ervil had the right to preach among us, and, if a few members decided to separate themselves and follow Ervil, he wouldn't stand in their way. Joel's tolerance and grace certainly exceeded our expectations.

We learned later that Ervil was just bluffing about the church, because his group used it only a few times. He had simply wanted the Firstborners to understand that he was in control.

Ervil's next move was even more shocking, however. One day he laid claim to all the buildings and land in Los Molinos, our Baja California colony. The place was now infiltrated with those who would antagonize and spread fear among our once-united group. Our worried members wondered if Ervil would evict them from their homes. It was a time of much unrest among Joel's followers. Our fears escalated during the week, when the men left the colony to work in the States. The women and children felt abandoned, vulnerable, fearful, and unprotected; it was a very trying time for the community.

In response to Ervil's claims, Joel brought it to Ervil's attention that the Baja land had been procured for the Church of the Firstborn colony and that he and Verlan held the titles.

Ervil argued childishly, stating it all belonged to him. Ever the peacemaker, Joel responded by saying Ervil could have the land if he could produce the legal papers of ownership. "In fact," Joel said disgustedly, "you can take any land that belongs to me, but I won't allow you to take precious land from these poor Mexicans."

Every word from Ervil's mouth revealed that he was going to pursue his own agenda. Obsessed by his lust for power, he became intoxicated by his own self-worth. Joel left the meeting saddened by his brother's unwillingness to comply. He knew now that there was no hope that the two would ever work together again.

CHAPTER THIRTY-ONE

My mother-in-law, Maud LeBaron, was afraid. She sensed that a death threat against Earl Jensen in a letter signed as the "Black Hand" was sent by her own son Ervil.

She was also upset about Ervil's attempts to steal Earl's wife Lawreve.

In addition, she was worried about Ervil's son Arturo, who had been living with her until Ervil suddenly took him away from school to bring Arturo under his control.

On Mexican Independence Day, the flag waved high above Colonia LeBaron grade school, but Arturo was absent. That same day, distraught over Ervil's irrational behavior, Maud wrote the first of several impassioned letters to Ervil, on September 16, 1971 (*The LeBaron Story*, pp. 201–210).

Ervil was making unceasing threats against Joel's Church of the Firstborn, which its leaders had begun taking very seriously. This situation easily might take a disastrous turn.

Maud couldn't sleep. Her mind reeled with fears of Ervil's sins against Joel's church. Maud began to write to Ervil, hoping to avert an inevitable bloodshed. Every sentence was laced with heartache. It was no easy thing for Maud to confront or chastise her beloved son. She begged Ervil to reconsider his wicked course and repent before it was too late. Yet in her mind, the only righteous path was to submit to Joel's claims of authority.

In her first letter, she revealed a lifelong secret about her own father who, like Ervil, had heard voices in his head and received revelations that misguided him. She feared that Ervil might become like her father. She wrote:

> My Dear Son Ervil ... I never thought to tell you before, but as a warning, I will tell you now. My father was as much like you as possible. He was faithful in the Church ... Something happened and he began to have revelations. It seems now that revelations run in the family. People talk commonly of your revelations ... the Lord told you to take over. It doesn't ring true.... If you love me, be humble ...free from the spirit of revenge.

Eight days later, on September 24, Maud made her most shocking plea when she revealed that her dead husband, Dayer LeBaron, had appeared to her with a warning that Ervil would soon have blood on his hands. She wrote:

> Dear Son Ervil, Your father came to my bedside and told me you were about to have innocent blood on your hands ... To imagine Dad gave you some authority is a lie—a preposterous lie. Something terrible will happen to you if you continue to work against Joel. I know who your father gave the authority to. He had no confidence in you; you know it. I'm afraid you have lost your mind—you have the spirit of revenge, and the spirit and desire to murder ... The sins of my father are being visited on your head. I'm sick about it ... You have been too arrogant. So was he. If you execute anyone as you have threatened, you will never amount to a pinch of nothing. Are you sure, dear, you are well; so many are losing their minds—you will lose yours if you don't repent and

I know it. God has revealed to me that you are gone ... The only sacrifice before God is a broken heart and a contrite spirit.

Still distraught, Maud decided to write to Ervil's cousin Conway LeBaron on September 26, 1971, hoping that he could steer Ervil back on track:

Dear Conway ... I knew when Ervil was here last that he had the wrong spirit, and I told Arthur that no one could use unrefined language and have the Priesthood of God.

She scolded Ervil on September 30, 1971:

Ervil Dear ... It is terrible the condition you and Dan and Conway are in ... Your father doesn't want innocent blood on your hands ... I demand that you honor your mother by respecting and coming before the church as a little child. Except you become as a little child now, you are lost ... something extreme is going to happen. You will lose your mind ... Somewhere along the way, you took too much glory to yourself. The only way out is to forget yourself in the best of good people ... and God will guide you in the rest.

Almost a month later, Ervil returned to the LeBaron colony. He ranted as he preached, accusing Joel of usurping power. He tried to convince Joel's members to believe and follow him. Maud wrote on October 27, 1971:

Son Ervil, ... By their fruits you should judge them. Your fruits are hardness of heart, revenge, wresting the scriptures, ridicule, character assassination, and premeditated murder, waste of money and time, and hatred ... I'm afraid each day for your life. You are naturally so handsome and sweet—but what might I expect? If anyone shoots, you will be to blame, so hurry and end the war.

Two days later, Maud was frightened by more rumors. A former police officer, Warren Foster, who had been loyal to Joel, had joined Ervil's band of dissidents. Ashamed that Ervil was stealing Joel's members and preparing for confrontation, she hurriedly wrote to him once again on October 29, 1971:

> *Dear Son Ervil, If you don't repent, innocent blood will be on your hands... Warren Foster got in too big a hurry to start executing. Did you too?... Please be a good boy because I know the Devil is after you like never before and is taking you fast.*

Upon hearing reports from frightened members that Ervil was spewing out death threats she saw the gravity of the situation. His anguished mother could see the handwriting on the wall. On October 30, 1971, she wrote:

> *My Dear Son Ervil... My father after teaching forty years in church... started receiving revelations for his own guidance. You look like him and act like him. He lost everything... The course you have planned ahead is abominable and you would know if you had the gift of the Holy Ghost. Right now you can right everything... You will fail terribly if you go further... For the sake of your great family you can't afford to forever be nothing. A disgrace.*

CHAPTER THIRTY-TWO

In Dr. Martinez's waiting room in Ensenada, I ran into my sister-in-law Gaye, whom I hadn't seen in some time. We had visited for ten minutes or so when a pretty, chic Mexican woman took a seat across from us. I wondered what she'd think with both of us laughing, making up for lost time. It seemed rude to yak away when this woman evidently knew no English. Gaye's older sister, Jeannine, who had run an errand, finally entered the office and took a seat next to Gaye. I greeted Jeannine, but I could tell immediately that she was feeling bad about something. "What's wrong?" I asked her.

Gaye cut me off before she could answer. "She's mad because I talked Joel into sleeping with me last night."

Jeannine retorted hotly, "You knew darn well it was my night!"

The two bantered over the unfairness of their sleeping arrangements. Jeannine wanted justice; once and for all she was going to make Gaye understand her position. She blurted out, "Listen to me, Gaye. You *knew* last night was mine. Joel slept with Kathy the night before, then Claudine the night before that. I just want Joel to be fair, that's all."

Too busy arguing over their nights, neither woman saw the horrified Mexican woman's jaw drop.

I cut in. "Jeannine that's enough. You can discuss this later, somewhere more private."

The look on the woman's face gave it away. She understood everything. Accusingly, Jeannine spoke to the Mexican woman. "You don't speak English, do you?"

The woman answered in perfect English, "Yes, I do."

Embarrassed by the situation, Jeannine lit into the woman. "Why didn't you speak up and say something?"

"I was too shocked," the woman answered defensively. "I was trying to understand your lifestyle. I was blown away when I heard you both fighting over one man."

The nurse spared us further argument, calling Jeannine into the doctor's office. My face must have been bright red from embarrassment, since I always do my best to avoid confrontations. I elected to retreat to the vehicle where I would wait for Gaye.

ONE NIGHT, AFTER SUPPER dishes were cleared up, I started washing the hands and faces of my smaller children. I wanted them to go to bed early so I could relax. My nephew Nathan, Joel's stepson, knocked on the front door. He didn't want to come in. "Mom said she needs to see you. She's walking over here now." He motioned down the road.

"Thanks," I answered, closing the door behind me.

I headed toward Jeannine to meet her in the road. She had her five-month-old baby in her arms. "Hi, what's up?"

"Please come with me to the beach," she pleaded. "We'll only be gone for an hour."

I had no idea what she wanted, but because of the urgency in her voice, I joined her on the two-mile walk to the beach. Her baby fussed continuously, and heavy fog settled around us. The crashing of the ocean waves made it necessary for Jeannine to speak loudly as she explained what she intended to do.

"I wanted you to be with me for this wonderful event that is going to take place, but you and I are the only ones who can know about it. I have prayed for weeks for some way I can be close to Joel every day. He is so busy with his church and his other six wives. I never get to talk to him or share my feelings with him. I feel so lonely and rejected. But, after much prayer, the Lord showed me how I can be with him forever."

I wondered what our going to the beach had to do with it. Her baby was cold. The thin receiving blanket definitely didn't block the damp breeze that whipped around us.

"Don't you think it's best we head for home?" I suggested. "Your baby is getting too fussy and cold."

"No, I just want you to stand here at the foot of this rocky cliff and wait for me."

I couldn't imagine why she wanted to climb the rocks ahead of us. "Let me hold your baby," I offered.

"No, I want her with me."

I felt uneasy; something didn't seem quite right.

At that moment, she dropped the bomb: "Irene, I am going to be translated. God is going to come for me while I'm standing on those rocks, watching the waves roll in."

Her words confirmed what I'd vaguely surmised. "Let me hold your baby," I offered again, fearing for the child.

"No, I want to hold my baby close to me. It will be the last time I'll see her in the flesh. It won't be long. The Lord informed me that I'd ascend into heaven between eight and nine o'clock tonight. I want you close by where you can keep an eye on me. As soon as I vanish, come and get my baby. I'll just lay her down in a safe place a moment before I'm caught up into the heavens."

I felt as though I'd just been hit on the head. What does a person do when someone goes over the edge? I knew Jeannine would finally give up when her translation didn't transpire, but I watched nervously as she made her way up the small rocky hill with a crying baby in her arms. Once near the top, she motioned for me to wait. I knew she wanted no interference from me.

Neither of us owned a wristwatch, but I was sure I waited for over an hour in the chilly damp breeze. I shook my head in disgust, laughing to myself. I thought we served a dependable God. Couldn't he at least show up for the baby's sake? Thick clouds of fog blew past, covering then uncovering the silhouette view of Jeannine.

Finally, I saw Jeannine making her way down the rocks, still carrying her squaling baby. She looked so dejected as she approached.

"What's wrong?" I asked.

Through tears of disappointment, she admitted the Lord hadn't come for her because of her unworthiness. "I had such hopes of being translated. Then I could be with my husband every minute, even when he's with his other wives. I had such great expectations, but I guess I'll have to perfect myself before the Lord allows it to happen."

She was more than crestfallen, cold, and disappointed as I accompanied her home.

WHEN I HEARD that Ervil was in town on August 15, I decided that I had to confront him. I was angry about his claims in the recent pamphlet *A Message to a Covenant People*. His message was full of lies, defaming Joel. If Ervil's name had been substituted for every reference to Joel, then it would have been true. So, I went over to Ruth Bateman's house where I saw Ervil's "Golden

Calf" parked in her yard. To my surprise, there sat Dan Jordan with her son-in-law Ervil at the breakfast table as Ruth busied herself removing the dirty dishes. I felt very uneasy from all I'd heard the past few months of Ervil's threats and power plays. Ervil's demeanor was not friendly. He knew I opposed him. Nevertheless, he insisted I take a seat on the empty chair beside him. But he intimidated me, so I took another.

As soon as I sat down, Ervil began his tirade. "How can you follow Joel and Verlan when they both have become traitors to the Kingdom of God?" He knit his eyebrows, giving me an icy stare. I didn't answer. I knew he wanted me to profess my allegiance to him. He continued speaking loudly. "Both Joel and Verlan are criminals." Giving his words emphasis, he doubled his right fist, then pounded on the table in rhythm with his words, "Verlan...and...Joel...will...be...put...to...death!"

His chilling words momentarily froze me. Though afraid to cross him, I summoned up my courage and spoke. "Ervil, they're your brothers! How can you say such a thing?"

He stared at me as though I were an idiot. "Ah, can't you see, God is no respecter of persons!"

Unwilling to listen to any more threats, I excused myself and went home. If Ervil would kill his own brothers, I wondered if I might be next.

A few nights later, Verlan secretly entered Los Molinos, staying undercover long enough to visit briefly with each of his seven wives. I expressed my fear, telling him of Ervil's threat against Joel and him.

"Wow," he said, his voice trailing off. "If he has Joel killed, our lives would really change. But, don't worry. Joel has promised us he will live to see Christ's Second Coming. If he dies without appointing a successor," he continued, "we'll all know he was just a good man and we barked up the wrong tree."

Somehow the belief had been circulated among the devout group that Joel would not die, because of this scripture: "...behold the life of my servant shall be in my hand. Therefore, they shall not hurt him..." (3 Nephi 21:10). I remember Bill Tucker and Verlan agreeing to how safe they felt when they flew to the mountains in Ossmen Jones's small plane with Joel. Both men believed that as long as they were in his presence they would not crash, because Joel was going to live to take them into the millennium.

Two days later, I found Joel in a small camper trailer, in bed resting. I greeted him warmly, sitting on the edge of his bed. I hadn't seen him for several weeks and felt fortunate to find him alone. Usually he was in the presence of one or more of his wives, making it impossible to have a private audience with him. I shared a bond with Joel. He was just a good guy with no flair or frills, just confident that he'd been appointed by God.

"What's up?" he asked.

I sighed. "Joel, I am just sick at heart. I've come to warn you about Ervil. I was at Ruth's two days ago when Ervil told me that both you and Verlan would be put to death."

I could see Joel's pain; he began to cry. He covered his face with his hands, trying to keep control of himself. When he could finally speak, he said, "They've got to be given enough rope if they want to hang themselves. Let them go ahead." He sighed sadly. "Let's see how far they'll really go."

I, too, had always thought Joel would be safe. Joel claimed to be the last prophet before the Second Coming of Jesus Christ. He had promised the church that he would take us into the millennium, that he would hand his faithful followers over directly to Jesus Christ upon his Second Coming. So I was completely surprised when Joel said, "I will be killed."

He had repeatedly consoled us by stating that he had a promise from his father, grandfather, and Jesus Christ himself that he would not fail. With his promise engrained in me, I couldn't accept his resolve. We had been taught that the words of Isaiah— "Behold my servant will prosper, he will be high and lifted up and greatly exalted...so his appearance was marred more than any man, and his form more than the sons of men. Thus he will sprinkle many nations. Kings will shut their mouths on account of him; for what had not been told them they will see, and what they had not heard, they will understand" (52:13–15)—applied to Joel.

"How can you say you'll be killed? You promised us you'd live until Christ came back."

"No, every testator that comes has to seal his testimony with his blood...just as Christ and Joseph Smith." He softly wept again. "I will be killed."

If Joel died, I concluded then he definitely was not the One Mighty and Strong, and his whole foundation based on that assumption would crumble. It would mean that he did not hold the first grand head of priesthood that Moses and all his predecessors held. It would mean that he was not the "promised seed of Joseph Smith by which all the nations of the earth would be blessed."

Joel had no clue that I walked out having questioned my faith in him. If he died, I knew we'd all been deceived. He had claimed he held the scepter, which gave him authority to redeem Israel and usher in Zion. I knew if Joel died, I had just wasted sixteen years believing in a false prophet.

More confused than ever, I hurried home.

CHAPTER THIRTY-THREE

On August 20, 1972, I backed the old green Chevy truck up against the side of a cement platform. The man who had filled three large butane tanks for me was loading them onto the truck. I watched traffic pass by on the highway in front of me while I waited and was pleased to see Joel's gray truck approaching. One of his wives was driving. He sat in the passenger's seat eating a banana.

I honked, hoping he would see me, but the vehicle went right on by. I had no idea it would be the last time I ever laid eyes on him alive.

EVENTUALLY THE DETAILS OF the murder of Joel F. LeBaron came to light from Ivan who was present at the scene and related the story to a group of family members.

On that fateful day, Joel stopped in Ensenada on his way from Los Molinos to Colonia LeBaron, where he was to attend the church conference.

Two of his wives, Cathy and Jeannine, and several of his children accompanied him in his pickup. They stopped at the home of Benjamin Zarate, where Joel had left his 1966 Buick, which he intended to tow behind his pickup.

Upon their arrival, they were met by Gamaliel Rios and Andrès Zarate, Benjamin's son. They told Joel and his wives that Benjamin had just moved to a new home. They also informed him that someone had taken the keys to his Buick. Andrès said he would drive Joel's pickup, with the family over to his father's house to go see if he could find the keys. This was only a pretext to leave Joel alone with Gamaliel so that Joel's family would not be present for the murder. But unbeknownst to anyone, fourteen-year-old Ivan, Joel's stepson, stayed behind, resting in Joel's Buick.

Gamaliel soon lured Joel into the empty house to discuss the church controversy.

Ervil, his cousin Conway, and Dan waited nearby in Conway's car, expecting Gamaliel to kill Joel and then join them. Conway was to drive them away in the getaway car. The three became nervous when they felt Gamaliel was taking too long, so Dan went in to do it himself.

A struggle ensued. Joel was struck with a steel wrench and a heavy wooden chair. Joel fought as he fell to the floor. Finally Gamaliel subdued him, and Dan shot Joel—by putting the pistol in his mouth. Then Dan shot him a second time in the forehead and blew more of the back of his skull away. (There was no confession as to whether Gamaliel or Dan did the shooting, but we all believed it was Dan.)

Ivan watched as Dan came out through the door and paused to see if the coast was clear while Gamaliel jumped out of a side window. Then both killers walked to the car and raced away.

Ivan had heard the shots, but stayed in the car, unsure of what to do. When Joel didn't come outside, Ivan went into the house and, to his horror, found his stepfather dead on the floor.

Soon, members of a small church across the street notified the police, who arrived with an ambulance, which took the body away. Ivan walked up and down the street crying uncontrollably, hoping to find his family, but eventually he gave up and returned to the house and waited until he was taken to a police station.

When the wives finally pulled up, Jeannine saw people gathered there. She made her way into the house, where she found a broken wooden chair and the floor splattered with her husband's blood. Cathy and Jeannine wept in despair. They knew that they had been conned into leaving so that the perpetrators could carry out Ervil's orders. Still crying and in shock they jumped in Joel's pickup and headed to the police station to inquire about the murder and to find out where their husband's body had been taken. As they pulled up, Ivan came running out and, though crying, managed to say, "They killed Daddy!"

MEANWHILE ERVIL'S ESTRANGED WIFE Kristina and a girl friend caught a ride to Ensenada with Steve Williams. She had separated from Ervil two years earlier and hoped to confront him about getting a legal divorce and some documents she needed.

Steven left Kristina and her friend at a motel while he went to a nearby store for coffee. The friend was nursing her three-month-old baby when Steve burst in the room. "An American has been shot and killed," he said. "I wonder if it's someone we know down here?"

Leaving the friend and her baby in the motel room, the two rushed outside to the car. They drove through town, stopping along the way to ask several people where they could locate a police officer. They soon found one who sent them to a substation. When they arrived, a policeman who had helped transport the body was still there. He took them to the chief of police, who consented to take them to identify the body. So, Steve and Kristina followed the two men to a rundown part of Ensenada.

Steve helped Kristina walk on a plank over mud; they were trying not to dirty their shoes as they entered what appeared to be a veterinary clinic. No staff member was there, but they could see a menagerie of caged animals everywhere outside, and they could smell animal waste and sewage from the yard. They entered a small, stark anteroom that reeked of mold and mildew. Steve led Kristina up to a partly opened door. Walking into the darkened room, he stood on a chair and pulled the chain to turn on the light. There Kristina saw her brother-in-law...her beloved prophet laid out on an old table. They couldn't believe his body was unattended. Steve cautioned her to stay back and not approach the body. "I don't think you need to see this up close." He shook his head in disbelief.

Kristina had a mind of her own. Steve couldn't have stopped her even if he'd barred the door. She knew she needed to witness this with her own eyes.

In spite of his violent death, Joel looked serene and peaceful. Blood was still on his face and head where he had been hit by some object and a bullet had hit his forehead almost dead center, a quarter inch above the beginning of his left eyebrow. Steve noticed the head tilted oddly backward so he rolled it to one side. The violence of the mushroom, hollow-point bullet had blown away pieces of the back of his skull.

Kristina trembled with disbelief as she peered closely into Joel's face. Her legs buckled, but Steve grabbed her before she hit the floor and led her back to the car. Kristina hesitated, not wanting to leave Joel's body in such an undignified resting place, even temporarily. To her it seemed so unworthy of him.

Kristina disclosed to the police that her estranged husband,

Ervil LeBaron, was probably responsible for Joel's murder. The chief of police called for backup and for a transport vehicle for the body.

Soon a patrol car and a police van, with metal seats on both sides, used to transfer prisoners arrived on the scene. The chief of police and two policemen rolled Joel's body off the table into a blanket. Carrying him out to the transport van, the chief of police chewed out the officers for delivering Joel's body to the wrong place. He then ordered it to be taken to the morgue in the center of Ensenada.

Still in shock, Kristina wailed, "If they've killed Joel, we're all going to die!" She wanted to leave right then and go back to St. George without confronting Ervil, but Steve insisted they continue on to Anna Mae's house, which was on the better side of town. Kristina tried to pull herself together, knowing she needed to follow through with what she'd come for.

Anna Mae's house sat at the top of an inclined driveway. When Kristina and Steve arrived, they parked on the slope directly behind Anna Mae's car. Having had some time to think on the way there, Kristina was now boiling mad. Steve had to help her walk up to the house because she was so distraught. He knew she needed privacy, and he didn't know Anna Mae, so he returned to the car to wait.

Even though both women had been sister wives and confidantes, Kristina was concerned about how Anna Mae would treat her now that she had left Ervil. Yet, she stormed into the house to confront Anna Mae face-to-face. She blurted out in agony, "Joel's been shot!"

"Has he?" asked Anna Mae calmly.

"He's dead, Anna Mae! He's been murdered!"

Now hysterical, she grabbed Anna Mae by the shoulders, looking for some kind—*any* kind—of reaction. Without emotion, matter-of-factly, Anna Mae said, "Well, Kristina, he was doing a lot of things wrong, you know."

She would never be able to forget those exact words. As they talked, Kristina happened to look out the back kitchen window and saw Ervil peeling out the back alley in his infamous "Golden Calf." It had been parked behind one of the outbuildings. Kristina knew the vehicle well since she had been at the dealership when it was purchased. She figured Ervil had been holed up in Anna Mae's house and sneaked out the back when she arrived. The rage she felt turned to fear.

While Kristina was inside the house, a car had pulled up to the driveway and boxed Steve in. Raul Rios was driving and another man sat in the passenger seat. Steve had met Raul several times on various occasions, so he recognized him immediately. Raul got out of his car and accosted Steve. "Who are you? What are you doing here?"

"I'm Steve Williams. We've met a time or two at church," he said, reminding Raul who he was.

Steve pointed to the large front window, where both he and Raul could see Anna Mae and Kristina. Steve explained that Kristina was Ervil's wife and they had come to visit.

"You're okay then," Raul commented, returning to his car.

While Steve was watching, the other man got out of the car and entered Anna Mae's house. Soon all three disappeared from view in the window for a few minutes. Then the man came out and he and Raul drove off, screeching around the corner.

Finally Kristina exited the house, got into Steve's car, and said, "The guy who came in the house was Raul's brother, Gamaliel, one of Ervil's men. I don't trust them. Let's get out of here!"

It was amazing that Steve and Kristina happened to be the ones who found Joel's body. They still get shivers when they think about it. Kristina totally forgot the reason she'd come to

Ensenada. Thoughts of signing papers and getting a legal divorce vanished. But Kristina's mind did wander back to the time Ervil had visited her in a hospital, after an auto accident. When she realized he was beside her bed, she screamed at him, "It's over, it's over, it's over! I never want to see you again—not in this life or the next!"

Nurses had rushed into the hospital room, demanding that Ervil leave. Soon her doctor cautioned her, saying, "How could you let yourself get so upset? You still can get paralyzed from the neck down if you're not careful."

It took her breaking her neck in a car accident to come to a final decision. She reasoned that if the hereafter was an extension of this life, she wanted out.

Kristina's mind shifted back to the present when she and Steve arrived back at the motel, where they picked up her friend and baby, then fled across the border heading for southern Utah. As it turned out, she never did see Ervil again.

JOEL'S BODY WAS PREPARED for burial, and a viewing was held at a mortuary in Ensenada. His numerous followers from Los Molinos, Ensenada, and San Diego came to pay their last respects. It was sad to see so many people weeping, not only because they had lost their prophet, but because their dreams had been crushed. They had all expected Joel to redeem Zion and present them to Christ at his Second Coming.

People were horrified when Anna Mae walked past the line of mourners, right up to the casket, a smirk on her face. As she walked away she muttered, "He deserved it."

After the viewing, Joel's body was flown to Casas Grandes, Chihuahua, then driven on home to Colonia LeBaron, where he received the biggest funeral ever held in the valley. Throngs of people filled the church and overflowed into the streets. Joel not only was well known as the prophet of a church, but also he was loved by many of the Mexicans who lived in the surrounding towns where he had done business.

Ossmen Jones, a lifelong friend to all the LeBarons and a dedicated member of the Church of the Firstborn, conducted the funeral, during which several Church leaders sadly eulogized their beloved prophet. They recounted his outstanding accomplishments and hoped that his dreams and expectations would still come to pass so that his sacrifice would not have been in vain.

A very long procession accompanied the body to the Galeana cemetery. Seeing Joel's seven wives weeping by his casket broke my heart. Just before they lowered it into the ground, his wife Priscilla fainted. And I'll never forget the crying and wailing of his numerous children.

That evening I reminded Verlan that both he and I had understood that if Joel died without leaving a successor, we had all barked up the wrong tree because he was mistaken. However, Verlan commented that he now had to carry on, because too many people were depending on him. He was determined not to let them down.

After long, late meetings with the brethren, trying to decide what direction to take the church now that Joel was dead, Verlan finally came to bed at three in the morning. I didn't hear him undress, but I felt him get into bed. He buried his head in the pillow and sobbed like a child. I didn't know how to comfort him, and I knew that my words couldn't console him at such a time, so I ran my fingers through his hair. As I did, he cried out, "My brother is gone! I have never in my life wanted to die, but now I wish I was in the grave with him." (My account of this was also used in *Prophet of Blood* on p. 143.)

*   *   *

IMMEDIATELY AFTER JOEL'S FUNERAL, Verlan and others notified authorities in Mexico and in the United States of Ervil's threats. The court in Ensenada still held other official accusations against Ervil and his assassins.

Having successfully blood atoned Joel, Ervil figured that the bulk of the Firstborners would naturally just fall into his lap, but instead he became more feared, even loathsome, in their sight.

Ervil intensified his writing and proselytizing campaign, threatening to destroy anyone who opposed him. And he still intended to use the LeBaron property in Los Molinos to fulfill his dreams of grandeur.

Verlan and his counselor Siegfried Widmar continued to urge the Mexican authorities to capture and punish those responsible for Joel's death.

In an effort to expedite Ervil's capture and eventual incarceration, his brother Floren printed a poster with Ervil's picture on it, offering a $10,000 reward to anyone who gave information leading to his arrest. Floren sent it to Ervil's followers, hoping they'd think hundreds had been distributed.

Somehow Ervil still believed he was invincible and decided to take the initiative before being arrested by the police.

On December 13, 1972, after thinking he had made ironclad arrangements with the Mexican authorities to quickly clear his name, he walked into the Ensenada police headquarters, accompanied by his lawyers, who requested that all charges be dropped. The law, however, required at least a seventy-two-hour investigation, so Ervil was temporarily detained.

As soon as word got out, the church leaders took action, compiling the needed evidence to press charges against Ervil for Joel's death. So Ervil was held for trial, upsetting and foiling his plans.

Ervil's own mother and three brothers—Verlan, Alma, and Floren—wrote to the governor of Baja California, requesting that he use his influence to assure that Ervil was justly punished and kept imprisoned so he could not continue killing.

During the trial itself, a voluminous amount of evidence was presented to prove how and why Ervil had masterminded Joel's murder.

Witnesses testified that he was in Ensenada at the time of the murder. Many testified that Ervil had bragged that he was going to kill Joel for being a false prophet and said that Joel must be put to death!

Ervil lied through his teeth, claiming to be innocent. He professed to be a noble humanitarian, stating that he was nowhere near the murder, let alone responsible for it. Most of the defense witnesses were Ervil's own family members, which further weakened his case.

Finally, the overwhelming evidence resulted in the court's determining that he was responsible for the murder. On November 9, 1973, Ervil was found guilty and sentenced to twelve years in prison.

At that time, the Ensenada authorities were still searching for Dan Jordan, Gamaliel and Raul Rios, Andrès Zarate, and Conway LeBaron. The police believed all these men had been involved in the assassination of Joel F. LeBaron.

While Ervil was in the Ensenada jail, he was informed that his number one supporter, Dan Jordan, was dead. But, shortly after Ervil's arrest an investigator, Pasqual Vallverde, told Siegfried that Dan Jordan was very much alive. In fact he had filled out job applications in Mexico City.

Siegfried was beside himself. Dan had fled after Joel's murder, but Siegfried had spent several thousand dollars of his own money trying to track him down. His goal was to see that both Ervil and

Dan were apprehended and brought to justice, so he urged Pasqual to search for Dan in Mexico City. Siegfried had once helped Dan get hired as a consultant in an engineering company that built cooling compressors. Dan had absconded one night, leaving more than three hundred thousand pesos (more than thirty-seven thousand dollars) in unpaid bills. If he was found, he could be legally detained for that as well as for the murder of Joel.

When I first heard that Ervil had finally been apprehended, I was relieved. With him in jail, I hoped I wouldn't have to spend my days and nights expecting to be killed at any moment. My children would be safe and we could live in peace. On the other end of the emotional spectrum, my anger toward him was indescribable. This psycho predator had robbed me, my children, and many others of peace of mind and security. He had robbed me of my sleep. He made it impossible for me to be near my husband, who had been forced to go into hiding. His threats had caused me to move several different times, trying to stay one step ahead of this madman. Yes, Ervil who claimed he was God's anointed one, who would bring peace and usher in the millennium, was now a jailed criminal.

I was relieved after the sentence, but as happy as I was that Ervil was behind bars, I still didn't feel completely safe. I knew we could still not relax. His Lambs of God were trained to kill traitors, which according to Ervil, included all of Verlan's family. Ervil's own children had been indoctrinated to be God's avengers, and I knew as loyal followers they wouldn't stop if he gave them the word to continue the killings.

Ervil used his stint in prison to his advantage. He did not have to waste his precious time traveling from state to state to visit his numerous wives. He could simply stay in one place and enjoy conjugal visits at his convenience.

He also preached to his captive cell mates, some of whom

looked upon him as brilliant. Others considered him a fanatical kook.

One inmate, Leo Evoniuk, a drug dealer who was serving eight years, studied the scriptures with Ervil throughout the day. He became convinced of Ervil's claims to greatness and soon began to help Ervil write pamphlets from their cell.

Ervil effortlessly converted Evoniuk to the belief that polygamy was a law of God. After all, Ervil proved it directly from the Bible. Ervil shared a secret with him that the world did not understand: Jesus Christ was a polygamist! He had married both Mary Magdalene and Martha.

When Ervil was convinced that Leo Evoniuk was sincere in his conversion, he arranged for a Mexican woman from among his converts to marry Leo.

The wedding was held in the prison, where Ervil sealed the woman to Evoniuk for time and all eternity. This thirty-eight-year-old bride who was willing to do Ervil's bidding became Evoniuk's second wife.

Soon, rumor had it that Ervil's followers were raising money to bribe the authorities to release him! Leaders from the Church of the Firstborn informed the Mexican authorities because the reports were reliable. They were assured that Ervil's case would be scrutinized and that Ervil would serve his term without escaping.

But, as always, Ervil found a way. The Mexicans call it *la mordida* (the bribe). So, on December 14, 1973, a higher court in Mexicali, Baja California, overturned the verdict and set him free, on the supposed grounds of irregularities and insufficient evidence.

CHAPTER THIRTY-FOUR

The members of the Church of the First-born were deeply saddened when Verlan announced at a conference that Floren would no longer be working with his brothers. He had forfeited his position as one of the twelve apostles. To this day, Floren believes that he is the only LeBaron brother who can fulfill his father's prophecy, "that through him and his sons, all the nations of the earth would be blessed."

He lived in Nicaragua for a couple of years and then moved to southern Mexico near Cancún, where he has been for over twenty-five years. He has a few followers who are awaiting the return of Christ, who believe in his teachings. Five of his wives have left him; nevertheless, he strongly believes he will fulfill the promise and that he will set God's house in order.

AT THE CLOSING OF OUR CONFERENCE we sang the hymn "We Thank Thee, O God, for a Prophet." Someone offered a closing prayer. No sooner had the crowd said, "Amen," when Jeannine walked up to the podium. Verlan looked upset, even though she insisted she only wanted to make an announcement. Because of some of her previous ideas, he didn't trust her. Verlan tried to avoid her request, but she pressed him further.

"I just want to welcome some of these people as guests to my house," she stated, perturbed, thinking he was denying her the opportunity to speak.

Verlan, still uneasy, capitulated and asked the audience to wait one brief moment because Jeannine had something to tell them.

"Brothers and Sisters," she said, "tonight all of you are invited to Esther Spencer's rock house for Joel's resurrection. Be sure to be there by seven thirty. Our prophet Joel will return to his people at eight o'clock sharp. Make sure you're there."

The crowd was aghast. Verlan now regretted that he hadn't followed his inner promptings. He hoped people would be smart enough not to participate in such nonsense.

I'd been with Jeannine eleven years earlier when I accompanied her to the ocean to be translated. I knew it was all just poppycock! Nevertheless, my inquisitive spirit drew me inside Esther's rock house, shortly after seven thirty. To my surprise, about fifty people were crowded together, seated on folding chairs around the room and on the floor. The partial silence was tainted with whispers, snickering, and doubtful looks from some in the crowd.

Jeannine's younger children, two daughters and a son, sat among the expecting and curious spectators.

I knew no one expected Joel to appear—except Jeannine and her gullible children. Her youngest daughter, Florence, kept falling asleep. Her head bobbed time and again until she was forced to lie down on the floor. Just before she closed her eyes, she cried out, "Mama, be sure and wake me up when Daddy comes back. I want to see him."

Hearing little Florence's sweet request angered me. I couldn't believe Jeannine had planted such false hopes in the minds of her innocent children. However, I kept my mouth shut for once. I didn't want to be accused of criticizing or trying to rain on Jeannine's parade.

The round blue clock on the wall held everyone's attention as time ticked by. It was now eight thirty, and Joel was late—as usual. Jeannine, who stood across the room from me, motioned for her sister Gaye to follow her into the kitchen. I could see by their facial expressions and body language that something was bugging them. After they conferred for about two minutes, Gaye returned to her chair and Jeannine wove through the weary bodies situated on the floor, making her way over to me. "Irene, would you please step outside for a moment?"

My gut feeling told me I was in trouble. We walked down the sidewalk out to the gravel road into the darkness.

"What's up?" I asked.

"I'm really sorry to have to say this to you. I hope it won't ruin our friendship . . ."

I braced myself. "No, go ahead and say whatever you have to say."

"I've prayed fervently every minute with great expectancy for Joel's return. When he did not show up at eight o'clock like I was told he would, I pleaded with the Lord to explain to me what was preventing his appearance. God spoke to me. I heard it clear as a bell. He said, 'Irene's negative doubting spirit is preventing Joel's return.' I'm really sorry to have to say this, but I must ask you to leave these premises."

"Okay, Jeannine, but I want you to know that you are deceived. Joel isn't returning! He is deader than dead!"

"No, Irene! He'll show up for sure when you leave. This I know for sure."

"Good night!" I said matter-of-factly, not only feeling snubbed but disgusted.

I was cold from the October chill in the air. I had no heat in my house except a fifty-gallon metal barrel that had been converted to a "heater." The fire had died down long before I had gone to the séance, so I slipped off my shoes and crawled into bed, fully clothed, beside my three smaller children. After a long stressful day, I was in dreamland in a flash.

In the darkness of my room, I was shaken awake. Groggy and momentarily frightened, I sat up wondering who was disturbing me. Jeannine's voice calmed my agitated spirit. "Please, Irene, I've come back to get you. I so want for you to be a part of this wonderful event. Joel loved you so much, and I know he doesn't want to return until you are present. Get up, come with me," she demanded.

Irritated by her contradiction, I blurted out, "Jeannine, I thought God was an unchangeable God! First he told me to go home because I was preventing him from executing his plans. Now you come back and say that he's changed his mind. What God is so indecisive?"

"Oh, Irene, please come. I still have an audience of about thirty-five people. They're tired and weary from the wait. You must come. The glorious moment will take place as soon as you join us."

Angrily I exclaimed, "Leave me alone! Go away! Supposedly I was the reason Joel didn't show up on time. Now with me absent you have no one to blame. What's going to be your excuse next time?"

"I'm so sorry you feel that way."

"Well, I'm not," I snapped. "God told you to have me stay away...and I am. Good night!" And I rolled over.

The following day I was informed that the crowd cleared out by ten o'clock.

CHAPTER THIRTY-FIVE

After searching the scriptures, Verlan, Alma, and others became convinced that Nicaragua was the appointed place for the saints to gather to await Christ's return. They were infused with joy when they read Isaiah:

> Then shall he give the rain of thy seed, that thou shalt sow the ground withal; and bread of the increase of the earth, and it shall be fat and plenteous: in that day shall thy cattle feed in large pastures.... And there shall be upon every high mountain, and upon every high hill, rivers and streams of waters in the day of the great slaughter, when the towers fall. (30: 23, 25)

They gathered from these verses that in Nicaragua they would be protected when the United States was burned and completely destroyed.

In November, Verlan thought it best to go to Nicaragua. Two thousand miles would separate him from Ervil. He could continue working on the new project there. The brothers—Verlan, Alma, and Floren—found and purchased land in the jungle, in the Bocay River area. They had investigated it diligently, deciding it would be an isolated and secure place where the saints could colonize. It would be a protected refuge away from the world, where they could raise their families in peace.

After Verlan left, I was heartsick to be alone again in Los Molinos. It seemed my whole life I'd been left to fend for myself while Verlan was away working to support his wives.

Verlan's dream had been to prepare a place before the destruction of the United States. As administrator of the new project, he hired a dozen or so men to plant several thousand trees. His hope was to have coconut, banana, avocado, and citrus trees producing by the time the group relocated in the jungles of Nicaragua. He wanted the group to be self-sustaining by having orchards, vegetable gardens, and enough small bamboo huts for protection from the rains when the members arrived. The new plantation in the jungle did not excite me. In fact, I was disheartened by the idea of moving two thousand miles away, where I knew I would be abandoned again and forced to live under someone else's control.

I knew Alma held a grudge against me. I'd never respected him and he knew it. I wasn't one to grab hold of his strict rules. At our last confrontation, he had demanded that I not wear pants. He said the Bible restricted women from wearing men's clothing. I strutted in my green and brown corduroy slacks and asked him, "Are these men's pants? Do they look like it to you?"

He held his ground. "Pants are for men, dresses are for women. You must obey the scriptures. When we make our move to Nicaragua, everyone will be forced to live by *my* dress code, or they will not be allowed to live among us. My duty as bishop is to see that the laws of God are enforced."

"Well, Alma," I quipped, "I think Christ is in big trouble then."

"Why?"

I tried to keep a straight face. "Well, he wore a long robe. It looks like a woman's to me, and," I couldn't resist adding, "from the pictures I've seen, it doesn't appear as though he was wearing men's pants underneath."

"Well, that was the custom in those days," he said, rebuking me.

"That's right," I said, hoping he'd get the point. "Our custom today is that women wear pants. And"—I couldn't help but laugh—"I'll bet you wouldn't be caught dead in mine!"

After much discussion among the members of the church, he'd finally capitulated by allowing women to wear jeans, but their blouses had to be long sleeved with a high neckline and flowing to cover their hips and buttocks.

On the trip Alma, Verlan, and others made to Nicaragua, Alma explained how they would clear the jungle and divide it into lots. Verlan suggested the fairest way to distribute the parcels of land was by numbering every lot. Those who drew a number that corresponded to the lot would be the new owners.

Alma agreed to the arrangement, but he warned Verlan that I was not welcome to live among God's people. Verlan objected. "There's no reason for me to live here if one of my wives is denied the right. What has Irene done that's serious enough to keep her from living among the saints?"

"Well," Alma said gruffly, "she'll have her radio, tapes, music, and novels. That rubbish will pollute the women. And I for one will not tolerate it!"

"If Irene isn't welcome to live in our new Zion, then you should take her before a church court and make your accusations. It's absurd, and I don't want to listen to such nonsense," Verlan said.

CHAPTER THIRTY-SIX

I bolted upright in my bed. My pounding heart made me gasp for air. My nightmare had seemed so real, but all I could remember was that a voice had warned me to move out of Los Molinos immediately. There was no possible way I could leave. I had no vehicle, no driver's license, no money, and nine children still at home. Kaylen was my oldest son at home. I had allowed Brent to go to Chihuahua with a friend. My two oldest boys, Andre and Steven, were working in San Diego in drywall to help support Verlan's large family. When it was convenient, they would drive across the border and come to the colony to see us on weekends. It broke my heart to see my boys leave home at such a tender age. As teenagers, they took on the responsibility that should have been their father's. Sadly, they lost their childhood.

I thought that my fear may have been triggered from the previous weekend when Steven had arrived from San Diego to visit. In spite of his young age, I looked to Steven for protection in these perilous times. In the night, I had been spooked when I heard a banging noise on the front porch; a five-gallon metal bucket clanged as though someone had kicked it. I bolted up in bed, my mind racing. I wondered, was it one of Ervil's "soldiers of God" sneaking around, looking to fulfill his orders to kill me? Stiff with fear, unable to move, I listened, trying to detect movement outside the bedroom window. My heart was in my throat, pumping so violently I could barely breathe. Finally I summoned the courage to make my way down the hall, feeling cautiously along the walls in the dark. I slid gently onto Steven's bed, which startled him. "Shh. It's just me," I whispered as I hugged him spoon fashion.

"Are you scared?" he whispered back.

"No..." I lied, but my trembling body betrayed me.

"What's wrong, Mom? I can tell you're scared to death."

Having endured that fright of my life, I realized it was just a false alarm.

My mind was heavy with thoughts as I fed breakfast to the kids crowded around the table. Later, I sent fourteen-year-old Kaylen outside to clean the yard. The memory of the voice weighed heavily on my heart. Throughout the day, in the midst of doing housework and caring for needy babies, I heard a voice in my head again: "Take your kids and leave immediately." I thought it was unfair that I was being asked to leave when there was no way I could possibly comply. I had no phone, no electricity, and no husband home who could help me. Verlan was lying low in Nicaragua, hiding from Ervil. Not a day went by that I didn't cry and pray that he would be protected by God. I hid my fears as I fulfilled my duties as a mother. I stood outside in the wind, hanging wet clothes. Then when they were dry, I gathered them in my arms and took them back into the house. I fed the brood boiled pinto beans and dry whole wheat bread and asked them to settle in their beds early. I was too beat to deal with the noise and confusion any longer.

Usually I zonked out when my head hit the pillow, but this night my mind ran to and fro and refused to settle. I didn't know if I was in imminent danger, or if my own fears had prompted the warning.

Desperately desiring to know what I should do, I pondered silently in the darkness. To my surprise, the voice spoke emphatically again: "Take your kids and leave."

I finally gave in to the tears of desperation, letting them fall unimpeded onto the pillow I embraced. I cried out to heaven for answers. Where was my husband? Where could I possibly hide with all my children? The antics of the whole LeBaron clan had severed the bonds between my former friends and family. The mere thought of going to the States, into a foreign environment, paralyzed me. I had no job skills, only a ninth-grade education and zero self-esteem. I had been an outcast among the Mormons as a child. Now I was one among my polygamous family.

Signing up for welfare was an absolute no-no. Fear of discovery had been well ingrained into my belief system. I'd been warned that I'd cause repercussions, possibly arrests, if I accepted money from the government. I'd been disowned by my own parents for marrying Verlan without their knowledge. Two of my brothers were living polygamy, which made it almost impossible for them to support their large numbers of wives and children. I knew there was no way that I could look to either of them for help.

Though my eyes felt heavy and my head ached from lack of sleep, I got out of bed early the next morning. I knew in my heart that I *must* find a way to leave Los Molinos that day. I thought about the Big Brown House in Ensenada that we had vacated when we moved to Los Molinos. If someone would drive me and my children the two and a half hours it took to get there, I thought I could survive in that house. As a further incentive, I recalled that the house had electricity and running water, which was a plus. With that thought in mind, I decided to go.

I left twelve-year-old Barbara to look after the kids, making sure they ate breakfast and did the dishes. Usually four or five young men in their late teens or early twenties drove the five hours to the Los Molinos colony on weekends from San Diego. It was pretty routine, because the weekends were the only opportunity they had to court their girlfriends. I recognized three new trucks parked beside the meeting house. Several young men were gathered in twos, trying to enjoy every moment possible with their girlfriends before they had to return to the States to work. Two were my nephews. I pleaded with both of them, plus another friend who joined in the conversation, to allow my children and me to ride to Ensenada. All agreed, but they said they couldn't wait long after the Sunday church meeting because they were going to leave immediately so they could travel together.

I ran home and started shouting orders. The four older girls tore the blankets from the beds and folded them. Two others removed clothes from the closets, hangers and all. We tied them tightly in an old sheet. We filled both my metal washtubs with dishes, pots and pans, and kitchen utensils. The kids were excited about this new adventure. They all cooperated, carrying the tubs of heavy dishes, bedding, two old suitcases, and my only good dresser outside. We hauled out two mattresses as well, and I grabbed some rope to use for securing the mattresses on the trucks.

Before I was completely ready, the meeting was over and three vehicles backed into my yard. The young teenagers loaded my meager belongings into the trucks, tying the load down tight. I counted the kids, making sure they were all accounted for and crowded in beside their cousins.

I kept with me my two smallest boys, two-year-old Lothair and four-year-old Seth, and we sat beside one of my nephews in his truck as we followed the other two in a caravan toward Ensenada.

The unheated house—cold, dusty, and uninviting—would be my temporary refuge. Everybody pitched in to unload the trucks. Noise from the boisterous kids rang throughout the empty rooms. We placed the two mattresses on the cement floor in separate bedrooms, then unfolded sheets and blankets and made up the beds. One of my nephews was kind enough to hook up my butane tank so I could start cooking for the kids. When the necessary tasks were completed, several of the older kids ran to the neighbors to see their former friends.

I had lived in that house before, sharing it with Verlan's two other wives, Charlotte and Lucy. Now, alone with my own children, it seemed more spacious than ever.

To my amazement, my insecurities found me longing for another wife for comfort and protection. I was so unprepared to live on my own. There was no one to fall back on in case of an emergency. My meager and sporadic budget of twenty to fifty dollars a week did no more than supply us with beans, rice, and homemade whole wheat bread. Cracked wheat, boiled, then mixed with a can of Carnation milk and a small amount of sugar was the main staple for breakfast.

My oldest child, nineteen-year-old Donna, had abandoned the cult the previous year. When word reached her of my move to Ensenada, she drove down from Los Angeles to see me. Insisting that I allow her to spend her own money, she set to work, trying to turn my bare house into a home. We measured the windows for curtains in the living room and my bedroom and then drove to town in Donna's car, which was a blessing in itself. She bought several throw rugs to help cover the cold cement floors. But the biggest surprise was the roll of linoleum we managed to cram into the backseat of the car, the upper portion jutting out through the open window. We unrolled and laid it on the kitchen floor with excitement. It looked beautiful and was warmer to walk on than the existing cement floors.

I had just started sewing the lacy material into curtains when Donna insisted that I accompany her to a nearby tree lot, where, to my great surprise and delight, she bought me a tall live spruce for Christmas. Her four younger sisters—Barbara, Margaret, Sandra, and Connie—had the privilege of selecting Christmas ornaments to adorn the tree.

Back at home, the children all experienced the excitement and joy of celebrating Christmas while decorating the tree. After buying peanuts, candies, and other goodies, Donna returned to the States to spend Christmas with her boyfriend, Marshall.

The following week, Douglas Fessler, a friend from Los Angeles, picked up Laura (Charlotte's daughter) and my son Steven in San Diego, and they dropped by my house in Ensenada. I'd met Doug a few months earlier while visiting Donna. He was headed down to Los Molinos to visit for the weekend. Curiosity and a sense of adventure had encouraged him to become familiar with Donna's half sisters. He hoped to begin a relationship with one of them, sparing her from the impending fate of polygamy.

Doug asked me if my sixteen-year-old son, Steven, could accompany them to the colony instead of spending the weekend with me. I could see that Steven was excited at the opportunity to return to see his half brothers and sisters again, so I let him go.

That night fog settled around the house, restricting my view. I couldn't even see the tall winery that stood kitty-corner across the gravel road from our house. The cold December air sent chills through my body. As was customary, I dressed all the smaller children in heavy sweaters in preparation for bed. Having no heat at all in the house, we had to fight the cold, which I resented. I slept in my jeans and long-sleeved blouse to keep warm.

At three in the morning, my toddler Lothair cried out for a bottle. His insistence drove me into the kitchen but I didn't turn on the light because I feared being seen by someone who might have been stalking me.

The light from the kitchen stove was sufficient, so I warmed up the sweetened cinnamon tea and then filled the plastic baby bottle. Catching a glimpse of something out of the corner of my eye, I parted the kitchen curtains. Two Mexican police cars were parked smack in front of the entrance into my yard. Their motors were turned off. I peeked just long enough to wonder what they were doing at this time of night. They seemed to be simply waiting in the darkness.

A strange foreboding came over me when I snuggled beside my son, listening to him suck on his bottle, as I tried to warm one of his legs that had become cold when he kicked off the covers as he slept.

I awoke early and lit the oven in the kitchen, leaving the door open so heat could escape and warm the room while the older kids dressed the younger ones. Through my open curtains, I saw my Mexican neighbor who lived behind me. He was on his way home from his night shift at the winery. I ran outside, waving as I called to him, "Rodolfo! Rodolfo!"

He approached me, but was not smiling as he usually did. "*¿Que pasa?*" I asked him.

Concerned, he confided in me. "Irene, last night two police cars were parked by your home. On my way to work I walked over by them to inquire if everything was okay. The officer said, 'Yes, we're just sitting here protecting the woman in the house.' 'Why?' I asked. They responded, 'Someone is trying to kill her.'"

Even though I had suspected it, the reality was too unbelievable to even comprehend. I'd barely moved to Ensenada because of a premonition. No one knew I was here alone except Verlan's other wives in Los Molinos.

"There must be some mistake," I sputtered, trying to sound trivial.

Rodolfo spoke gravely. "I'm worried about you. If you need me for anything, send one of the kids over and I'll come immediately."

A half hour later, my oldest son, Andre, drove into my yard, bringing his car to a screeching halt. He and my longtime friend Juna (pronounced Janae) Wakeham jumped out of the vehicle and ran inside to meet me as I opened the living room door. Juna was white with fear. "He's done it, Irene! Ervil attacked Los Molinos! We don't know all the details."

Andre cut in, "Verlan Jr. phoned the Ensenada police when he got wind of the raid. They were supposed to come out here to protect you last night. Did they?"

"Yes, I guess that's what they were up to." I fired questions repeatedly, trying to get more details. I needed to know whether Steven had been hurt.

Juna spoke up disappointedly. "No one knows anything yet. Let's go to the police station and see if they can tell us what happened. I heard a dozen or so people were shot and two are dead. But I'm not sure that's accurate."

I burst out crying, thinking that one of those dead might be Steven. I sent my kids over to Rodolfo's, got into the car with Andre and Juna, and headed for the police station.

The three of us drove the six miles into downtown Ensenada. I hurried into the police station with Andre and Juna at my heels. Andre spoke Spanish fluently, so he asked the most pertinent questions: Did they know who was dead? Was his brother Steven killed? Were any of the dead Verlan's wives or children? Was Doug Fessler dead?

But the police chief didn't know any details. He had been inundated with calls from frenzied reporters from all over the U.S. and Mexico, demanding details of the raid. The overwhelmed officer conveyed what little news he had of the attack. Between his constant phone calls, he tried answering our questions, covering the receiver with one hand.

For a split second, when the calls died down, he pointed to two eight-by-ten black-and-white photos on his desk. My stomach turned when I glanced at the pictures.

"Who are these men?" he probed. "Do you know either of them?"

All three of us sadly admitted that we did. I pointed to the first photo and said, "This is Ervil LeBaron, my brother-in-law." And then to the second. "The other guy is his bodyguard, Daniel Jordan."

"Who are you?" he asked, looking me in the eye.

"I'm Irene LeBaron."

"Oh, my! You're the woman my buddies were sent out to guard last night. You'd better leave your home immediately. Go somewhere and hide, because we can do nothing more for you."

The phone rang three times without his answering it. He was determined to finish his sentence first. "You'd better go now," he warned, finally picking up the receiver. With his free hand, he waved us out of the police headquarters.

On the way home we were too distraught to think straight. We'd received absolutely no information from the authorities, and we didn't know if any of Verlan's family was dead or alive. I mentally berated myself over and over, sickened that I had let Steven go to Los Molinos for the weekend. I'd never forgive myself if he was dead.

Among the three of us, we discussed how we could leave and where we might run for safety. We definitely needed another vehicle to transport the numerous children. First we drove toward the Big Brown House. Just as Andre was driving off the highway onto a gravel road, we heard loud, quick blasts from an oncoming vehicle's horn. I spotted the familiar dark blue former potato chip truck coming from Los Molinos.

"It's Ray Dambacher!" Andre and Juna yelled in unison.

When Andre pulled over and stopped beside the vehicle, all three of us jumped out. I could see Pat Mackey in the driver's seat, so I knew something was amiss. He descended from the truck and hurried toward us.

I cried out, sobbing for an answer. "Is Steven dead?"

"No. Steven is a hero. He helped save several houses from burning."

I felt relieved, but faint from all the stress I had endured the last hour. "Are any of Verlan's wives or children dead?" I asked.

"No, no. But I've got Ray inside the truck on a cot. He was mowed down by a shotgun blast. I'm transporting him to San Diego, where I can get him to the veterans' hospital."

I'd known Ray for several years. I climbed into the truck and found Ray delirious and moving in constant pain with tears running down his cheeks. When he felt my hand on his, he blinked. I could tell he had a hard time focusing. Maybe his pain delayed his memory for a moment or two.

"Ray?" I heard my voice crack from sadness. "Are you okay? It's Irene. Can I help you?" I spoke again. "Ray?" My words finally registered in his ethereal world.

"I've been shot." He grabbed my blouse. "Please don't leave me." He tried unsuccessfully to turn back the gray blanket that covered his body. "Help me," he ordered weakly, trying to lower the blanket again.

I peeled the cover back, but I was not prepared for what I saw. His legs and stomach were completely marked with pellets of buckshot. He reminded me of a dead duck my brother had once brought home. I forced myself not to cry, knowing that if I did, Ray would become more upset. He had too many worries already. Pulling the cover back into place, I gently patted his face. "You'll be okay. Wait here; we'll be right back to go with you."

Pat, Andre, and Juna also saw his condition and sensed the urgency. Leaving Juna to console our wounded friend, Andre and I rushed to our house, which was only about three minutes away.

I loaded five of my youngest children into Andre's car, grabbed one change of clothes for each child, and then we hurried back to the van. We evacuated the car and the children loaded themselves into the van. I seated all the kids on the floor on a blanket, next to the cot, and I kept vigil at Ray's head, my hand in his for comfort.

Juna and Andre returned to the house to pick up Kaylen, Barbara, Margaret, and Sandra. The kids had barely had enough time to gather a few belongings, which they put in the trunk of Andre's red car. He and Juna sped to catch up to us, just as we were leaving Ensenada, ready to hit the main highway to San Diego.

My soothing words calmed Ray's delirium, but the two and a half hours to San Diego, watching him suffer, seemed like a lifetime.

Not wanting to be detained at the border, we gave the least possible amount of information. We declared our citizenship. When Ray didn't answer, I spoke for him. "He's very sick. We are on our way to the hospital."

"What's wrong? Does he have stomach problems?"

"Something like that," I responded. "I understand lots of people return with Montezuma's revenge." With that answer, he waved us through to the good ol' USA.

With a few instructions from Ray, we finally found the veterans' hospital, pulling up to the emergency annex. I ran in, demanding a stretcher. Minutes later, Ray was under a doctor's care. I was heartsick to leave him alone, but I had to take all my children to Juna's. She had offered us refuge until we could figure something else out. The fear in Ray's eyes when I left him still haunts me today.

Ray recovered with time. His near death experience did not cause him to lose hope in his newly found faith.

CHAPTER THIRTY-SEVEN

L ittle by little we pieced together the details of the raid on Los Molinos.

Ervil's paranoia had escalated. In his most recent delusional revelation, God had spoken emphatically to him concerning his brother Verlan. Ervil confided in one of his followers that he'd been told to "kill the son of a bitch!"

Shocked at God's vocabulary, the stunned follower asked, "Were those God's exact words?"

Ervil replied, "Absolutely!"

Ervil gave strict orders to his followers to carry out God's commands. He promised the group that he sent on a mission to kill that Verlan would be in Los Molinos and that he would fall into their hands.

"Just do your part by throwing fire bombs at his homes so they'll burn," he said solemnly. "Open fire with your shotguns. We'll blast the son of a bitch right into hell." Then he chuckled, stating unequivocally, "God has wondrous plans of retribution." The plan was to strike all seven of Verlan's homes, burning each one and shooting out every window. So he informed his commandos that they were to go to Los Molinos on a special mission and burn down the buildings, which Ervil claimed rightfully belonged to him.

The group Ervil chose to carry out this plan consisted of Don Sullivan and some of Ervil's own children, stepchildren, sons-in-law, and even his future wife, Rena. His shocked followers listened intently as Ervil explained the orders from God, who promised that Ervil's brother Verlan would be in the colony and that He would deliver Verlan over to the Lambs of God so that he could be blood atoned.

These soldiers left to carry out Ervil's orders, believing they were doing the will of God.

THE DAY BEFORE THE RAID, when Steven had accompanied his half sister Laura and Doug Fessler to Los Molinos for the weekend, Charlotte graciously welcomed Steven and Doug, giving them a place to sleep for the night. The following morning, Doug was anxious to show off his new Toyota to Laura's family and friends, so they made arrangements to drive around town to visit friends and then go to the beach.

Steven, who was cautious since Joel's death, warned Charlotte. "I heard a rumor yesterday that your mother from Salt Lake City called someone in San Diego. They said to get word to those in Los Molinos because Ervil had ordered a raid."

Charlotte considered Steven's words, but since she saw no other indications of trouble, she overlooked the warning.

Steven noticed several cars gathered at Bud Chynoweth's house, one of Ervil's loyal followers. He recognized the vehicles belonging to other dissidents and felt uneasy. Even though he was only sixteen years old, Steven still felt vulnerable, not trusting Ervil's bunch since Joel's murder. Wanting comfort and protection, he chose to stay at Charlotte's where he could be with family.

But he joined the group for the day's activities. Their first stop was at the Castro home, where Laura delivered a letter, which Fernando Castro Sr. and Ossmen Jones sent to warn the people of possible danger from Ervil's followers.

That evening, on December 26, 1974, Doug, Laura, Steven, and a couple other teenagers were occupied playing board games. Steven, feeling too worried to concentrate, wandered outside to see if there was any unusual activity. He wondered if Ervil's flunkies were up to no good. He noted that it was about ten o'clock.

Moments later, he heard commotion and could see in the distance that the tower house, a three-story framed building not far from my now-vacant house I had abandoned a few days earlier, was on fire.

Steven rushed back into Charlotte's house to warn them. Little did Steven know that as soon as the tower house was ablaze, Ray Dambacher had immediately taken charge. With the help of several dozen men, he had formed a "bucket brigade," dipping water from a nearby well and passing the buckets down the line as the group rallied to douse the roaring flames.

Two young brothers, Fernando and Joel Castro, used shovels, flinging sand and dirt onto the structure, hoping to quench the fire. For a few minutes, they focused their efforts in hopes of saving the burning building.

Moroni Mendez, only sixteen years old, was up on the second level fighting the flames. Horrified, the onlookers below watched as Moroni slumped over and tumbled down the exterior flight of stairs, crying as he fell, "I've been shot in the legs!"

Because of the crackling fire, no one had heard the gunshots. But now bullets flew into the crowd from all directions.

Ray Dambacher tried to dodge the bullets by getting out

of the light from the fire and into the shadows. However, the engulfing flames from the building lit up the night scene clearly, revealing the group of firefighters as brightly as if a spotlight had been directed on them. As Ray took his first quick steps to safety, he felt the stinging pain in his side and both legs. He had been blasted with a shotgun.

Because of the noise and pandemonium below, Fernando Castro Jr., from his position near the stairs, had no idea they were being attacked or what peril they were in until a bullet zinged into his leg. He yelled frantically to his brother Joel, begging him to jump off the balcony of the burning building. Joel obeyed his brother, leaped to the ground, and rushed toward a stack of adobe bricks where he intended to be safe. But before he reached cover, he too received a shot in his right leg. A second later, another bullet exploded into Fernando's right hand. Bleeding, but too afraid to stop moving, he limped to safety behind an adobe wall.

Cries from women and children drowned out the blasts from the guns as bullets sprayed into the horrified crowd. But Mark and Duane Chynoweth, Don Sullivan, Eddie Marston, and the others relentlessly carried out their leader's commands.

The Firstborners stumbled, grabbing their wounds as they fell to the ground. Moroni's pitiful cries were soon silenced when one of Ervil's commandos walked up to him, placed a gun near his chest, then pulled the trigger.

The Lambs of God yelled for retreat, running to two different vehicles. Several attackers piled into a GMC truck and others scooted into a Fiat. The vehicles left in different directions, making their way through town, throwing firebombs and shooting into the houses.

Edmundo Aguilar was caught completely off guard when the soldiers attacked. Groggy from partying the previous night, he slept so hard that he was oblivious to the shotgun blasts and screams from the frightened crowd. He was jolted out of a deep sleep, however, when a Molotov cocktail flew through his window, shattering the glass and landing beside him on his bed. Flailing his arms against the burning bomb, he leaped from his bed. He hurried toward the window, throwing the bomb outside, when a gun blast came through the window. The shot knocked him unconscious, wounding him terribly.

The killers raced through town, shooting and throwing firebombs, believing in Ervil's vision that Verlan would be delivered into their hands.

The last house they attacked was Charlotte's. The GMC stopped directly in front of her home, opening fire at both doors and blasting every front window. They completely emptied their shotguns Mafia style as they sprayed her house with bullets and threw their firebombs. The Lambs of God jeered, mocked, and laughed jubilantly. Their voices rose in shouts of victory as they drove away, hoping that Verlan had been killed as Ervil had promised.

They didn't know Verlan had left Los Molinos two weeks before and was safe in Nicaragua.

In the aftermath, five of the wounded were helping others, but ten wounded people lay in the darkness, unable to stand or help themselves. Benjamin Zarate, while trying to aid his fallen comrades, had been shot in the neck. Before he could react, a second bullet grazed his head. His wife, seeing he was still alive, whispered to him urgently to pretend he was dead. Moroni, clinging to life with a bullet in his chest, began crying again. The confused and wounded group was immobilized—until they heard Ray Dambacher's blue delivery van approaching.

Despite their severe injuries and blinding pain, Ray and others loaded in the worst of the despairing wounded. Benjamin took the driver's seat. He had never driven a vehicle with a gear shift, so Ray, though in excruciating pain, shifted while Benjamin steered. The terrified group made their way down the main street, hoping to aid other wounded victims. When they ran into Steven and fifteen-year-old Humberto Rascon who knew how to drive a stick shift, Steven insisted that Humberto drive them to the clinic.

Later, Steven recounted the attack, telling how he and Doug had hurried out of Charlotte's house to investigate when they heard shots and surprised cries through the darkness. Steven knew it was Ervil's people, so they ran back into Charlotte's house, shouting warnings to her: "It's the Ervilites! They're here to destroy us!" Steven then told Doug to stay with Charlotte and her kids to help protect them while he ran swiftly through the dark to Don Juan's house. There he grabbed a .22 rifle, shoved twelve bullets into the magazine, then ran outside accompanied by Don Juan's son Humberto. Hearing screams and shouts, they threw themselves prostrate into a small trench in the orchard close to the street. They saw several homes ignite when the firebombs hit. They heard the glass shatter as the attackers shot out windows in several homes along the main street.

Steven watched the truck approach. He could see the attackers from about forty yards away. He hugged the ground, keeping himself concealed from the headlights of the truck as it turned a corner coming toward him. He lay still with his gun cocked, holding his breath, praying no one would detect him. As soon as the truck left the town and headed up the road to the main highway, the boys scampered out of their hiding place and ran to Charlotte's burning house. Humberto boosted Steven onto the roof, where the flames leaped higher and higher. Steven tore off his wool jacket and began beating out the fire. As he made his way across the roof, he threw to the ground numerous Molotov cocktails. When the fire was out, he jumped down and ran to Susan's house (Verlan's sixth wife) and extinguished the flames that threatened to consume her front door. Humberto hoisted Steven onto the roof, where he grabbed three burning bombs and threw them to the ground. With his coat, he then beat out the fire, which was burning the tar paper roof. By the time Steven and Humberto reached Lillie's house (Verlan's seventh wife), her front door and frame were burning. Her roof had also caught on fire above the door. Both boys scaled the wall onto the crackling roof and beat the dancing flames until they were extinguished.

By now, it was evident to Steven that every house of his father's had been targeted. When he finally arrived at Beverly's house (Verlan's fourth wife) the fire had already been extinguished with water from the sink.

Steven ran down the road toward my evacuated house, hoping to save it from burning, but someone had already extinguished the blaze.

Just then, Ray and Benjamin drove up in Ray's van, screaming for help. Inside were several wounded victims. Benjamin was in bad shape and Ray himself was badly wounded. Humberto got in the driver's seat, put the truck into gear, and headed off to the Mexican clinic twenty minutes south of the colony to get medical aid.

The Buen Pastor Clinic overflowed with victims of the attack. The small hospital was unprepared and unequipped for so many wounded. Fearing more attacks, a staff member called the police to go to the colony. They worked frantically to save the wounded, but sixteen-year-old Moroni Mendez died shortly after he arrived.

Back in the raided town, Steven went to Esther's house (Verlan's fifth wife), where the Aguilar family was living. He ran to the blown-out six-foot picture window and found the glass in hundreds of pieces inside and out. Hearing an unusual noise, Steven turned and felt chills of fear racing through his body when he found nineteen-year-old Edmundo Aguilar, who had been shot in the head, his body jerking and convulsing. Steven could see Edmundo's injuries were beyond his limited skills, so he left to get help.

Manuel Rascon, who had been in the small town of Guerrero, saw the flames in the distance from the highway as he was returning home. He met Steven running down the gravel road and insisted that Steven get into his vehicle. They drove back to Esther's house, where Edmundo lay in agony. An older woman who had been shot in the shoulder came out of her hiding place in the closet when she realized the boys were there to help her. Manuel and Steven helped both of them into the car and Manuel rushed them to the clinic, but, sadly, Edmundo also died a short time later.

By now, Steven was beginning to grasp the magnitude of the raid. He scurried through the fields to Charlotte's house, yelling several times. No one answered. He ran into her backyard to investigate, calling out into the darkness. Charlotte and Doug answered him from a small orchard thirty yards away. Steven briefly told them what had happened, informing them about the wounded. He learned that Doug had driven his car into the orchard when the commotion had first started. He offered to take Steven up to my abandoned house, two blocks away. It had been saved, but the tall tower house that sat just beyond my home was a smoldering ash heap.

Setura Castro stood by the road in a group of about fifty or sixty distraught women and children, weeping and moaning. They feared the attackers would return. When Steven told them about the wounded and how much of the town had been destroyed, they became more frightened. Not waiting to hear the rest of Steven's report, the group—gripped with fear—ran weeping toward the ocean to the salt flats, hoping to save their lives.

At daybreak, Ossmen Jones, his son Larry, and Fernando Castro Sr. flew to Los Molinos after word had reached them of the raid. Their small plane circled the colony, buzzing overhead, taking note of the ashes of the three-story tower house and charred homes. The victims who survived the destruction from the night before were absolutely terrified, seeing the plane circle and then land. They hid in their homes screaming and praying that they'd be delivered from more violence. They all thought that Ervil's henchmen had returned in the plane to finish them all off. The scene was pure pandemonium.

When the plane landed on the salt flats, Steven and a group of men drove down to investigate. They wanted to help protect the women and children who were hiding near the ocean sand dunes. Steven was surprised when he realized it was Ossmen Jones and Fernando Castro Sr., the two men who had sent a warning to them the night before, a warning that had not been circulated. Therefore no one knew of the impending threat. The uninformed colony was completely unprepared for the surprise attack. They were absolutely caught off guard.

Several government soldiers arrived in trucks. Some went to calm and protect the emotionally distraught group who had taken refuge near the ocean. The soldiers convinced the crowd to return to their homes, following them with a promise of protection.

Later that morning, news reporters from the United States and Mexico swarmed the colony. Cameras flashed for hours as women and children willingly shared their stories, pointing out the burned spots on their homes, and the gunshot holes. They wept as they recounted the screams and agony of the wounded.

With the level of destruction created by the Lambs of God, it was a miracle that only two people died and only thirteen others were wounded. My son Steven was a true hero. Had it not been for him, five of Verlan's homes would have burned to the ground. I was so proud and I loved him for his courage and strength to act under pressure.

When Verlan returned from Nicaragua to attend the funerals, he looked tired and haggard. Verlan had believed wholeheartedly that his brother Joel was a prophet of God. Now he was dead and Ervil had clearly lost his grip on reality. Verlan wondered how his brother could be so insane as to want to wipe out some of his own family. He was sickened that his dear mother had to endure so much pain. I sensed Verlan's disappointment. His brothers, Ben, Ross, and Alma, had shamed the family, but Verlan had tried for years to redeem the LeBaron name. Now Ervil was infamous—a black-hearted brother who was out to destroy the last shards of the LeBaron legacy.

Verlan's responsibilities to his wives and children also weighed heavily on his mind. I sensed sadness and disappointment that he couldn't spend more time with us. Mostly it pained me to see him so jittery, always having to look over his shoulder, always wondering if he'd be cut down by Ervil's henchmen. My heart ached for Verlan. He kissed me sadly and told me how appalled he was by his brother's behavior. "I'm so sorry that I can't stay with you. I feel so bad that you're in such a perilous situation and I can't be here to protect you and the children."

We hugged warmly, wondering if it would be the last time we would see each other. Life was so uncertain.

After he left to attend the funerals and comfort his flock of believers, I felt so abandoned and alone, especially during the holidays when we should have been celebrating as a family. I'll forever be grateful that I listened to my prompting and fled ten days earlier with my children to Ensenada. I was grateful that my children and I were safe with my friend Juna in San Diego.

I was especially saddened to hear of Moroni Mendez's death. He had helped load my belongings into a pickup in preparation for my departure from Los Molinos. In gratitude I had given him a Spanish Bible and also a dresser. He'd warmly expressed his thanks, and that was the last time I saw him alive.

Had we still been living in our house in the colony that night, I'm sure my children would have been standing out front watching the three-story house burn. I myself would have been out trying to fight the flames in the bucket brigade. I learned that my adobe home had been riddled by shotgun blasts and Molotov bombs had charred my front door and burned part of my roof. I knew our lives had been saved by my being obedient to the voice that had warned me to leave ten days earlier.

VERLAN WAS OVERWHELMED WITH FEAR and concern for his families. Since all his homes had been targeted in Los Molinos with firearms and riddled with shotgun pellets, I remained in hiding in San Diego with my ten younger children at my friend Juna's home while Verlan attended the funerals in Los Molinos of the two young men who were killed during the raid.

It was chaos with so many children and nowhere to run for safety, but we had to take action. Verlan returned after the funeral and took me back to Ensenada, where we quickly spent thirty minutes grabbing bedding, dishes, utensils and clothing. We took only the bare necessities, knowing I had to leave space in the camper for the children. Our main concern was that some of Ervil's soldiers would be lying in wait. Nevertheless, we repacked the truck again in San Diego, making sure he left room for the children, then we left at five in the morning for Colonia LeBaron.

The fifteen-hour trip heightened my depression. We all kept our eyes open, hoping our enemies would not detect us. We felt so vulnerable wondering if we'd make it to our destination without encountering any trouble. During our trip, Verlan confided to me that he was weary from the death threats and overwhelmed with so much responsibility. During our conversation he informed me that we would be in the LeBaron colony for only a week, and then he was moving us to Nicaragua, where we would be concealed and safe.

I cried despairingly, feeling as though I were being taken to the end of the earth, away from all that was familiar... away from friends and family into the unknown. As it was, I saw very little of Verlan; he'd been on the run because his life was in peril. I knew I'd be left alone months at a time if he took me to Nicaragua. I felt I could not cope with the fears and responsibilities of my children without his help. Lucy had willingly moved to Nicaragua a year earlier. I knew she and her children would be a comfort to us, but my soul screamed against the plan. I needed stability and a future for my children. None of my family in Utah was capable of taking on all of us. They had large families themselves, and our different religious views had severed our bonds, so I did not reach out to them.

I cried every day throughout our seven-day trip through Mexico and Central America. The farther we drove, the more desperation I felt. The kids were so tightly packed in the camper that they complained about claustrophobia and we were forced to stop often for them to stetch their legs, vomit, and catch a breath of air.

Once we arrived on a small farm called the "Arenal" that

Verlan had purchased in Nicaragua, we unloaded our few belongings into a three-room wooden structure, with a tin roof and dirt floors, where Lucy also lived.

Soon I found myself knee deep in the nearby running creek, where the natives taught me how to scrub my dirty clothes on large rocks, then spread them on nearby bushes to dry. Verlan didn't come back to see me for four months. He returned just long enough to take our older boys back to the States to pick pine nuts. He didn't even spend the night with me.

When the pine nut season was over, he returned with his first wife, my sister Charlotte, and Susan, to also live with us.

All the children were thrilled to see one another and they felt like they were in paradise. They swam in the creek and grew vegetable gardens. They hiked and enjoyed the beautiful rolling hillsides. They even found a parrot and a monkey that became their pets. They felt secure and their anxieties about Ervil's threats subsided. They were happy that at least four of Verlan's wives were together. I spent over two years in this foreign country, where we battled ticks, diarrhea, intestinal worms, and loneliness.

Verlan's dream of forming a new religious colony failed when other church members did not join us because a revolution began in Nicaragua. Verlan made several trips and moved us back to Chihuahua to the LeBaron colony, where we were subject to face the dangers again.

CHAPTER THIRTY-EIGHT

By 1974, Neomi Zarate had become fully disenchanted with Ervil. She deeply resented that he had coerced her to leave her husband and enter into the forced marriage with Bud Chynoweth—for whom she now had born three sons.

Of course, the marriage fell apart. Neomi felt trapped, displaced, used, nothing more than a pawn in Ervil's schemes, as she and even her sister were both married to Bud. Neomi had begun voicing her dissatisfaction.

Every time I saw her, she was miserable about her situation, coerced to make a new life with a family who were strangers to her and didn't speak her own language. She was relieved when she could speak Spanish with me. I had given her some of my maternity smocks and tried to comfort her.

For a few years now, she had witnessed Ervil's threats and mistreatments against the Firstborners. She felt very vulnerable due to the ways that Bud and other men blindly followed Ervil's every wish. There was so much talk of revenge and "the sword of justice" falling upon the condemned that death hung in the air like the summer heat.

Neomi fumed about Ervil killing Joel, saying that if he carried out any more threats, she would "not remain quiet." (See my account as cited in *Prophet of Blood*, p. 174.)

Ervil could not risk waiting to see if Neomi was serious. The voices in his head insisted that Neomi must be silenced so the "work of God could move forward."

In January 1975, Ervil's wives Vonda White and Yolanda Rios left Los Molinos taking an unsuspecting Neomi with them. The three women drove toward the San Pedro Mountains until dark, when Vonda stopped in a dry wash and told Neomi to get out of the car.

Perplexed but not suspecting, Neomi complied and climbed from inside the vehicle. Without warning, Vonda shot her several times with a .38 revolver. Then her sister-wife Yolanda helped Vonda lift Neomi's corpse, which they slung awkwardly into the trunk.

The two women climbed back in the Dodge and searched the hills for a secluded area far away from the road. The women took turns digging in sandy dirt until long after dark. When finally satisfied the grave was large enough, they deposited Neomi's dead body in the freshly-dug hole and covered it with dirt. They left Neomi in that lonely place and headed for home.

Vonda reported Neomi's death to Ervil confirming that his orders had been carried out. Ervil was overjoyed. "You don't know how pleased the Lord is that that traitor is dead!" (*Prophet of Blood*, p. 174).

SEVERAL OF ERVIL'S FOLLOWERS were disappointed that Ervil's prophecy about Verlan's death had not transpired when they tried to kill him in Los Molinos. Not wanting to appear as a false prophet, Ervil revealed a supposedly *fool-proof plan*. He informed his hit men that they should "blood atone" Verlan's mother-in-law Rhea Kunz (Charlotte's mother). Certain that Verlan would attend her funeral, Ervil revealed that the Lord would surely deliver him into their hands (*Prophet of Blood*, p. 180).

In April 1975, my aunt Rhea, who lived in Draper (thirty minutes south of Salt Lake), received a phone call from a woman named "Bonnie." She told Aunt Rhea that she was LDS and wanted to learn more about Mormon fundamentalism, but she was afraid to be seen with polygamists in public. She asked if Rhea would be willing to meet her at a horse-riding stable just north of the area where Rhea lived. Aunt Rhea was a serious defender of polygamy, a sergeant of salvation who drilled us about our responsibility to live the Principle and urged souls into line. She jumped at any chance to preach plural marriage. So Rhea agreed to meet this investigator, in spite of the nighttime appointment and unusual location, since the riding club was conveniently close to her home.

Yet the meeting did not unfold as Rhea had anticipated, she explained to me two months later, at a family reunion in June 1975. Shortly after her departure, Aunt Rhea had had a strange feeling that she was being followed. She stopped briefly at a gas station to wait for cars to pass. She said she had to calm herself before deciding to drive onward in the dark. When she saw the property where the stables were located, an eerie feeling of foreboding came over her. She said that she "felt scared to death that something bad was going to happen" and she decided against keeping her appointment. So she turned her car around and quickly made her way through the dark night back home.

Aunt Rhea didn't learn the full truth about that night for another three years, not until Lloyd Sullivan confessed Ervil's murder plot to detectives. Lloyd also told Verlan the details, which Verlan shared with Rhea. "Bonnie" wasn't there. Lloyd had been lying in wait for Rhea with a pistol, ready to kill her.

After hiding in a ditch for some time he became alarmed when Aunt Rhea didn't arrive. He began to fear that *he himself* had been set up by the Firstborners, which made him too jittery to continue. He lunged out of the ditch and ran to the car where Ervil's son Arturo and Don Sullivan waited. Arturo rebuked him, yelling, "You're a chicken shit! A traitor!"

Later, Dan Jordan also berated him, "You're just a damn coward!" Lloyd wasn't prepared for the hostility he received for all his efforts.

Yet Ervil was more embarrassed than angry. During the moments when Rhea was to die, Ervil was elsewhere at the LeBaron safe house in Salt Lake, always ample distance from his own murder plots. Yet he paused from speech, listened to a voice in his head, then falsely prophesied to his co-conspirators, "I heard a shot...she is dead" (*Prophet of Blood,* p. 180; *The 4 O'Clock Murders,* pp. 139–140).

However, Aunt Rhea lived, and confirmed that Ervil was a liar. When she heard about the horrific plans for her demise, she gasped and sighed over and over—how "fortunate" she was that "the spirit of the Lord had warned her to leave that night, or she could have been killed."

CHAPTER THIRTY-NINE

In 1974, Ervil had sent yet another warning to my uncle Rulon. He sent him a copy of his Society of American Patriots pamphlet, along with a personal letter. He demanded that his pamphlet be distributed to the members of Uncle Rulon's group. Ervil also instructed him to hold a monthly meeting to teach Ervil's "civil law." He criticized Uncle Rulon for "willfully engaging in carrying on psychological warfare against him, one of the foremost champions of liberty of all time. You are charged with criminally disregarding and disobeying minimal law." Ervil told my uncle that if he didn't carry out his instructions, the Society of American Patriots would "bring further attention to your case and as a matter of due process, through our legal counsel. We have *very impressive* methods of causing the rights of honorable men to be recognized, respected, and upheld."

Making sure all Mormondom understood the magnitude of his holy position, he sent copies to Spencer W. Kimball, president of the LDS Mormon Church, as well as to four major fundamentalist factions. He figured that once they had read and understood his powerful document, there would be no further excuse for them to reject him as God's anointed.

★　　★　　★

ERVIL MAILED THE FIRSTBORNERS and other fundamentalist groups an eighty-seven-page pamphlet titled *Hour of Crisis—Day of Vengeance*. The cover alone was unsettling, depicting an unsheathed sword. The troubling threats sent chills of fear through everyone who read it:

> The most flagrant and criminal violations must be stopped first. The one single violation of the law, which God hates more than any other, is the crime of ecclesiastical treason among His own people.... God has said that He would bare His holy arm, or the military power of His kingdom, in the eyes of all nations and that He would do terrible things that they don't expect in order to make His name known.

Though he distributed it as widely as he could, *Hour of Crisis* had been directed specifically to the Church of the Firstborn and stated:

> The time has now come when the judgments of God...are to be poured out without measure, beginning upon this criminal and apostate organization.... All who remain in the midst of such wickedness will be utterly destroyed root and branch and will be burned as stubble.

Verlan knew Ervil's threats couldn't be taken lightly, so he notified every authority he could think of—the police, the FBI, the leaders of the LDS Church, and every fundamental faction he was aware of. Verlan was told by authorities that a crime had to be committed before they could charge Ervil.

The Church of the Firstborn members lived in terror, always vigilant. We felt like sitting ducks fearing for our lives. No one knew the gravity of Ervil's threats better than we. But before we had time to digest the *Hour of Crisis—Day of Vengeance*, Ervil distributed more blatant warnings in his second pamphlet, titled *Contest at Law*.

A short time later, I was with Verlan. We had traveled from the colony in Los Molinos across the border. While driving through San Ysidro, California, I happened to glance up and catch a glimpse of Ervil in a phone booth. Positive that it was him, Verlan pulled up behind Anna Mae's car. He wanted to confront Ervil. Ervil looked up from his conversation, then turned his back to us and kept right on talking on the phone. He shuffled his feet nervously. I'd have given anything to have read his mind; I'm sure he thought we'd come to kill him.

Verlan walked up to Anna Mae's car beside her open passenger window. "Hi," Verlan said, startling her. "I haven't seen Ervil since he killed Joel."

Not refuting what Verlan had said, Anna Mae gave a nervous laugh. "It's not about who killed Joel, it's about doctrine." She then stated her complete faith in Ervil and her belief that he was God's anointed prophet.

Ervil hung up the phone and got in his car, avoiding any conversation with Verlan.

Before he drove away, and making sure Ervil could hear, Verlan hollered, "You're a real chicken shit!" In their youth that was the worst insult they were allowed to say.

SINCE THE INCEPTION OF THE NEW CHURCH, Ervil had taught that marrying a mother and her daughter was definitely prohibited in the Old Testament. Several of the fundamentalist groups nevertheless disregarded the commandment and did it anyway. Ervil was adamant when he was introduced to a polygamist who openly bragged about his situation being married to both a mother and her daughter, trying to convince Ervil that it was a wonderful principle. He soon found himself in a confrontation with Ervil, trying to justify his position. He became very indignant, deriding Ervil for calling it sin. Ervil pulled out his Bible and read Leviticus to him: "And if a man take a wife and her mother, it is wickedness: they shall be burnt with fire, both he and they; that there be no wickedness among you" (20:14).

Ervil spoke with such vehemence it frightened the new investigator. He left the LeBaron colony immediately after Ervil warned him that he had broken a law that deserved the death penalty.

DESPITE THE BAD OPINION that Verlan and many others had of Ervil, he seemed to be lucky at gathering wives. Even sixteen-year-old Rena Chynoweth, who had once written that he gave her the creeps, finally was coerced to become his thirteenth wife. Ervil had proposed many times, telling Rena that it was God's will for her to marry him. Finally, Ervil sent Dan Jordan to give her a message that it was either marry him or she'd be cast into hell.

Intimidated, fearful, and vulnerable, she complied. On February 3, 1975, believing she was serving God, she allowed Dan Jordan to seal her to Ervil for time and all eternity as his thirteenth wife. However, little did she know that technically she was Ervil's fourteenth wife.

Ervil had made it clear that he would not tolerate a man engaging in the unlawful marrying of a mother and a daughter, yet it's ironic to me how Ervil seemed to break the rules when they pertained to himself. Rumors circulated, affirming that Ervil was indeed sleeping with his mother-in-law Thelma. The fact that she traveled with him gave way to suspicions. When she was in his presence, her eyes focused on him with total adoration. She sat at his feet for hours imbibing every word that came out of his mouth. She idolized Ervil and everyone suspected that he was more than just her beloved prophet.

Delfina asked Ervil on countless occasions if he'd married Thelma. She became convinced because of the things she saw when Thelma was in Ervil's presence. When she confronted Ervil, he angrily denied it. Yet, Delfina's son Isaac told her it was common knowledge that Thelma was Ervil's wife because they were sleeping together. Then, later when Thelma was confronted by Detective Ron Collins, she confirmed the fact that she had indeed married Ervil LeBaron. This is just one more piece of evidence to prove how unscrupulous Ervil LeBaron was. He bent all the laws and made new rules to accommodate himself. He disregarded God's law, yet tried to convince Lorna to return to him after several separations when she became privy to the secret.

THERE WERE MANY FACTIONS and splinter groups throughout Utah that frustrated Ervil. He could not tolerate any man who claimed authority or leadership over any fundamentalist group. He was furious when he visited the fundamentalist Merlin Kingston, who was the leader of the Davis County Cooperative. Ervil heard of their wealth and he resented that the group would not bow down and recognize him as God's anointed one. He made a point to visit Merlin and held nothing back in their subsequent conversation. He made threats in no uncertain terms. Merlin was to pay tithes to him; if he didn't, Ervil promised there would be bloodshed. He even threatened to burn several businesses owned by the co-op. Merlin immediately warned the other fundamentalist groups to be on the alert.

★   ★   ★

ROBERT SIMONS, A LONER POLYGAMIST PROPHET, owned a sixty-five-acre ranch in Grantsville, Utah, which Ervil coveted. The Simons had been LDS Mormons until Robert had experienced serious psychological and mental problems which resulted in his divine call as the "one true prophet" and his divorce from wife Mary Jane Anderson. Robert also had a great interest in the American Indians, imagining himself as the prophet who was supposed to lead them.

Robert had been excommunicated from the Mormon Church. He, like many other self-proclaimed prophets, sought power and believed that he was the long-awaited One Mighty and Strong. Therefore he set out to prepare for the millennium, and he embraced polygamy.

Robert wedded Samantha McKinnan and her beautiful twenty-nine-year-old daughter Linda. Beguiled by prophecy, polygamy, and power, Robert sought preeminence.

Ervil claimed it was a crime for a man to marry a mother and a daughter, quoting Leviticus 20:14. Ervil wanted to convert the Simons for three reasons: to eliminate the competition, acquire Robert's ranch as "tithing," and woo his young wife for himself. Ervil fell in love with Linda and secretly proposed. Robert was furious when Linda told him of Ervil's intentions. He wrote a letter to Ervil as one prophet to another, in which he denounced him, openly challenging Ervil's power and authority.

Ervil wasn't one to be challenged or reprimanded. Given the contents of the letter, he concluded that this false prophet must be put to death. Consulting with his minions, Ervil soon developed a plan.

Lloyd Sullivan, still a devout follower of Ervil, contacted

Robert, pretending to have defected from Ervil's group and flattering Robert with a story that he was considering Robert as the true prophet. Lloyd also claimed that he had contacts with Native American chiefs, who knew about Robert and wanted to meet him. Robert was duped, and a day was set for the pow-wow (*Prophet of Blood* pp. 187–191; *The 4 O'Clock Murders*, pp. 132–134).

Early in the morning on April 23, 1975, Ervil's stepson, Eddie Marston, and Mark Chynoweth, drove south of Price, Utah, and turned off on a dirt side road that they marked with an old tire on a fencepost. Looking around, they chose a spot where they would kill Robert. The two then erected a pile of rocks as a landmark for the designated spot. Next they dug a grave on an inconspicuous hillside. They hid their vehicle a short way down the dirt road beyond where they'd piled the rocks. Then they sat down to wait.

In the meantime, Lloyd Sullivan had convinced Robert that the meeting with the Indian chiefs was set. But only he and Robert had been invited. Samantha waved good-bye to her husband as he and Lloyd drove away.

The two finally arrived after dark at the intersection marked by the old tire where Lloyd turned the car onto the isolated dirt road. Robert could hardly contain his anticipation, although briefly distracted by the strangeness of the deserted area. He couldn't help commenting to Lloyd that if he didn't trust Lloyd, he might wonder if he was being lured into a trap to be killed. But Robert's belief in his own prophetic role was stronger than his doubt or fear.

At the pile of rocks, Lloyd stopped the car, leaving the bright headlights on. Both men got out of the car and Robert walked out into the light, assuming the rock pile was an Indian marker.

From their hiding place in the shadows, Eddie and Mark closed in with a shotgun and a .357 magnum. Eddie took aim and the still night air exploded with a shotgun blast.

Eddie, Mark, and Lloyd carried Robert's body to the shallow grave. They removed his wallet, jacket, and wristwatch. Then they scrunched him into the hole, where they emptied a bag of lime over his body, as Ervil had suggested, believing the lime would quickly decompose him. The three took turns shoveling dirt into the grave and onto the gravel to hide the evidence. Eddie dug another small hole for Robert's Timex, which later would be found by a metal detector. When they had finished their fiendish deed, they drove two hundred miles to Ogden and reported to Ervil, who lavished praise on them for the good job that they had done. Finally, they stripped Robert's wallet of its valuables then burned it along with his jacket.

CHAPTER FORTY

Leonard Vest, one of the Arizona converts to Joel's new church, came to the new ensign in Colonia LeBaron. He and his sons, Nathan and Dean, stayed at our home during the church's two annual conferences. I lived in a four room adobe house with Charlotte and Lucy, and at the April conference they slept in their sleeping bags on our lawn. In the evenings, I enjoyed visiting with the Vests. It was comforting to me to have them as new members, which we deeply needed.

Long before Ervil's crazy rampages, I sewed clothing for him. One morning, Dean found me at my Singer sewing machine making a shirt for Ervil. He got excited and admitted he could never find a shirt with sleeves or tail long enough for him. He was a big man, standing six foot eight, and weighing 260 pounds. His bushy brown beard seemed to elongate his face, yet it accentuated his big blue eyes.

Dean asked if I would be willing to make him a couple of shirts. If I would, he'd buy me material to make something for myself. He gave me money to buy four yards of a red-and-gray plaid that I used to make myself a pretty dress. I cut out two shirts, both gray, and finished them by lamplight after my four kids and my two sister wives had retired with their children. For fun, I tried on the huge shirt I'd made for Dean. It fit me like a dress. I remember how the tail of the shirt hit my knees. I had a good laugh.

Shortly after conference, Leonard and his son Nathan became disenchanted by the rigid rules they encountered. When they learned of the murders of Mauro Gutierrez and John Butchereit, who had been loyal disciples of Joel, they picked up and moved as far away as they could—to Alaska. But Dean stayed; he had been exposed to just enough religion to pique his curiosity. He had served two tours of duty in the U.S. Navy, including some time in Vietnam, so military action was his forte. He had a metal plate in his head where he had been wounded.

He had met Ervil at the inception of the church, and, later, when Ervil broke away from Joel's Church of the Firstborn, the two met again. Dean fell for Ervil's militarylike civil law practices for God's new kingdom, and Ervil, seeing Dean's potential, appointed him to be his military leader. Dean was soon privy to the secret activities of Ervil's church, the Lambs of God. He helped to plan and make preparations, including teaching his soldiers how to make Molotov cocktails for the December 26, 1974, Los Molinos raid in Baja against those of us who remained loyal to Joel.

Back in 1970, Dean's wife, Emily, had joined him in San Diego, where they made their home. A keen judge of character, she saw through Ervil immediately. She not only detested Dean's new prophet, she mistrusted him, and most of his cronies

When Joel was murdered in 1972, Emily had endured enough, and she separated from Dean. When she learned of the killings in the Los Molinos raid in 1974, she gave Dean her final ultimatum. It was either Ervil or she. Dean was so converted to Ervil that he hesitated, so she moved away to Seattle.

Missing Emily and enduring several altercations with the flunkies in Ervil's group finally forced Dean to make a decision. He concluded that he'd had enough and decided to move on to better things.

However, he was concerned about the consequences of leaving the blood-atoning Lambs of God. Sure enough, unbeknownst to him, early in 1975, Ervil had already noted signs of his defection. In fact, Ervil was planning his execution.

Ervil confided in Don Sullivan, telling him that God had revealed that Dean Vest had to be blood atoned to save his soul. Ervil's tenth wife, Vonda White, who had murdered Neomi Zarate, was now assigned to execute Dean, and Don furnished the Colt .38 for the job.

Not having spent time with Vonda for a while, Ervil drove to San Diego to deliver the pistol to her himself. He carefully instructed her how to carry out the deed.

On June 16, 1975, Dean intended to leave for Seattle to see Emily and their daughter who both had been in a minor auto accident. He went to the house in a suburb of San Diego, where Vonda White and Linda Johnson lived; he often spent time with them and their children. When he entered the house, Linda was away at her job and Vonda was feeding their children.

Dean shared the details of his wife's accident with Vonda, then he informed her he was leaving for Seattle as soon as he could gather together a few of his belongings. Vonda asked him to check out her washing machine that was giving her trouble. He was glad to look at the washer problem for her and she expressed her appreciation; then she suggested that he clean his hands at the sink.

While Dean rinsed his soiled hands, Vonda finally mustered up enough courage to obey Ervil's order. Trembling with anxiety, she aimed the .38 pistol into Dean's back. Then she shot him, two times. He tumbled forward onto the kitchen sink.

She later confessed, "I was scared clear out of my wits, but... I knew it was a command of God" (*The 4 O'Clock Murders,* p. 150).

However, what followed might seem like the work of a cruel, calm executioner.

Dean had fallen on the kitchen floor, where she shot him again, delivering what Ervil liked to call the "coup de grâce," in the head.

She had followed Ervil's instructions to the letter to avoid the wrath of her husband and leader if she disobeyed.

When she was sure Dean was dead, she wiped off the gun and then placed it by Dean's body. She went upstairs and cleaned herself up to remove any spots of blood from her clothes. Then she quietly called the police, stating that she and the children had heard what she thought were gunshots downstairs.

When the investigators came, it didn't take them long to question the truth of Vonda's story. First they noted small blood spots on her white sneakers, pants, and shirt. When asked about the bloodstains, Vonda claimed that earlier Dean had had a nosebleed, and while helping him, some blood must have dripped on her. When they talked to the children they learned that Vonda had come upstairs after they heard the sounds of shots.

Vonda stoically denied that she had killed Dean Vest. Nevertheless, she was held as a suspect for murder and questioned while laboratory tests were completed.

The lab technicians found the blood sample too small to confirm its source. Also, the investigators were unable to connect any traces of gunpowder to her. Because the evidence was insufficient they had to let her go, but she was asked to remain in town for a while.

However, Ervil sent Anna Mae to drive Vonda and her family to Colorado. There, Ervil praised her for a job well done and assured her of her reward in heaven, calling her an "elect lady."

However, even if Ervil might have thought it to be so, I can't understand how any "elect lady" would consider having her own son put to death. But Ervil and Vonda took literally the words of Deuteronomy:

If a man have a stubborn and rebellious son, which will not obey the voice of his father, or the voice of his mother, and that, when they have chastened him, will not hearken unto them: then shall his father and his mother lay hold on him and bring him out unto the elders of his city and to the gate of his place; . . . and all the men of his city shall stone him with stones, that he die: so shalt thou put evil away from among you; and all Israel shall hear, and fear (21:18–19, 21).

Like many youngsters with raging hormones, searching for his identity and not sure where to look, Vonda's son Craig tended to be forgetful, and this disobedience was looked upon as "open rebellion."

Vonda threatened that if Craig didn't "straighten out," she would have to deal with him in accordance with Deuteronomy.

When Craig realized he could be killed, he immediately fell into line!

CHAPTER FORTY-ONE

Ervil had bragged to his followers that he would use his daughters as "blessings" for those who did his bidding. And in several cases he kept his word. Without even considering the implications or effects upon the girls, he bartered them off as property in trade for favors to men who were older, unappealing, and married to women with several children. Ervil didn't care that this traumatized each daughter and her mother; he simply gave away the daughters of his wives Delfina, Anna Mae, Mary Lou, and Rosemary to men who served his purposes. He gave five of his daughters to Dan Jordan alone: one girl, Sara Jane, ran away to Chihuahua City after a short time with Dan, trying to leave the insanity behind, yet the lasting effects of the nightmare marriage caused her continuing emotional breakdowns for the rest of her life from which she never completely recovered.

The most tragic case of all was my beautiful fifteen-year-old niece Rebecca (Ervil and Delfina's daughter). She was tall and slender, with long brown hair the color of caramel. She had beautiful large and expressive eyes that everyone noticed; she walked with a stately grace and was happy by nature. She had a wonderful sense of humor, and her laughter could be heard whenever a funny situation unexpectedly arose from the humorless life she lived. She made the best of many bad situations, as she was used by wife after wife to babysit their children.

When barely sixteen, Rebecca was "given" against her will to Victor Chynoweth as a reward for his financial backing. Ervil's older daughter Alicia kept in contact with her sister Rebecca, especially when she learned of her unhappy marriage to Victor. On one visit, Alicia immediately saw the whole picture in the sadness and despair written on Rebecca's face. Alicia encouraged her disenchanted sister to attend beauty school, to carve out some kind of future for herself. She wanted Rebecca to become independent and self-confident.

Rebecca seized upon the idea and enrolled in beauty school; however, Victor pulled the rug out from under her. He would not allow his plural wife to be "a law unto herself." He had seen the brewing tensions between Rebecca and his first wife, Nancy, and feared that if Rebecca gained her independence, he would lose her permanently.

But living in plural marriage was not working out for Rebecca, who was always second or third in decisions about her own life. As the second wife, she was put in a situation where she was a thorn in Nancy's side—who as Victor's first wife, was the favorite and dominant wife. Nancy bossed Rebecca around as if she were a child. Their conflict became more intense when Rebecca gave birth to her first child. While in the hospital, Rebecca determined that Nancy would not have any control over her there. So she named the baby Victor Jr. and made sure it was recorded on the birth certificate—to show that she had a right to exercise authority over her own life and her child, that Victor and Nancy could not enforce their will on her, especially when giving birth and becoming a mother herself. Nancy was enraged because she had planned on having a Victor Jr. someday.

When Rebecca returned from the hospital to Victor and Nancy's home, they gave her the silent treatment. Victor turned cold toward her for "provoking" Nancy, whom Rebecca felt was cruel. The conflict naturally escalated, because Rebecca wouldn't accept Nancy's authority over her. For punishment, Victor would not allow Rebecca to leave the house or contact her family for weeks.

After months of being controlled by them, the now seventeen-year-old Rebecca finally rebelled, refusing to take further orders from Victor or Nancy. Pregnant once again, she wanted to leave Colorado and take her young son to Mexico to live with her older sister, Sylvia Esther, in Colonia LeBaron. The emotional stresses were wearing her down, causing her to feel frustrated and irritable much of the time. She sought comfort in food and began to gain weight as well. At the same time, she continued to try to defend herself, which they viewed as "mental."

Worried that Rebecca would flee, Victor seized her little boy and placed him in Nancy's care. Rebecca threatened to report Victor and her father to the authorities if Victor didn't return her son (*The 4 O'Clock Murders*, p. 161). She demanded to see her father, who was in Dallas, but instead Victor called him. When he told Ervil that Rebecca was threatening to go to the law, Victor and Ervil determined that she was nothing but trouble. Ervil told Victor that he needed to "get her under control" because Ervil didn't want disgruntled Rebecca running to the law about her stolen son and spilling any details about their murder plots. Ervil feared his daughter knew too much.

So, Victor separated her from her son by sending her to Dallas alone. Once Rebecca arrived in Dallas, however, Ervil realized he had made a mistake. Still fuming over her disobedience, Ervil took matters into his own hands. He knew he had to comply with God's commands in dealing with rebellion, even if it came to destroying his own flesh and blood. So, Ervil wasted no time in issuing his orders. Rebecca must be eliminated.

He designated his stepson Eddie (Anna Mae's son) along with his wife Lorna's brother Duane Chynoweth to carry out the despicable deed. Duane was Victor's youngest brother.

By phone from Sullivan's office, Ervil ordered Eddie and Duane to "take care of her." Victor bought a tent to be used as cover for digging Rebecca's grave, which Duane and Eddie "practiced setting up in the warehouse" (*Prophet of Blood*, p. 231).

However, Rebecca was told she would soon be "free." She was jubilant that her father had finally changed his mind, allowing her to pick up her infant in Colorado and go to Mexico. She could hardly wait to reunite with her son, then put as much distance as possible between herself and Nancy and Victor.

Yet Eddie and Duane had definite orders from Ervil to see that Rebecca never made it to the airport. As Ervil later told Don Sullivan matter-of-factly, "She couldn't get along and the Lord ordered to send her a one-way ticket" (*Prophet of Blood*, p. 230).

It was a lovely spring day in April 1977 when the men picked up a happy and pregnant Rebecca in Ervil's brand new Ford LTD. They drove her to the outskirts of Dallas, then turned off the streets into a remote area. I have often wondered what Rebecca thought when the car didn't proceed to the airport, taking her instead to a dead end.

Eddie retrieved the rope he had conveniently hidden beneath the car seat. He and Duane then jumped in the backseat beside the surprised young mother. Duane restrained her and Eddie forced the noose over Rebecca's head. She thrashed around, putting up the fight of her life. Eddie spent his strength tightening the rope until his hands and wrists ached from the exertion.

Seeing that Eddie needed help, Duane joined in. The assassins pulled the rope taut from both ends until Rebecca quit resisting, went limp, and stopped breathing altogether.

They lifted her lifeless body from the backseat and carelessly threw it into the trunk. Then they drove back to report to Ervil.

Later, Ervil drove the LTD to the appliance shop, where Lloyd Sullivan noticed that the back of the car seemed to be lower than usual.

When Sullivan questioned him, Ervil sarcastically asked, "Do you think Rebecca is in the trunk?" Sullivan was stunned by the question. "Open it and see for yourself," Ervil challenged.

Sullivan caught the keys that Ervil threw at him and opened the trunk. He cringed when he saw Rebecca's dead body streaked with blood that had oozed from her nose and mouth. Sickened by the scene, he whispered, "How could you have done this? She's your own daughter!"

Even as he asked, Sullivan knew the question was needless. Ervil had taught all of his followers the words of Matthew 10:37: "He who loves father and mother more than me is not worthy of me, and he who loves son or daughter more than me is not worthy of me."

Ervil ordered Duane and Eddie to dispose of the body. Just before they drove away, Ervil cautioned them, "If anyone asks—Rebecca ran off... Delfina's gonna come back and wonder where Rebecca's at, so if she wants to know, she ran off to Mexico with a lover" (*Prophet of Blood,* p. 229).

They took a pick, a shovel, and the tent and headed for Oklahoma with Rebecca's corpse, only stopping along the way for large bags of ice to keep her body cold and limit the odor and decay. Once they found a hidden spot, they set up the tent Victor purchased, which had the floor cut out of it. They couldn't risk hikers catching them in the act, so they wanted to appear to be camping. They took turns digging Rebecca's grave inside the tent, which took them several hours into the evening. Waiting until they were sure that no one was in sight, the two walked down the small hillside, pulled Rebecca's body out of the car, and lugged it back up to the freshly dug hole. They covered her body with dirt, making sure it was buried deep enough. Then they covered the site with debris.

Her grave has never been discovered. When the exhausted gravediggers returned, Ervil was incensed upon seeing his dirty car. He showed no remorse whatsoever over the murder of his own daughter; Ervil was furious that his new car was splashed with mud. He ranted, calling the boys "stupid idiots." When he checked the tires, he saw even more mud and feared it could be used as evidence. He reprimanded Eddie and Duane for being so incompetent, then turned to examine the trunk of the car. He saw Rebecca's blood had stained the trunk mat, and he raved that they'd left still more incriminating evidence. He grabbed the bloody mat and threw it into a trash barrel. He lit the contents with a match and made sure everything burned to ashes.

Ervil was still dissatisfied. He ordered Eddie and Duane to wash his car inside and out and to buy new tires for the car. But, still fearful of being implicated, Ervil refused to drive the LTD. He sold the car and replaced it with another—same make, year, and color.

Upon hearing of Rebecca's death, I fell apart, half in shock. She was only seventeen years old, and four months pregnant with her second child. She was young, beautiful, full of determination and spunk. My heart was wrenched. I could not comprehend her death nor the sick mind that ordered it. I'd witnessed the years of neglect she received from her father as a child. She was treated as less than most because she had Delfina's blood coursing through her veins. She had been emotionally starved and deprived of education, never having any but her most basic needs addressed. Now, on top of seventeen years of abuse, my precious niece met the end of her short unhappy life by being "blood atoned."

I hated Ervil, more than I could bear to express; he was evil. His satanic tendencies caused suffering, deprivation, misery, torture, or death for increasing numbers of people. Yet he was too gutless to do the dirty deeds of death himself, so he manipulated and ordered others to do his killing. In Rebecca's case, he had forced his own stepson and brother-in-law to carry out the dastardly act of her murder.

CHAPTER FORTY-TWO

As soon as Ervil had his brother Joel assassinated, he began contacting all the fundamentalist Mormon splinter groups, demanding that they join his church and, of course, pay their tithing monies to him. The Allreds' Apostolic United Brethren was first on the list, being a juicy apple to be plucked.

The next real threat came in 1975 in a pamphlet Ervil had titled *Response to an Act of War*. Handwritten on the back of his new recruiting tract was a personal note to my uncle Rulon. In this warning Ervil urged Rulon to "repent and live the constitution of the political kingdom of God lest the sword of the Lord fall upon you . . . the day is at hand. Repent ye therefore or suffer destruction at the hand of God! There shall be left neither root nor branch" (*The 4 O'Clock Murders*, pp. 137–138).

Sufficiently concerned, Uncle Rulon went to the police. He asked them to seriously consider the threats and extortion demands being made on the Mormon splinter groups.

At the same time, Uncle Rulon ignored Ervil's threats, refusing to join or pay him. Ervil became indignant and sent another warning to the Allred group, offering them one last chance to comply with his demands. Still Rulon ignored his outrageous commands.

Rebuffed by Uncle Rulon's disobedience and bolstered by the success of his previous murderous victories and his miraculous release from jail, Ervil began to plan the blood atonements of other men he considered to be false prophets who also were ignoring the Lord's commands received through him.

Ervil's wives Rosemary Barlow and Anna Mae Marston rented a mailbox in South Pasadena, California—P.O. Box 1412, which Ervil used to promote his new organization, the Society of American Patriots.

In another pamphlet the Society of American Patriots indicated that Ervil M. LeBaron, God's servant, would soon run the world. Ervil also referred to himself as a martyr and rebuked Jimmy Carter for distributing posters and allowing the press to use Carter's picture as though he were Christ coming to save America. He warned Carter that when he took the presidential oath, he would be exalting himself as a false god, which carried the death penalty.

The FBI and Secret Service took interest in the threatening accusations, believing Ervil was capable of killing Carter if given the opportunity. Ervil's ambiguous pamphlet was written purposely to confuse those who read it, but the Secret Service knew it was a threat, though it was difficult to prove in court.

ONLY DAYS AFTER REBECCA'S MURDER, on April 20, 1977, with several of his followers gathered in the safety of Thelma Chynoweth's home (Ervil's mother-in-law),he outlined the next big hit (*The 4 O'Clock Murders,* p. 166).

His brother Verlan, now an archrival, would be killed while attending the funeral of the disobedient Rulon C. Allred—who obviously would have to be killed first. Supposedly, one death would lead successfully to the other. Three teams would possibly be required to accomplish the two murders. The first team would kill Dr. Allred in Salt Lake City and escape the state. The second would wait for his funeral, where they would stalk and kill Verlan. If they failed to kill Verlan at the funeral, a third team would drive to El Paso, Texas, where Verlan often traveled or stayed with Siegfried Widmar, Verlan's closest counselor in the church.

Ervil explained that he wanted two "pretty women" to handle the hit of Dr. Allred. So, he designated his new wife, Rena Chynoweth, and Ramona Marston, one of Dan Jordan's wives, for the first death team who would kill my uncle Rulon.

Why did Ervil pick women for such a horrific task and perhaps the most visible murder? Women were more malleable and obedient to Ervil, and they were far more expendable in his scheme of things.

Don Sullivan, Eddie Marston, and Jack Strothman were to kill Verlan a few days later at Rulon's funeral. If for some reason the mission failed, John Sullivan and Mark and Duane Chynoweth were to wait in El Paso, Texas, hoping to encounter Verlan at Siegfried Widmar's home.

On May 10, 1977, just past four thirty, Rena and Ramona entered Uncle Rulon's chiropractic office in Murray, Utah. Rena carried a .25 automatic pistol, Ramona a .38 revolver. Both women were disguised with wigs and heavy coats. Three people were waiting in the reception room, an old couple and a middle-aged man. Ramona sat down next to the middle-aged man, Richard Bunker, who was reading a magazine. She placed her purse, with the pistol hidden inside, on her lap. Rena paused at the door with her hand on the pistol inside her blue parka, then entered the hall leading to the examining rooms. Uncle Rulon came out of one room and entered a lab area. As he turned to face Rena, she recognized him from the description she'd been given. She drew the gun and fired. He exclaimed, "Oh my God!" as all seven bullets seared into him. He fell to the floor.

Ramona stood up with her gun drawn while Rena walked back into the reception room, still holding her pistol. Neither the old couple nor Bunker moved, so both killers stepped outside and shut the door. Bunker finally reacted, opening the door, to get a better description or a license plate number, but the armed women pushed their way back inside to make sure Allred was really dead. This caused Bunker to resist them in a scuffle, fearing for his own life. He pushed Ramona's arm against the door frame as Rena aimed her pistol at him. Fortunately for him, all the bullets had been fired. Both girls were shoved outside, and again the door was closed.

By then Uncle Rulon's wife Melba, who was his receptionist, was kneeling over him. The girls exchanged pistols and reentered. Rena fired a shot toward Bunker, who scampered into a bathroom. Then she approached the dying doctor. As Melba confronted her, Rena fired a final shot, which actually missed and went into the floor, but Uncle Rulon was dead enough.

The two shooters left in a stolen Ford pickup to an appointed rendezvous in a parking lot where Eddie had brought their station wagon and Ramona's baby. When Don arrived, he took their wigs and coats, which he later threw into a random Dumpster. The murderers fled to Denver, and the men went back to the hotel, where Jack joined them to celebrate. Then the men drove to Wyoming to wait for their next assignment.

When Bunker was sure the two female killers had left, he cautiously exited the bathroom to join Aunt Melba beside Uncle Rulon's body. She kept whispering his name repeatedly, but he couldn't answer. Bunker felt beneath Uncle Rulon's bloody shirt, checking for a heartbeat, but it was too late. The seven shots from Rena's pistol had silenced him forever.

★   ★   ★

I HAD ALWAYS ADMIRED and loved my uncle Rulon. From childhood he was not only my mentor, but my father figure, my religious leader, and my confidant, even after I married Verlan. His death created a deep void in my life. I wanted to run to him, even after his death. My heart needed his loving acceptance. I knew that his murder had been arranged by Ervil. Now my family connection to the LeBarons would cause the members of the Allred group to ostracize me. The emotional pain of my own situation in this mess was almost unbearable. Most of Rulon's followers were my aunts, uncles, and cousins. I knew his death would sever my relationships with them forever. Still, I wanted to attend his funeral to make a statement to my relatives that I honored and loved my beloved uncle.

Verlan accompanied Siegfried and Ossmen Jones to Salt Lake City even though they knew their lives were in danger. Verlan had told me he thought Ervil might send someone to kill him at the funeral. But he gave me permission to go, cautioning me to be wise by distancing myself from him for the trip. Though disappointed that we couldn't travel together because it would endanger me to be with him, I went to Las Vegas, where I met up with my sister Becky, who drove me to Utah.

On the day of Uncle Rulon's viewing, several hundred people filed past the open casket to pay homage to their revered leader, father, and friend. I don't believe that Uncle Rulon ever had a single enemy—other than Ervil. He was so kind, patient, and forgiving. All who met him couldn't help but love him. I was astounded to see so many grown men weep openly before his casket, not wanting to leave, but they were forced along by the pressing crowd. His numerous children took turns standing beside his casket while throngs of well-wishers offered quiet condolences.

Becky pushed ahead of me confidently. We stood before the casket, tearfully peering into the face of our beloved uncle. We mentally whispered our good-byes as we passed the lines of cousins and aunts standing at attention. We could feel their icy stares, the anger and hatred they felt toward us, wondering how we dared show up.

Becky had been a black sheep for years. She had abandoned the polygamist lifestyle and married a gentile. She had been the talk of every family gathering. The family whispered to one another, asking whether they could see her "worldly spirit." They criticized her hat, high heels, and voluptuous breasts. In fact, they said a woman with a set of "knockers" like hers certainly intended to entice or lure men. They said the only reason God had given her six daughters was because of her unrighteousness, so she was not blessed with any sons. Furthermore, any woman who was divorced and lived in the wicked city of Las Vegas deserved God's punishment.

Becky was rejected for abandoning the group, but I was shunned even more after my outlaw LeBaron in-laws caused my uncle's cruel and untimely death. Some cousins refused my handshake or embrace. Those who knew that my name was LeBaron, acted as though I had pulled the trigger myself.

My eyes wandered over the crowd. I spied Verlan, Siegfried, and Ossmen entering the room. At one time, Uncle Rulon and other Allreds had respected and loved Verlan. They considered him the most likeable LeBaron, the one who could redeem the LeBaron family name. Verlan admired Rulon and asked him to perform his plural marriages. Verlan's warmth and congeniality was infectious. However, now that his brother Ervil had ordered Uncle Rulon's assassination, Verlan was treated with suspicion; people who had once admired him now looked upon him with disdain. When I caught Verlan's eye, he smiled at me. That tiny gesture gave me the courage to endure my relatives' icy stares of condemnation.

It didn't occur to them that Verlan LeBaron was also on Ervil's hit list, nor could they have fathomed that Verlan had been stalked for years. In all the publicity about Ervil's war on rival fundamentalist factions, people missed this finer point of Ervil's insanity: He used Uncle Rulon's death to lure Verlan. It was more than revenge; it was a means to another end.

Becky didn't care that Verlan had told me to distance myself from him. She grabbed my arm and pulled me through the crowd. When we finally reached him, she put me on one side and plunked herself down on the other, sandwiching Verlan between us. She laughed quietly, telling Verlan that she and I were there to protect him from being killed in case anyone showed up.

How I loved Becky. She didn't need anyone's acceptance because she accepted herself—that was sufficient for her. She urged me to ignore my family's self-righteous opinions and actions. During the years Verlan worked in Vegas, I spent a week or two at a time with Becky. We really bonded, never discussing religion; we accepted each other as sisters. Our unconditional love and acceptance for each other was the glue that bound us so tightly together.

After the viewing, Verlan and Siegfried spent hours talking with local authorities, revealing Ervil's threats and the danger that they themselves feared from him—and not only them, but any members in their Church of the Firstborn. We all were considered traitors by Ervil because we didn't follow him, so we all deserved his death penalty.

The following day, May 14, 1977, Uncle Rulon's funeral was held at Bingham High School in order to accommodate the impressive crowd of almost three thousand mourners. Becky and I took our seats in the center of the school auditorium as friends and family filled the seats. From the rear of the auditorium, Verlan caught my eye, giving me a wave of recognition. His two friends stood by him, hoping to keep him safe in case Ervil's hit men tried anything.

Rulon's numerous children stood by his seven lovely wives. We'd all grown up together, laughed, played, and spent many a weekend together. We had attended their religious meetings every Sunday at their father's homes during our youth. When I beheld the tear-stained faces of my cousins, I was cut to the core. I realized then how one man's death could cause excruciating pain and grief impacting so many people.

I was touched as sixteen of Uncle Rulon's sons sang the beautiful Mormon hymn "I Know That My Redeemer Lives." I cried silently as they sang, thinking how these wonderful sons had been robbed of such an exemplary father. I reminisced how as children we swam in the creek and played baseball and hide-and-seek together. Twenty of his daughters harmonized in a song written specially for the occasion. The auditorium was filled with love for this holy man who had truly lived his religion and stood by his religious principles.

Rulon's brother Owen begged members of the Allred clan not to seek vengeance for Uncle Rulon's death. His oldest son, Louis, reminded the crowd that his father was "wealthy in love, not in money" (*Prophet of Blood*, p. 246). Their youngest brother, Clarence, prayed for the family, especially his wives and children. My dear aunt Beth, Uncle Rulon's youngest sister, read a poem called "The Family Doctor." Another brother Marvin stated how Rulon had brought more than six thousand babies into the world, half of which he had delivered for free.

When the funeral ended, the mourners formed a procession, driving to the Sunset Lawn Memorial Park in Salt Lake City, where my dear uncle Rulon was laid to rest.

Verlan and Siegfried had met with the police the day before, cluing them in about Ervil's murderous rampage, so nine police cars and many policemen had been dispatched to keep guard during the funeral and check license plate numbers or watch for suspicious vehicles. The presence of all those police is what saved Verlan's life.

Ervil had long plotted Verlan's murder at Uncle Rulon's funeral, so he had ordered Don, Eddie, and Jack to attend the funeral, where they were to ambush Verlan with guns. First they drove by, stalking Verlan but they were very nervous. It was dangerous to kill Verlan because if they succeeded they could easily be shot by police on the scene, but if they failed then they could be killed by Ervil for not following his orders. Either way, it was do and die. This was a typical double bind that Ervil placed on his followers.

As they surveyed the situation, they realized it would be impossible to take Verlan out among throngs of people peppered by police. If they went inside the building to kill Verlan, it would mean killing other people as they fired in a crowd, and the police would immediately return fire.

Scared stiff, yet determined, they approached the site again with loaded firearms ready. However, again, the throngs of mourners and numerous policemen were too intimidating. It would be suicide, Don told Eddie and Jack; it was crazy. Don voiced their mutual conclusion—they weren't going to do it.

They realized they had botched God's revelation to Ervil. Dejected, they drove back to Dallas, fearing for their lives when they would have to face Ervil's wrath.

Meanwhile the other hit team staked out Siegfried's home in El Paso, but Verlan didn't show up, so they aborted that mission as well.

Unbeknownst to both hit squads, Ervil himself had fled to his hideouts in Mexico in case something went wrong.

CHAPTER FORTY-THREE

After Ervil's latest killing spree began, we became convinced that he would not quit until he had annihilated all those who opposed him. He was determined that no one was going to push him aside! His inflated pride convinced him that Verlan, who had been given the office of patriarch and the presidency in the Church of the Firstborn, had to be cut down. And not only Verlan. With unrelenting vengeance, Ervil began to pursue any person who would not uphold and support him. His continual revelations from God convinced him that he, and not any other brother, was the rightful prophet and head of the church.

Caution drove Verlan and Siegfried, Verlan's counselor in the church, into hiding. Before he left, Verlan said, "Look, I know Ervil intends to kill me. I've just got to lie low for a while."

I knew Verlan feared for his life, and rightly so, but his decision sent rage pulsing through me. "How can you just leave me and our children here in Colonia LeBaron like sitting ducks, with absolutely no protection?" I asked him.

"You'll just have to have faith and pray that God will protect you," Verlan said. To convince me, he reluctantly gave me his prized shotgun and a box of bullets. "Use this if you have to; you'll be justified."

Apparently Verlan thought it wouldn't hurt to put a bit of faith in firearms as well as in the Almighty, but I wasn't convinced that either would be able to protect us from his power-crazed brother. Besides, I would never have willingly let him go if I'd known then that I would not see or hear from him for six months.

NIGHTS WERE THE WORST. The uncertainty, the waiting, nearly drove me mad. I felt I could not cope with the impending violence. At dusk one evening, I ran across the gravel road and then held down a section of loose barbed wire, taking a shortcut through the fence. I made my way to my best friend, Linda Liddiard's house. Both of us had thirteen children, and we had endured poverty, polygamy, and countless disappointments. I still had ten children at home.

As required, I knocked and identified myself at the same time. Keeping the rules would assure my safety, because most people in town had guns to defend themselves. "It's Irene, let me in."

As the door opened, Linda's frightened youngsters scattered down her long hall, running to hide.

"What's up, Linda?" I asked, seeing fear in her eyes.

"We got a phone call saying Ervil's group will be here any minute to blast us with dynamite. Irene," she said, trembling, "he's determined to kill us all."

By now, Linda was trying to calm her frightened children, who had overheard her. She grabbed pillows and blankets from the two adjacent bedrooms, throwing them into the hall. She instructed the older kids to bed down beside the smaller ones,

and added, "We're safe here in the hall because there are no windows, and these thick adobe walls will protect us."

Despite our fear, both Linda and I tried to reassure the upset
children. "Be quiet and go to sleep. You'll be okay," I said.

I ran home, tearing my blouse as it snagged on the barbed
wire. I couldn't wait to take my own children in my arms, but I
wondered if I was capable of protecting them.

I spent a miserable night. Thoughts of sleep fled as I listened
to my pounding heart. *Whom would I grab if we had to flee for our
lives? Would I take the baby and leave the other nine to fend for themselves? Whom would I take and where would I run?*

My agitated mind could not keep on facing death every
moment I was awake. I had to come up with a plan. The next
morning, I walked three blocks to my ex–sister wife Helen's
rock home. In a rush of words, I told her of my concern for
my children's lives and that I needed help. She agreed, and we
walked together out of the house and through her backyard. She
unlocked a small feed room adjacent to the goat corrals. Once
inside, I scoped out the space. I could move a few bales of hay
and, by stacking them a little higher, make a little more room in
the shed. Helen offered a twin-size mattress that was stored on
top of the hay. With a promise from Helen to tell no one, relief
flooded me. I had a hiding place for my brood of children. We
would be safe.

Helen drove me home. I loaded two sleeping bags, several
blankets, and four pillows into her car. She did me the favor
of unloading the bedding in the shed, making it ready for me
to use.

Shortly after dark, I sent out my tribe of kids by twos. They
moved quietly down the road, through a broken wooden gate,
to our hiding place. Margaret took Seth, and Barbara walked
with LaSalle into the night. Sandra and Connie left with others

about four minutes later, carrying two quarts of drinking water. All the children had complained of being too fearful to go ahead without me. "Being quiet and keeping our hiding place a secret will keep us safe," I told them. "I'll be right behind you. Don't be afraid."

Following minutes later, close behind my children, I held the hand of my youngest child, three-year-old Lothair. I hugged the shotgun with my free hand as I paced along the gravel road, praying no one would detect our presence.

Once in the darkened shed, I put three smaller kids beside me on the narrow mattress. The two older boys slept in sleeping bags, while the other five crowded onto the blankets on the floor. I looked around hoping to find something to use as a potty when I spied an empty gallon-size metal paint can. I knew it would be perfect. I cautioned the children to whisper. We did not want to be discovered by anyone.

The constant bleating and milling around of the dozen or so goats prevented us from falling asleep for quite a while. Finally, after praying to God for our safety, I soon heard sighs and deep breathing from the children. I checked at the head of the mattress, feeling to make sure I had quick access to the shotgun, in case of an emergency. My mind pinballed, unsettled from the predicament I'd found myself in. An overwhelming sense of hopelessness engulfed me. I could handle death, but my precious children didn't deserve to be caught up in a religious war, especially among brothers. I listened to the goats' movements, their playful antics and occasional butting. My eyes hung heavy with sleep, but my mind refused to settle down. I wished there was a way I could run with my children far away to a place where no one could ever find us. I endured a stressful, sleepless night.

With the first rays of morning light, I knew I had to wake the children and get them back into my adobe house before our safe haven was discovered. Once home, we stayed inside, always on the alert, unable to relax. The kids kept on the lookout for any strange vehicles or unusual activity.

At night we resumed our ritual. Each night after prayer, tucked safely in the goat shed, I thanked God that we had made it through one more day. I ached as I observed the changes that had come over my children. The little ones, especially, seemed paralyzed with fear and clung to me as though I were their life line in a stormy sea. Their need for constant reassurance, the fear-filled nights, and my inability to protect the ones I loved wore me down emotionally and physically. Besides, even for self-defense, I knew I could never pull a trigger and kill someone. I felt like a hypocrite. Here I was, pretending to be strong and protective, when I knew I was scared spitless. But my cheerful facade was all I could offer my children to ease their terror and give them hope.

For two weeks we went to the shed every night. For two weeks I endured the questions from the children: "Are we going to be safe, Mother?" "Can't we go somewhere else?" And the question that hurt the most was "When will Daddy come home?" How could I answer them when I didn't know myself?

I ran to Linda's each day for comfort. The two of us would break away about four o'clock to the only refreshment stand in town. Going there for our daily Coke kept us energized and boosted our morale. We had to act confident, hiding our fears and concerns as we continued to run our overcrowded households. Our bonds of friendship kept us both focused on our responsibilities and gave us the motivation to cope. I knew that no man could begin to understand the devastation of being alone, vulnerable, and unprotected. Living under death threats with the huge responsibility of rearing numerous children plagued us and wore us down. I knew I would never feel safe or experience peace until Ervil was apprehended.

JUST BACK FROM NICARAGUA, Verlan surprised me one day with an invitation to accompany him to Dallas. He went on to explain we were going there to look for housing for some of his wives and children, although we didn't discuss which wives at the time. I hesitated to leave the children, afraid something would happen to them while I was gone. For months I had yearned to spend uninterrupted days with my husband, but now I felt torn. Did I dare leave my children in the care of others in these frightening times?

Verlan assured me that they would be as safe with Lucy as they would be with me. He had already made arrangements for her to be in charge and to sleep with my children to avert their fears. He assured me he needed my help to get the family situated, and then he gave me fifteen minutes to throw some clothes into a bag while he gave orders to the children.

The four-hour trip to El Paso was the longest stretch of time I had spent with Verlan in several months. Despite my concern for the children, I relished each moment with my husband as sacred, a gift from God. How fortunate I was to be chosen out of all his wives to accompany him on a four-day trip.

He parked his white Chevrolet pickup in long-term parking at El Paso International Airport, and we hurried inside to the counter of Southwest Airlines. Verlan bought two round-trip tickets to Dallas. As we walked to the gate his eyes never stopped moving, scanning the crowd to make sure no one was following us. Every few seconds he turned to look over his shoulder, fearful that one of Ervil's henchmen was pursuing him. I longed for his touch, just to hold hands and snuggle close to him as we took our seats on the plane. Once we'd buckled our seat belts, I leaned into him. "I'm too nervous, Irene. Please don't demand that I pay attention to you in public. I'm shut down emotionally." He sighed. "After being absent for six months, I didn't even take the time to make love to anybody. I left them all disappointed and angry. All the pressures and problems have left me depressed. Affection and intimacy aren't even a part of me right now." He patted my knee and then stated wearily, "I hope you'll understand."

I tried to, but my mind couldn't even go there. I thought, *I am a human being...a woman...and I am passionate and hungering for my husband.* It exasperated me. What the hell did I care if he had disappointed the other wives? They were his problem, not mine! When would I ever be able to show him affection? It seemed as though there was always an excuse. "Don't show affection in front of the other wives," he would say, yet somehow they were always around. And now I couldn't even show affection in public? If not now, when?

The intense desires I'd felt over the years resurfaced as the plane rose into the sky. I wanted to be loved for me, to be needed, and desired. Why couldn't he run into my arms without reluctance or hesitation? But no. All my attention and affections depended on whether it was "my" night. I always had to wonder if I was next on his rotation list. Like a crystal ball, he consulted it to see who might be there that night to please him. I felt like a number, a tool in furthering his dreams of grandeur. And I'll never forget his words to me on our wedding night: "Irene, you are the *key* to plural marriage. No matter how many wives I get, you will always be the key." How I hated to be a *damn key*! I wanted to be pursued, to feel the sparks as he enveloped me in his arms. I'd always regretted that I wasn't his source of sexual discovery. The act of lovemaking had been tarnished from my first encounter. As his large frame loomed over me, my mind asked a thousand questions: *Will he enjoy me as much as he did my sister? Am I adequate? Is he comparing my every move to hers? As my love for him grows, will he feel pangs of love for me in return? Or am I just the key to his future world, populated with throngs of plural wives and children?*

Interrupting my reverie, Verlan pointed out the window, "Look, that's the outskirts of Dallas below. We'll soon be landing."

Erv Lowther, a church member and friend, met us as we descended the airport escalator. We shook hands, greeting each other. I noticed Erv's toupee was askew, and his yellow trousers were as bright as his smile. "You'll love Dallas," he said as if he thought he was convincing me.

"She doesn't know all our plans yet," Verlan said apologetically. "I figured I'd tell her after she had a chance to look the place over."

"What are you talking about?" I asked.

Verlan smiled uneasily. "We're going to find a place to rent," he answered. "You get to take first pick from the two apartments because I am leaving you to oversee Susan and Lillie, who will share the other apartment."

"How will you ever support us here?" I asked, shocked, since he could barely support us in Mexico where he owned his own homes.

"Erv has several businesses set up around town, and he's agreed to let all three of you work for him. You'll be selling jewelry in hotel lobbies. It will be good experience for all of you."

Erv's habit of pulling his trousers constantly up over his protruding stomach was beginning to get on my nerves. I wondered how he could run a business if he couldn't even keep his pants up.

Once in Erv's black Lincoln Town Car, I relaxed, trying to be open to this crazy idea as Erv drove us to a large Holiday Inn.

"This is where I want you to work, but first I'll show you the ropes. I know if you can care for a dozen or more children, you're capable of selling lots of jewelry."

We both followed Erv down the long corridor beyond the reception desk. Twelve feet from the registration counter was a large table covered with a red cloth. Various pieces of silver-and-turquoise jewelry were arrayed artistically on the tabletop. A pretty bleached blonde, whose attire (or lack of attire) surprised me, was standing at the table. Her firm breasts were only partly covered. I wondered if she was trying to sell the jewelry or herself. Erv embraced the stranger and then introduced her, "This is my wife, Judy."

After the tour of Erv's three workplaces in prominent hotels, we returned to pick up Judy. The table was emptied, and the jewelry was packed in a heavy black case. Then we accompanied our friends to their large sprawling ranch house in the suburb of Richardson.

The following morning, Erv retrieved his newspaper from his front lawn, and he and Verlan sat down together and scanned through the rental section. A yellow highlighter marked available town houses near Erv's home. He knew that none of us three wives owned a vehicle, which would make it necessary for him to pick us up each day for work. It was going to be a challenge for Erv to reach out to Verlan's family in this perilous time, but he felt compelled to help him.

Erv rented two affordable town houses side by side. I would live in one with my eight youngest children. Lillie and her three children would share the other town home with Susan and her four kids.

★   ★   ★

WITH EVERYTHING IN ORDER, Verlan, we three wives, and fifteen children left Mexico in two pickups with campers. Our personal belongings, clothes, dishes, and bedding were stashed beneath a sheet of plywood, which was used as the base for a bed. The kids were all excited about the adventure. It gave them a renewed hope, believing they would be safe in a big city.

The fifteen-hour trip to Dallas was a nightmare. Verlan drove one truck while Susan and I took turns driving with Lillie. That made it possible for Susan and me to have some private time with Verlan. Only a plural wife can understand how rewarding it is to snatch even a few minutes with her husband. Lillie felt upset that she didn't get a turn, but of the three of us she was the only one with a driver's license. Verlan promised that he would give her the first night when we arrived, regardless of whose turn it was. We all had to make sacrifices to keep one another happy; my heart ached for all of us. Verlan especially looked devastated. I could tell he was weighed down emotionally, and when it was my time alone with him, he revealed his dilemma.

He'd endured Susan's complaints, seeing her tears and cries of desperation. He admitted sadly, "She's afraid of this new environment I'm taking you all to. She's especially hurt that I'm making all of you work to support yourselves. I'm depending on you to watch over her, and Lillie." He shook his head. "You know there is so much temptation in this wicked world. Please keep an eye on my children for me also."

I'd waited for more than six months for an opportunity to hash out my problems, but I had enough compassion not to dump them on Verlan now. My heart went out to him. His life was in danger. He was on the run and still had multiple families to worry about. I knew he would break down emotionally if I vented my true feelings, so I just listened to his fears and concerns. My hopes and aspirations were slowly slipping away, unnoticed by Verlan, as I tried to bury my heartache and uncertainty.

In his absence, Verlan's two Mexican wives, Esther and Beverly, had found other men to love them, but Verlan still felt obligated to financially support his children. Beverly moved to Mexico City with her five children. Esther returned to Baja California to live next to her parents with her five children and a new lover. Verlan was distraught that he had lost three of his wives. "I can't understand why God allowed my family to fall apart when I have tried so hard to make it all work. I've been so proud of all my wives. It's strange. But I·thought things were going pretty well with everybody. Still, I guess I don't blame them for leaving; I was gone so much of the time."

We were left at the mercy of Erv, in houses with no furniture. With Erv's advance money, garage sales soon provided a few beds and necessary furniture. Had I known what I was in for, I would have rebelled. My fourteen- to sixteen-hour workdays started when Erv came for me at six thirty every morning. I helped him set up the jewelry display on two six-foot tables and then stood on my feet all day long selling while my varicose veins tortured me. We never closed up shop before eleven o'clock at night. By the time I got home and settled into bed, it seemed it was time to wake up again. I had no time for my children. Fourteen-year-old Barbara cared for my entire brood for the rest of the summer. She and twelve-year-old Margaret were the sole caretakers of all three wives' children. I worried every day, all day, about the children's safety.

As strenuous as the job was, I found solace in the fact that I loved selling. The interaction with people fed my empty soul after years of isolation in Mexico. I took pride in the fact that I could so easily convince someone to buy jewelry. For years, I'd felt emotionally incapable of expressing myself. Now, through conversations with total strangers, I began to feel validated. My ego was really stroked when, on two different occasions, strangers offered me a job. One gentleman watched my performance for over an hour as he relaxed in an oversized chair in the lobby. During that time, I'd convinced three men in their thirties to buy a necklace, something none of them had ever worn before. Their first reaction was "Absolutely not!" But, in no time, I'd secured one around each of their necks. Between their reflections in the mirror and my insistence that the different-colored necklace suited them perfectly, they bought it. The spectator took note of my persuasive skills and offered me a position with him to sell insurance. For one fleeting moment, I entertained the idea, wishing I had the courage to run away and be on my own. But how could I? I didn't own a vehicle, let alone have a driver's license. The unfamiliar culture in Dallas was scary enough without my entertaining any ideas that I could make it in the big world alone with eight of my children. The very thought paralyzed me.

Before the summer was over, all three of us attention-starved and neglected women were being pursued by interested men, testing our loyalty to Verlan. Of course we all felt guilty. No one had committed adultery yet, but our love-starved minds and bodies entertained such shocking ideas.

I felt it my God-given duty to call Verlan and have him come rescue all of us before three more wives abandoned him.

CHAPTER FORTY-FOUR

Delfina's recurring breakdowns exceeded the number of her nine children. She existed from moment to moment, chain-smoking in hopes of calming her frazzled nerves. She finally quit counting the months since she had seen Ervil. After all, he had abandoned her emotionally years earlier, right after he had married Mary Lou.

Ervil convinced his daughter Alicia to travel to Mexico to Colonia LeBaron to get her mother and three siblings and take them to his newest home in Mississippi. Delfina, of course, rebelled when Alicia explained her motive for being there. Delfina knew darn well that she would be abandoned again in some place far out of her comfort zone. She understood very little English and didn't think she could cope with an unfamiliar environment.

Alicia was loving, yet firm, insisting that she would not leave without her mother and promising to take Delfina to a safe haven in the U.S. Alicia knew it was a risk to try to cross the border with her mother and three siblings without any legal documents, but fair-skinned Delfina and three towheaded children easily made their declaration of citizenship "American" and crossed the border into El Paso, Texas, without raising any suspicions.

The three children were excited to stop at a McDonald's for the first time, where they ate their first hamburgers and fries. The group then wasted no time in getting on Interstate 10 East, headed for Jackson, Mississippi.

Once in Jackson, and without Alicia, Delfina felt she had exchanged abandonment for imprisonment. She was virtually a slave to Ervil's numerous children and a couple of his wives. Most of the cooking became her daily chore. The house was overcrowded with teenagers, who tried to boss her around. She had been forced into a situation that she abhorred. Not only did she hate her husband's religion and resent his wives, but she now loathed him as well.

Ervil avoided Delfina. The two shared no more physical contact, and their few conversations were brief and to the point. When Ervil had heard enough of her ranting and tearful accusations, he distanced himself even more. Yet whenever she could, Delfina begged Ervil to allow her to visit her daughter Rebecca. She had been out of contact since Rebecca was given to Victor Chynoweth in marriage.

When Ervil saw that Delfina wasn't going to quit hounding him, he tried to silence her by telling her the lie he'd been circulating, that Rebecca had run off with a lover, disappearing into Mexico. When Delfina heard the story, her heart told her it was a lie. She knew her daughter well enough to know that Rebecca would never venture into the unknown, especially after being isolated all her life.

Relentless in her demand to know the truth, she wept and fought with Ervil, begging for him to level with her. Her other daughter Lillian, who was married to Mark Chynoweth, pleaded with her mother to remain silent, warning her that she was jeopardizing her life. Finally fearing that she might be killed, Delfina decided to play their game. She asked to be rebaptized into the Lambs of God Church, committing her allegiance to Ervil as a prophet and promising to uphold their cause.

After her submissive request, Lillian and Mark told her they planned to take her to a movie, but first they had to run a quick errand to the warehouse, promising to return in twenty minutes. Delfina suspected she was being lured away to her death. When they left, Delfina knew it was now or never. She had no time to change her house slippers. Her apron was wet from preparing the evening meal. She grabbed her small daughter Delia and fled out the front door. They ran a block to a convenience store, where, crying pitifully in her broken English, she begged a clerk to help her. Seeing that she was desperate, one of the clerks hid her in a storeroom, where Delfina's daughter helped translate their predicament. Having compassion on Delfina, the clerk took her to the bus station where she intended to travel to El Paso and on into Mexico.

Before boarding the bus, Delfina called her mother, who was in San Diego. By sheer chance, police officers happened to be interviewing her mother there, so they arranged to have an investigator meet Delfina in El Paso. Already familiar with Ervil's violence and needing more evidence to detain him, the FBI flew Delfina and her daughter Delia to Salt Lake City.

Soon she was also reunited with her sons Isaac and Pablo, who were legally placed in her custody and given new identities.

The information Isaac provided and Delfina's courageous revelation of Ervil's doings and plans ultimately led to his arrest and conviction.

Tragically, Delfina's brush with death sent her again into a private mental hell. She suffered from insomnia and spent many nights chain-smoking, listening to every noise, wondering if she would be found. She knew her fate would surely be death. She feared it, yet longed for the peace it would bring. Reality was too harsh, yet she hung to it for the sake of her children.

CHAPTER FORTY-FIVE

Once again, one of Joel's widows caused a scandal throughout the Church of the Firstborn. It had been five years since Joel's death when Jeannine convinced her eighteen-year-old daughter that a righteous man would descend from heaven to marry her. She informed everyone of the particulars. In fact the groom's name was John Franklin, a sinless soul, who merited a young woman as select as the late prophet Joel's daughter. The mother and daughter were both absolutely convinced that John Franklin would appear from heaven and the prophet Joel himself would rise from the grave to perform the ceremony. Wedding invitations were distributed throughout Joel's group and many were mailed to other splinter groups.

Verlan was sickened when he received his invitation. He knew this would just bring more ridicule and condemnation to the already scandalous LeBaron group. Curious spectators arrived at the church on time, to witness the "heaven-ordained" wedding. They watched as the disillusioned bride in her flowing white gown was finally brought to tears from embarrassment. After two hours, it had become evident that the bride had been jilted. Not only did the groom leave her standing at the altar by herself, but her late father Joel didn't attend either. Of course the *no-show* was attributed to the disbelief and skepticism of the attending saints.

In spite of the absurdity, I told Verlan that at least it was one wedding that the bride and groom didn't have to wait till *death do us part.*

ERVIL'S PROPHECY FORETELLING that all Mormon factions, as well as the LDS Church, would crumble by May 3, 1977, had not transpired. The day had come and gone—and the lack of events caused Lloyd Sullivan, third in command of the Lambs of God, to lose all faith in Ervil once and for all. Four years earlier, when he confronted Ervil about the prophecy timeline of "A time and a time, and a time and a half," Ervil had explained to Lloyd and his other commandos that it meant in three and a half years their troubles would be over. Not only had the prophecy failed, but his supreme leader, Ervil himself, had abandoned his flock and fled to Mexico.

Disillusioned, broke, and depressed, Lloyd hid for several months from the police and his accomplices. He spent endless hours reevaluating his troubled life. He listed every one of Ervil's failed prophecies. He read through hundreds of pages of his writings, in which Ervil quoted scriptures proving he was a servant of God. When he finished Lloyd came to the painful conclusion that Ervil was not a servant of God but a son of perdition. He sent letters to other cult members explaining his new viewpoint.

In September, the authorities snared Lloyd in a bust. Among his personal belongings were his own writings of disbelief in Ervil. The investigators felt that with this information they soon would have a break in the case.

When he was interrogated, Lloyd confessed his dissatisfaction with Ervil but refused to elaborate. He was extradited to Utah and at first he did very little talking. Yet he was determined not to go down with his partners in crime, so he became an informant for Dick Forbes, the investigator. He knew it was to his own advantage, because he would never feel safe until Ervil was incarcerated. Soon, Lloyd was free, out on bail, and living in Denver.

Unbeknownst to his fellow Lambs of God, he sent a letter to Verlan. When Verlan received the letter, he wondered if Lloyd was sincere or if the communication was just another setup. Lloyd begged forgiveness from every member of the Church of the Firstborn: "I was a victim of one of the greatest deceptions ever perpetrated upon any member or members of the human race. I feel humbly to apologize to each of you and beg forgiveness for any wrong I have been guilty of" (*The 4 O'Clock Murders*, p. 212).

He later sent an impassioned letter to his son Don and his cousin John: "I led you to this man because I was sincere and was truly deceived by him. Now let me lead you away from him and his bloody tenure. I testify to you in the name of the Lord God of Israel that from all that I can find out through prayer, research and study, this man is Satan!" (*Prophet of Blood*, p. 281).

In early February 1978, Verlan left his hiding place and came to see me and the children. The loneliness and long absences were wearing me down. I longed to set aside all our fears and hoped that we could communicate and laugh once more as husband and wife.

We sat at the table together and Verlan spoke quietly, not wanting to frighten the children. "I received a letter from Lloyd Sullivan. I think he's sincere, but it could be a setup."

Dreading his answer, I asked, "What did he say?"

"He said he's repented from ever getting involved with Ervil. He wants to see me in person to ask for forgiveness."

"Why you, Verlan? Aren't you afraid it's just a ploy?"

"He feels that since Joel appointed me patriarch of the church, he owes his apologies to me."

"Please don't go. I don't think you can trust him."

Verlan sighed. "For some reason, I believe he's sincere. I've already contacted the authorities in Salt Lake City and the FBI. They want me to set up a meeting with him in Denver."

Upon leaving, he pulled me into an embrace; we kissed, clinging to one another hungrily. Both of us knew there was a probability that we would not see each other again.

On February 13, 1978, an agent promising security met Verlan at the Denver airport and then drove him to the local FBI office. The agents made it plain that they desperately needed Lloyd's testimony, but officially they were unable to ask it of him. If Verlan was killed, they'd be held responsible.

Verlan felt this was a job he had to do, not only for the authorities, but for Lloyd. He felt if Lloyd told him the truth, maybe more lives could be saved.

Verlan was taken to an upscale hotel, where authorities registered him under a fictitious name. When Verlan called Lloyd he communicated his mistrust and asked if Lloyd would submit to a pat down.

"I'll show up naked if it makes you feel better," Lloyd replied. With that, Verlan pushed his fears aside and met Lloyd in the hotel lobby.

Verlan was surprised at how genuinely happy Lloyd was to see him. The two seated themselves inside the hotel restaurant. Lloyd asked Verlan if he was being protected, and Verlan told him there were undercover agents nearby.

After they'd eaten, the two moved to big chairs in the open lobby and continued to converse.

They met the following day also. Verlan took careful notes, writing down every pertinent detail. The longer they talked, the more certain Verlan became of Lloyd's sincerity. He could sense Lloyd's desire to repent for any involvement with the Church of the Lamb of God.

This was only Verlan's second encounter with Lloyd. He'd seen him shortly after his baptism into the Church of the First-born. At that time Lloyd and his son Don and both their wives discussed the priesthood that Ervil was trying to usurp from Joel. Seeing that Lloyd was taking Ervil's side, Verlan warned him, insisting it would be a great mistake to follow Ervil. Lloyd showed his colors, vowing that if he did convert to Ervil, he'd help destroy those who opposed him. At the time, Verlan felt that Lloyd could be a dangerous man.

In Lloyd's confession, he told of his blind obedience, his complete submission to Ervil. He'd been forced to sever all other ties, showing complete loyalty to his new prophet. Thus Lloyd, believing he was following a man who was God's anointed for all the earth, was soon caught up in Ervil's obsessive delusions.

He'd joined Ervil in hiding and their paranoia escalated. They believed they were being persecuted by their enemies. Lloyd was convinced he was special because Ervil shared his revelations from God almost daily with him. He assumed he was a confidant and friend of the great One Mighty and Strong.

So convinced was he that Ervil's visions and utterances were from God, he finally surrendered his own will to do the bidding of the Lord's anointed. He would help Ervil cleanse the earth. When God spewed forth orders to kill, Lloyd would obey without question.

Explaining how he'd been duped, he convinced Verlan he wanted to confess all he knew, even if it implicated him or sent him to prison. His guilt consumed him because he knew others were marked for death. If Ervil's "soldiers" were not apprehended, more innocent people would be killed.

As Lloyd gave Verlan a detailed account of his involvement with Ervil, Verlan felt great empathy for Lloyd. His sorrowful words conveyed deep regret as he shared his testimony. He knew his confession would brand him as a traitor and he would likely be blood atoned.

Nevertheless, Lloyd agreed to confess all he knew to the authorities. So, accompanied by his lawyer, he met with prosecutor Dave Yocum and confirmed his involvement in many of Ervil's blood atonement missions. He admitted that in the plan to kill my aunt Rhea Kunz, he became spooked and abandoned the mission. He related how he had accompanied Eddie Marston and Mark Chynoweth in killing Robert Simons. He stated he heard Ervil's announcement that Dean Vest should die. He recalled Vonda White's confession to him, concerning the details of how she shot Dean. He retold about her involvement in Neomi Zarate's case, how she had described to Lloyd the incident of Neomi's death, admitting she had pulled the trigger. The most awful, grisly account was that of Rebecca's death, Ervil's own daughter. Eddie Marston had confessed to Lloyd that he had strangled her while Duane Chynoweth held her down in the backseat of the car. Eddie had complained that his hands and wrists ached for days from applying so much force and pressure.

Lloyd claimed Ervil had sent him to Jackson, Mississippi, because he wanted him out of the way while my uncle, Rulon Allred was assassinated. Lloyd confirmed Ervil's plan to lure Verlan to the funeral where he would be killed by his soldiers.

After confessing to the authorities, Lloyd's greatest fear was that he and his family would be blood atoned. He had made a blood covenant with Ervil, which, if broken, carried the death penalty. When Lloyd led police to the shallow grave in the mountains where Simons's body had been buried, any doubts they may have had about him were erased.

*   *   *

SHORTLY THEREAFTER, on a police raid on a LeBaron safe house in Denver, Colorado, Vonda was arrested. She was soon back in California facing murder charges.

This time, on April 24, 1978, she appeared in San Diego for a preliminary hearing on the murder case of Dean Vest. Now, in addition to the original evidence, Lloyd Sullivan was available as an incriminating witness.

According to Verlan, who told me the terrible details of Lloyd's confessions, Lloyd gave a graphic account of all the exploits of Ervil LeBaron's cult and of the control that he exerted over his blood-atoning warriors. He testified about the revelation Ervil proclaimed, dooming Dean Vest to be sacrificed. He then related how Vonda had confessed and admitted exactly how she had killed Dean.

Considering the possibility that Lloyd might be killed before Vonda's trial, the judge allowed Lloyd to be taped as he testified about the murders of Neomi Zarate, who had also been shot by Vonda, and Rebecca LeBaron, who had been strangled by Eddie Marston and Duane Chynoweth. To all who heard the facts, the testimony was both astonishing and damning.

Vonda was arraigned, bond was set at $350,000, and she was inescapably detained in the county jail.

Most unfortunately, while all were anxiously awaiting Vonda's trial, Lloyd Sullivan had the gall to up and die of a heart attack.

On July 19, 1978, Vonda's trial began on charges of both murder and conspiracy, which complicated matters because conspiracy obviously implicated other conspirators.

Lloyd's previously recorded testimony was read to the jury. Isaac LeBaron (fifteen-year-old son of Ervil and Delfina) served as the primary witness by testifying to what he had heard, and he also quoted Vonda, hoping to show her callousness. He testified that Vonda had said her own son Craig had been "bad," and "If he doesn't straighten out, he's going to be put to death."

Ervil's sixth wife, Linda Johnson, who lived in National City and had been Vonda's roommate, presented herself as a hostile witness. She took the Fifth Amendment twenty-eight times when asked about her relationship with Ervil.

At that point the judge stopped the trial because of insufficient evidence to support the conspiracy charge, which made a new trial necessary.

Vonda's next trial—begun almost eleven months later—ended after all the revamped evidence and compelling testimonies were presented, and prosecuting attorney Gary Rempel made his closing statement.

On May 13, 1979, the jury found Vonda White guilty of murder. Almost a month later, she received the maximum prison term, life imprisonment. As far as I know, she never gave up her belief in Ervil; she remained convinced he was a true prophet. In fact, she allowed her children to be raised in Ervil's cult.

CHAPTER FORTY-SIX

Two years after my uncle Rulon's murder, Ervil and his wife Lorna were arrested. The Mexican police found them in their hideout near Atlixco, in a small town south of Mexico City.

In the United States, investigator Dick Forbes was notified of their capture and that Ervil was being expelled from Mexico as an "undesirable." The FBI was waiting for Ervil as he walked across the bridge separating the two countries. On June 1, 1979, Ervil was arrested and taken to the Webb County Jail in Laredo, Texas.

Dick Forbes was euphoric that Ervil had been apprehended. He and his companion, Gary Pederson, had flown in from Salt Lake City, and another detective, Wayne Fowler, from National City, California, joined them to get more information about the Dean Vest case. The detectives began interrogating their captive in the jail of the U.S. marshal's office. Forbes read Ervil his rights, then listed his outstanding warrants. There were three, one from Price, Utah; one from San Diego; and one from Salt Lake City. After Forbes had read his statements, Ervil was taken before the U.S. judge in Laredo, where he was arraigned for "unlawful flight." His bail was set at $100,000, and Ervil was returned to his cell.

While in Laredo, the three detectives held several interviews with Ervil. At first he remained silent, except to answer yes or no. But Forbes pressed him for answers. Finally, Ervil admitted that he was a prophet and the leader of the Church of the Lambs of God. He also unabashedly declared that he was the "anointed one" who would bring about the millennium, bragging that he was the only person on Earth designated to lead God's kingdom and prepare a worthy people to meet Christ at his Second Coming. Ervil also admitted that he had written many of his church's publications.

Forbes was excited when Ervil admitted that he had written the threatening pamphlets, *Hour of Crisis—Day of Vengeance, Response to an Act of War,* and several others. Ervil took pride in claiming to be the author. He had always flaunted his writing skills, so I'm sure he felt superior to his interrogators.

Wanting to hear it from Ervil's own mouth, Forbes asked him if traitors or those who were disobedient to the law of liberty would be put to death. To set him straight, Ervil replied, "Once the person fully understands the law, then willfully disobeys, he brings judgment upon himself."

At one point, Ervil rose from his chair, stating that he had no more to say.

Lieutenant Fowler told Ervil that he didn't have to talk, but he wasn't allowed to leave. Both Forbes and Pederson talked about the murders of Joel F. LeBaron, Robert Simons, Dr. Rulon Allred, Dean Vest, and Ervil's own daughter Rebecca.

Ervil sat as though oblivious to their accusations, revealing his unwillingness to listen. He stared at the floor. The detectives interrupted Ervil's silence, asking if he was still following what they were saying. He nodded yes as they continued. After an hour and a half, Fowler and Forbes ended their questioning and began packing up, indicating their intention to leave. Ervil congratulated the two men, using his habitual flattery. He praised them for being "brilliant" men who knew how to do their job. A smirk crossed his face as he finally rose to the occasion and began responding to their final positions.

"I do want to tell you some things that may help you to understand," Ervil began (*Prophet of Blood*, p. 327).

To their amazement, Ervil proceeded to ramble on for several hours, explaining his religious beliefs and those of his followers. He said he had summed it all up in his pamphlet *The Law of Liberty*. The detectives were taking notes during the session and also taped his long-winded speech. Ervil's preaching seemed to be nothing more than an opportunity to show his sense of importance by inflating his ego. He made it clear that he was the head of every government the world over. He said every president and leader who didn't subject themselves to his authority was a criminal.

On June 11, 1979, Ervil arrived in Salt Lake City and was held and arraigned for trial.

During the time that Ervil was in jail in Utah, he wrote a July 9 letter to Walter Mondale about the "deplorable state of the union" and "government officers whose thinking is distorted by religious fanaticism," implying President Jimmy Carter. Seeking sympathy, he explained his dilemma, claiming that he was falsely imprisoned. For some reason, that letter was never mailed, but he did mail other writings (*Prophet of Blood*, p. 298).

Ervil was enraged by every leader who claimed authority— from the president of the United States to the pope—and all who would not acquiesce to his authority.

While in prison, Ervil allowed only two or three people to interview him. Two detectives from National City spoke with him first. They pressed him about the murder of Dean Vest in 1975, but Ervil refused to answer their questions. As always, he began preaching to them, often quoting the Bible. They saw firsthand Ervil's fanatical teachings, and they quickly came to understand how he could tie anyone up in knots when it came to religion.

At one time, Laurie Beckland, from the *San Diego Tribune*, tried to interview Ervil for a story, but his incessant ranting over the scriptures provided her with no facts and nothing that would interest her readers. When she left, she couldn't remember any of the religious doctrines he'd tried to teach her, but she knew she'd never forget his foul breath, which, for her, overpowered his confusing rhetoric. To my knowledge, Beckland was the only reporter to ever interview Ervil.

Finally on May 12, 1980, his trial began in Salt Lake City. Judge Ernest F. Baldwin presided in the Third District Court. The jury consisted of three women and nine men. Special prosecutors were led by David Yocum who gave the opening statement. Evil was charged with ordering the murder of my uncle, Dr. Rulon Allred, and attempting to kill my husband, Verlan, for vengeance and money. Yocum alleged how "pecuniary gain for Ervil is his belief that he was commanded by God to kill and take over Allred's church and Verlan's church and their tithing and membership and eventually take over the world" (*Prophet of Blood,* p. 333).

Unable to afford a lawyer of his own choosing, Ervil accepted a team of court-appointed lawyers led by John Hill. He declared that Ervil "was only a religious leader. He was a theologian . . . a preacher," thus could not be blamed for the actions of others in his church who became radically violent (*Prophet of Blood,* p. 333).

The prosecution called forty-three people as witnesses. Among them were the following:

Richard Bunker—the man in Dr. Allred's office
Don Sullivan—Lloyd's son who aided the assassins and stalked
　Verlan

Jack Strotham—who aided the assassins and stalked Verlan
Bonnie Sullivan—the widow of Lloyd Sullivan
Owen Allred—Dr. Allred's brother
Verlan LeBaron—the brother whose death Ervil ordered
Conway LeBaron—Ervil's cousin and confidant
Esther Spencer—Ervil's sister
Merlin Kingston—a leader of the Kingston group
Carol Jensen—the widow of Earl Jensen
Melba Allred—the widow of Dr. Allred
Isaac LeBaron—Ervil's son

These witnesses told all they knew, that though Ervil was not at the murder scene, he had given the assassination orders and then fled to Mexico. The evidence was overwhelming!

The four defense witnesses were Ervil's wife Lorna Chynoweth and her mother, Thelma Chynoweth, and Alex Chynoweth along with Bill Rios (Ervil's brother-in law), all of whom were LeBaron family members, which fact did not help the case.

At the conclusion on May 28, the jury deliberated for only three hours before returning with the verdict: guilty of first-degree murder and conspiracy to commit murder. The jury was allowed to go home for the weekend but was to return on Monday to decide if the punishment would be life in prison or death.

Unfortunately, right after the verdict was read, Siegfried Widmar, who had worked so hard to get Ervil arrested, tried, and punished, gave a televised interview stating that Ervil had commanded at least eight additional murders.

Two of the jurors learned of Siegfried's interview. When they reconvened on Monday, the defense claimed that the jury had been prejudiced and could not pass sentence. In Utah, the death penalty requires a jury. Since the jury was now unable to proceed, the judge sentenced him to prison for life.

On June 2, 1980, Ervil was incarcerated in the state prison at Point of the Mountain.

We all hoped that his imprisonment would end the violence, but Ervil made it his business to prolong the anguish, even after his death in 1981. He ordained his sons to carry on in his stead, so between Ervil's order and the continued workings of his followers, twenty more people were "blood atoned" after Ervil died.

A YEAR LATER, my son Kaylen, whom I was visiting in San Diego, answered the ringing phone. He said hello and stood still for a few moments. Then he jumped up, waving the receiver and shouting, "Thank God! Thank God!"

He slammed down the phone and grabbed me by the waist. "Mom, Mom, Uncle Ervil is dead! He's dead! It's all over the news. They found him on the floor in his cell during their three in the morning watch. They say he died of a heart attack."

I'd never felt such euphoria, and the tears on my cheeks expressed only sheer joy. I felt absolutely no sorrow for this psycho-mastermind who'd cut short the lives of eight of our family and friends. Finally... my murderous brother-in-law had been stopped. We were free!

His death merited a celebration. Kaylen jumped in his truck and drove to the 7-Eleven. He came home with five different flavors of Häagen-Dazs ice cream and two large packages of chocolate chip cookies.

Kaylen and I howled, danced around the room, and shouted at the top of our lungs—in between spoonfuls of ice cream and bites of cookies. The date was August 16, 1981, one of the happiest days of my life. I called all my children, expressing my relief and satisfaction, and we rejoiced together.

Two days later, August 18, 1981, at approximately two o'clock in the afternoon, I lay sprawled on the floor with my head on a pillow, just relaxing. A cross breeze blew in through the screen door as the phone rang. Kaylen, thinking I was sleeping, answered on the second ring hoping not to disturb me.

"What? *What?*" he yelled. "Are you *sure*? Is he *dead?*"

I sat up, wondering what or whom my son could be talking about. Kaylen covered the mouthpiece. "Mom, Daddy's dead. The Red Cross just verified it. He was killed in a head-on collision by Mexico City."

His words pierced me like a dagger. What a transition in just two days—a death that liberated so many from suffering, and another death that robbed my children of their father. Verlan had lived in constant fear, hiding not only in Mexico and the U.S. but in Nicaragua as well. He had spent almost ten years looking over his shoulder, sleeping fully dressed, never able to let down his guard.

For the first time, I felt guilty that we had celebrated Ervil's death because I realized that his family was feeling the same heartache, loss, and devastation as we were.

Though Verlan was never able to be everything I'd hoped for in a husband and father, I was glad he was finally free of the burdens and fears he'd carried for so long.

Soon I realized I, too, was free. I didn't know exactly what I'd do or where I'd go, but for the first time, I could make my own plans and decisions without repercussions. Finally after years of living in fear and being controlled by a religious cult, my future stretched out before me, inviting me into a new adventure...called life!

EPILOGUE

This must be concluded with a brief summary of events either orchestrated or caused by Ervil LeBaron and this cult insanity.

Before Ervil's last arrest, trial, sentence, and death, he ordered the following crimes:

September 1971—Earl Jensen received the "black hand" life threat by Ervil.

August 20, 1972—Joel F. LeBaron was murdered by Dan Jordan and Gamaliel Rios. Ervil and Conway were also in the getaway vehicle.

December 26, 1974—Ervil's soldiers raided Los Molinos. As a result, Edmundo Aguilar and Moroni Mendez died, and thirteen others were wounded.

January 1975—Neomi Zarate was murdered by Vonda White, aided by Yolanda Rios (both were Ervil's wives).

April 23, 1975—Robert Hunt Simons was murdered by Ervil's stepson, Eddie Marston, aided by Mark Chynoweth and Lloyd Sullivan.

June 16, 1975—Grover Dean Vest was murdered by Vonda White.

April 1977—Ervil's daughter Rebecca was strangled with a rope by Eddie Marston and Duane Chynoweth, Ervil's brother-in-law.

May 10, 1977—Dr. Rulon C. Allred was assassinated by Rena Chynoweth, Ervil's thirteenth wife, aided by Ramona Marston, Ervil's stepdaughter.

WHILE IN PRISON, among other items, Ervil wrote the *Book of New Commandments,* in which he listed some fifty people who should be blood atoned. Verlan told me that not only his, but both Charlotte's and my name were on the list. Ervil had also ordained his son Arturo Morrel LeBaron to be his successor as "worldwide patriarch," and he had ordained at least six other sons as "high priests" to perpetuate the Lambs of God cult, and continue the blood atonement killings.

When first locked up, Ervil lived with the general population. But when he tried to form a following inside the prison, he was put in a solitary cell.

Because most of his original followers eventually defected—including leaders and several wives—he received fewer and fewer visitors, so his depression and mental illness intensified.

Finally on August 16, 1981, Ervil was found dead in his cell, evidently from a heart attack.

Ironically, two days later, on August 18, 1981, my husband Verlan and his friend John Adams died in a tragic car accident in Mexico.

Many hoped that their deaths would end the feud and the blood atonement, but they did not. Even after Ervil's death, the madness continued.

After Ervil's demise, Arturo succeeded him as the One Mighty and Strong patriarch.

In 1983: Isaac LeBaron, Ervil's son, committed suicide on June 17.

Two of Ervil's daughters by Delfina—Lillian (married to Mark Chynoweth) and Delia—committed suicide, as did nine of my nephews, nieces, and close relatives.

Two or three of Leo's troops were killed in the autumn when they made a raid on Arturo's gang in La Joya, their hideout ranch in Mexico. During the confrontation, ten-year-old Norma LeBaron, Ervil's daughter, was shot in the leg.

Lorna Chynoweth, Ervil's wife, was blood atoned by her own son Andrew and Andrès Zarate, who had received orders from Arturo LeBaron (Ervil's son by Delfina). Her body has never been found, nor have any of the Lambs of God been tried for her murder.

Leo Evoniuk murdered Arturo in December in La Joya. Then Heber became their head patriarch.

In 1984: Gamaliel Rios was assassinated by Heber in La Joya. His body was never found.

Gamaliel's brother, Raul Rios, was also executed by Heber's men.

Yolanda Rios, Ervil's wife and a sister to Gamaliel and Raul, was murdered by Heber's men.

Heber and his followers became drug runners and car thieves.

Patricia LeBaron's baby, fathered by her half brother Heber, died and was buried along the roadside.

In 1985: Andrès and Alex Zarate disappeared, allegedly murdered by Heber's followers.

In 1986: Andrew LeBaron was murdered by Heber's men in the summer. His body has never been found.

On November 5, Heber held up a bank in Dallas, was arrested, and then released on $50,000 bail. He jumped bail and fled to

Mexico. There he was deposed and Aaron became the last of the patriarchs.

In 1987: Jorge LeBaron, Mary Lou and Ervil's son, was murdered by Douglas Barlow.

Mary LeBaron, Dalila and Nephi Marston's daughter, was killed by her husband, Heber LeBaron. (How ironic that Mary [also known as little Maria] survived the horrific automobile crash near Ensenada that claimed both her parents' lives only to be blood atoned as an adult.)

Sandra LeBaron, thirteen years old, was killed by her brother Richard.

In 1987: Leo Evoniuk was murdered on May 21 by Heber LeBaron and Douglas Barlow (Rosemary's son). His body has never been found.

Daniel Ben Jordan was murdered on October 16 while deer hunting in Utah. His killer was Heber, who was aided by his half sister, Patricia LeBaron, whom he had taken for one of his wives.

In 1988: Duane Chynoweth, Ervil's brother-in-law, and his eight-year-old daughter Jennifer were assassinated at four o'clock in the afternoon on June 27 by Richard LeBaron, aided by Patricia. At the same time Mark Chynoweth (who was both Ervil's brother-in-law *and* son-in-law) was killed by Heber, aided by Cynthia LeBaron and Natasha; and Eddie Marston (Ervil's stepson by Anna Mae) was murdered by Douglas. They were all killed by Aaron LeBaron's orders.

In 1991: Natasha LeBaron, Lorna's daughter, was strangled with a wire by fourteen-year-old Thomas, one of her younger half brothers who followed Aaron. She was buried in a grave that she thought she'd dug for someone else, and her body has never been found.

★   ★   ★

RENA CHYNOWETH WAS ACQUITTED for Dr. Rulon Allred's murder, but in July 1990 she appeared on *The Sally Jessy Raphael Show,* where she admitted to being his killer.

Ramona, who aided Rena in Dr. Allred's murder, eventually surrendered to the authorities. She was only put on probation.

Heber and Patricia LeBaron, and Douglas Barlow, are serving life sentences without parole for the four o'clock murders.

Aaron LeBaron was sent to prison for forty-five years for masterminding the four o'clock murders.

Richard and Cynthia, both children of Linda Johnson, surrendered and eventually testified. They provided the information needed to convict others, so Richard was sentenced to only five years and Cynthia was granted immunity.

Delfina was a brave heroine through it all and has now peacefully passed on.

To me it's sad that the blood of those unfortunate souls who were atoned will continue to seep through the pages of history.

WORKS CITED

- Anderson, Scott. *The 4 O'Clock Murders.* Hardcover edition, New York: Doubleday, 1992, pp.182, 184, 267, 271, 274, 277, 279–280. Paperback edition, New York: Dell, 1994, pp. 339–341, 346–347, 352, 415, 420–422, 431.

- *The Bible, King James Version.* Leviticus 20:14, 1 Peter 2:9, Numbers 15:32–36, Deuteronomy 13:6–9.

- *Book of Mormon.* Salt Lake City, Utah: The Church of Jesus Christ of Latter-day Saints, 1958. 1 Nephi 1:1–4, 1 Nephi 12:23, 1 Nephi 4:12–13, 17, 18.

- Bradlee, Ben Jr. and Dale Van Atta. *Prophet of Blood: The Untold Story of Ervil LeBaron and The Lambs of God.* New York: G. P. Putnam's Sons, pp. 65–67, 92, 99, 174, 229, 231, 240–241, 246.

- *Doctrine and Covenants.* Salt Lake City: The Church of Jesus Christ of Latter-day Saints, 1963. Sections 85, 132, 132:61–62, 135:3.

- *Journal of Discourses.* Volume 1, p. 83; Volume 3, p. 226; Volume 3, p. 247; Volume 4; pp. 49–50; Volume 4, p. 375.

- LeBaron, Verlan M. *The LeBaron Story.* Self-published, printed by Keels & Co., Inc., 1981, pp.61, 201–210, 233, 247.

- *Priesthood Expounded.* Originally published by the Mexican Mission of the Church of the Firstborn of the Fullness of Times, August 1956. Peace Publishing Co., Chihuahua, Mexico. (1991 Revised Ed. by Harvard Pratt Stubbs, pp. 15, 32, 57–58).

- Tanner, Jerald and Sandra Tanner. *The Changing World of Mormonism.* Chicago: Moody Press, 1981, pp. 241, 490, 497–498.

- Young, Brigham. *Manuscript History of Brigham Young, 1846–1847,* comp. by Eldon J. Watson. Salt Lake City, Dec. 20, 1846, p. 500; Feb. 24, 1847, p. 500.

ERVIL MORREL LEBARON
1925–1981

Wives	1. Delfina	2. Mary Lou	3. Joy	4. Anna Mae	5. Lorna†	6. Linda	7. Kristina	8. Debbie	9. Rosemary	10. Vonda	11. Teresa	12. Yolanda†	13. Rena
Children	Sylvia Esther	Elsa	No children	*Children with Nephi*	Andrew	Anthony	Daughter	Son	*Children with Ralph Barlow*	*Children from previous marriage*	Gladys	Sandra†	Erin
	Sarah Jane	Jorge†		Marston	Tarsa	Cynthia	Daughter	Son	Janice	Craig	Norma	Danny	John Ryan
	Alicia	Patricia‡		David	Aaron‡	Richard			Cheri	Audrey	Jenny		
	Lillian*	Benjamin		Edward	Natasha†				Douglas‡		Bertha		
	Arturo Morrell†	Virginia		(Eddie)†	Monique				Annalee	*Ervil's children*			
	Rebecca†	Ruben		Ramona	Bridget				Ellen	Evelyn			
	Isaac*			Fay	Jared					Janet			
	Paul				Joshua				*Ervil's children*	Mimi			
	Delia*			*Ervil's children*					Nathaniel	Nathan			
				Kathleen					David				
				Heber‡					Eva				
				Marilyn									
				Celia									
				Anna									
				Hyrum									
				Adine									

*Suicide
†Murdered
‡Life in prison

ABOUT THE AUTHOR

IRENE SPENCER lives in Northern California, with her husband of twenty-one years, Hector J. Spencer. During the twenty-eight years of her first marriage to a polygamous husband, Irene gave birth to thirteen children (all single births). She also adopted a newborn girl, who became her ninth child.

Irene has 123 grandchildren and 60 great-grandchildren. Among her many talents, she is an accomplished seamstress, a great cook, and fluent in Spanish, and she has traveled to twenty-three foreign countries and twenty-three states speaking about polygamy and related issues.